INTRODUCTION TO TOURISM STUDIES - TEXT BOOK

DR ANSHUMALI PANDEY

Contents

Prologue

Tourism is a dynamic and multifaceted field that transcends geographical, cultural, and economic boundaries. As one of the fastest-growing industries in the world, tourism not only fosters global connections but also plays a pivotal role in cultural exchange, economic development, and environmental sustainability. It is a realm where the pursuit of leisure meets the quest for knowledge and understanding, offering opportunities for exploration, interaction, and transformation.

This textbook, *Introduction to Tourism Studies*, is designed to provide students, professionals, and enthusiasts with a comprehensive foundation in the principles, practices, and potential of the tourism industry. It delves into the theoretical underpinnings of tourism, examines its historical evolution, and explores its various forms and functions in contemporary society.

Through structured modules, case studies, and practical examples, this book seeks to bridge the gap between academic knowledge and real-world application. Topics such as destination management, sustainable tourism, cultural heritage, and emerging trends are addressed to prepare readers for the challenges and opportunities in this vibrant sector.

As you embark on this journey through the pages of this book, may you develop a deeper appreciation for the power of tourism to unite, educate, and inspire. It is my hope that this resource will not only enhance your understanding of tourism but also ignite a passion for contributing meaningfully to its future.

Dr. Anshumali Pandey

CHAPTER I

TOURISM CONCEPTS

Introduction:

Welcome to the study of a dynamic group of industries that have developed to serve the needs of travelers worldwide – tourism! Tourism is the business of travel. Whether we are travelers or we are serving traveler's needs, this exciting and demanding group of visitor services industries touches all our lives.

In this chapter you will understand the different perspectives on the study of tourism, know the meaning of the term 'tourism', 'visitor', 'tourist', 'excursionist', 'transit traveler' and the difference between travel and tourism. You will also come to know of different definitions adopted by different countries on the term 'tourist'.

Changing Facets of Tourism:

Human beings are innately curious concerning the world in which we live. We yearn to know what other places look like - what the people, their culture, the animals and plant life, and landforms may be elsewhere. Today, higher levels of education and the influence of television and other communication media have combined to create in us a much greater awareness of our entire world. We are now in global economy and our industries must be globally competitive. We must think globally. Material prosperity in many countries, with accompanying higher standards of living, has made travel attainable for hundreds of millions of us. Although travel can be undertaken for many reasons, the most common are pleasure, business, and study. In this block we explore the multiplicity of social and economic phenomena that bring about and are created by this vast worldwide industry.

The subject of travel is exciting and fascinating. Human beings have been moving from place to place for about 1 million years. Our early ancestors, Homo erectus, originated in eastern and southern Africa. But remains of these same forms of early humankind have also been found in China and Java (Indonesia). It has been estimated that migrations of this type took about 15,000 years, but this is a brief span of time in the long history of humanity.

Various theories have been proposed regarding the motivation for such amazing journeys. Foremost is that these wanderings were in search of food and to escape from danger. Another theory is that people observed the migrations of birds and wanted to know where the birds came from and where they were going. Recently, in the most dramatic discovery of its kind ever made, the preserved body of a man dubbed the "iceman," who died 5,000 years ago, was found in the ice in mountainous northern Italy. Some of the scientists studying his body and accoutrements have concluded that he was returning to his home in what is now Switzerland from a journey to the south of what is now Italy.

Since the times of the wanderings of ancient peoples, we have been traveling in ever-widening patterns about the earth. From the days of such early explorers as Marco Polo, Ibn battute, Christopher Columbus, Ferdinand Magellan, and James Cook to the present, there has been a steady growth in travel.

Tourism is one of the world's most rapidly growing industries. Much of its growth is due to higher disposable incomes, increased leisure time and falling costs of travel. As airports become more enjoyable places to pass through, as travel agency services become increasingly automated, and as tourists find it easier to get information on places they want to visit, tourism grows.

The Internet has fuelled the growth of the travel industry by providing on line booking facilities. It has also provided people with the power to explore destinations and cultures from their home personal computers and make informed choices before finalizing travel plans. With its immense information resources, the Internet allows tourists to scrutinize hotels, check weather forecasts, read up on local food and even talk to other tourists around the world about their travel experiences for a chosen destination.

This new trend has made the tourism job very challenging. The holiday makers want a good rate of return on their investment. They are to be lured with value additions and improved customer service. This also put emphasis on the regular flow of manpower with specific skills at the appropriate levels to match and cater to global standards. The success of the hospitality industry comes from provision of quality rooms, food, service and ambience. There is no doubt that fitness has increasingly become a larger part of everyone's life. And business and leisure travelers alike look to maintain their fitness goals while away from home. Awareness should be created about the environment and education. A collective effort and co-operation with powerful networking are the need of the hour. People should be acting as the watchdogs of the society as far as environmental issues are concerned. Eco-tourists are a growing community and tourism promotions have to adopt such eco-practices which could fit this growing community.

Another growing trend in the tourism scene is the Incentive Market and the scope of the destination to attract conferences and convention traffic. Here the prospects are better for those destinations where state of the art infrastructure has been developed along with a safe and clean image.

Tourism today is much more than just developing products. It is more about quality, insightful thinking and ability to have global information about technology, partners, contacts and responding quickly to global and regional trends. The fundamental task before tourism promoting is to facilitate integration of the various components in the tourism trade as active participants in the nation's social and cultural life. There is a long road ahead. All must work towards a society where people can work and participate as equal partners. Tourism should be a vehicle for international cooperation and understanding of the various civilizations and a harbinger of peace.

From the foregoing we can see how fast the face of tourism is changing and how challenging the job of travel agencies is now. There is therefore a need for proper training of the personnel working in the industry through thorough and detailed study of the subject A unified approach to the subject is also needed since at present people from different fields have been studying tourism from different perspectives.

Different Approaches to study Tourism:

Tourism commonly is approached through a variety of methods. However, there is little or no agreement on how the study of tourism should be undertaken. The following are several methods that have been used:

Institutional Approach:

The institutional approach to the study of tourism considers the various intermediaries and institutions that perform tourism activities. It emphasizes institutions such as the travel agency. This approach requires an investigation of the organization, operating methods, problems, costs, and economic place of travel agents who acts on behalf of the customer, purchasing services from airlines, rental car companies, hotels, and so on.

Product Approach:

The product approach involves the study of various tourism products and how they are produced, marketed, and consumed. For example, one might study an airline seat - how it is created, the people who are engaged in buying and selling it, how it is financed, how it is advertised, and so on. Repeating this procedure for rental cars, hotel rooms, meals, and other tourist services-gives a full picture of the field. Unfortunately, the product approach tends to be too time consuming, it does not allow the student to grasp the fundamentals of tourism quickly.

Historical Approach:

The historical approach is not widely used. It involves an analysis of tourism activities and institutions from an evolutionary angle. It searches for the cause of innovations, their growth or decline, and shifts in interest.

Managerial Approach:

The managerial approach is firm oriented (microeconomic), focusing on the management activities necessary to operate a tourist enterprise, such as planning, research, pricing, advertising, control, and the like. It is a popular approach, using insights gleaned from other approaches and disciplines. Regardless of which approach is used to study tourism, it is important to know the managerial approach. Products change, institutions change, society changes, this means that managerial objectives and procedures must be geared to change to meet shifts in the tourism environment. The Journal of Travel Research and Tourism Management, leading journals in the field, both feature this approach.

Economic Approach:

Because of its importance to both domestic and world economics, tourism has been examined closely by economists, who focus on supply, demand, balance of payments, foreign exchange, employment, expenditures, development, multipliers, and other economic factors. This approach is useful in providing a framework for analyzing tourism and its contributions to a country's economy and economic development. The disadvantage of the economic approach is that whereas tourism is an important economic phenomenon, it has noneconomic impacts as well. The economic approach does not usually pay adequate attention to the environmental, cultural, psychological, sociological, and anthropological approaches.

Sociological Approach:

Tourism tends to be a social activity. Consequently, it has attracted the attention of sociologist, who has studied the tourism behavior of individuals and groups of people and the impact of tourism on society. This approach examines social classes, habits, and customs of both hosts and guest. The sociology of leisure is a relatively undeveloped field, but it shows promise of progressing rapidly and becoming more widely used. As tourism continues to make a massive impact on society, it will be studied more and more from a social point of view.

Geographical Approach:

Geography is a wide-ranging discipline, so it is natural that geographers should be interested in tourism and its spatial aspects. The geographer specializes in the study of location, environment, climate, landscape, and economic aspects. The geographer's approach to tourism sheds light on the location of tourist areas, the movements of people created by tourism locales, the changes that tourism brings to the landscape in the form of tourism facilities, dispersion of tourism development, physical planning, and economic, social, and cultural problems. Since tourism touches geography at so many points, geographers have investigated the area more thoroughly than have scholars in many other disciplines. Because the geographers' approach is so encompassing dealing with land use, economic aspects, demographic impacts, and cultural problems, a study of their contributions is highly recommended.

Interdisciplinary Approaches:

Tourism embraces virtually all aspects of our society. We even have cultural tourism, which calls for an anthropological approach. Because people behave in different ways and travel for different reasons, it is necessary to use a psychological approach to determine best way to promote and market tourism products. Since tourists cross borders and require passports and visas from government offices and since most countries have government-operated tourism development departments, we find that political institutions are involved and are calling for a political science approach. Any industry that becomes an economic giant affecting the lives of many people attracts the attention of legislative bodies (along with that of the sociologists, geographers, economists, and anthropologist,) which create the laws, regulations, and legal environment in which the tourist industry must operate, so we also have a legal approach. The great importance of transportation suggests passenger transportation as another approach. The fact simply is that tourism is so vast, so complex, and so multifaceted that it is necessary to have a number of approaches to studying the field, each geared to a somewhat different task or objective.

The Systems Approach:

What is really needed to study tourism is systems approach. A system is a set of interrelated groups coordinated to form a unified whole and organized to accomplish a set of goals. It integrates the other approaches into a comprehensive method dealing with both micro and macro issues. It can examine the tourist firm's competitive environment, its market, its results, its linkages with other institutions, the consumer, and the interaction of the firm with the consumer. In addition, a system can take a macro viewpoint and examine the entire tourism system of a country, state, or area and how it operates within and relates to other systems, such as legal, political, economic, and social systems.

The Importance of Managerial Perspectives to the Study of Tourism:

Now due to higher disposable incomes, increased leisure time and falling cost of travel, the Tourism industry has shown a very high growth and since tourism is a service industry it comprises of a number of tangible and intangible components. The tangible elements include transport system- air, rail, road, water and now, space; hospitality services accommodation, food and beverage, tours, souvenirs; and related services such as banking, insurance and safety and security. The intangible elements include: rest and relaxation, culture, escape, adventure, new and different experiences. As there are number of bodies involved the need arises for a management of services related to this industry and so the study of Tourism acquires a great practical necessity and usefulness. Tourism industry is very fast growing and this industry involves activities and interests of Transport Undertakings, Owners of Tourist Sites and Attractions, Various tourist Service Providers at the tourist destinations and Central and Local Government, etc. Each of these serves both the resident population and the tourists and their management must reconcile the needs of tourists with the needs of the resident population. So it becomes important to study tourism from the perspective of Management, since the management of various bodies in this industry in invaded.

What is Tourism?

When we think of tourism, we think primarily of people who are visiting a particular place for sightseeing, visiting friends and relatives, taking a vacation, and having a good time. They may spend their leisure time engaging in various sports, sunbathing, talking, and singing, taking rides, touring, reading, or simply enjoying the environment. If we consider the subject further, we may include in our definition of tourism people who are participating in a convention, a business conference, or some other kind of business or professional activity, as well as those who are taking a study tour under an expert guide or doing some kind of scientific research or study. These visitors use all forms of transportation, from hiking in a wilderness park to flying in jet to an exciting city.

Transportation can include taking a chairlift up a Colorado mountainside or standing at the rail of a cruise ship looking across the blue Caribbean. Whether people travel by one of these means or by car, motor coach, camper, train, taxi, motorbike, or bicycle, they are taking a trip and thus are engaging in tourism. That is what this block is all about-why people travel (and why some don't) and the socioeconomic effects that their presence and expenditures have on a society. Any attempt to define tourism and to describe its scope fully must consider the various groups that participate in and are affected by this industry. Their perspectives are vital to the development of a comprehensive definition.

Four different perspectives of tourism can be identified:

1. The tourist:

The tourist seeks various psychic and physical experiences and satisfactions. The nature of these will largely determine the destinations chosen and the activities enjoyed.

2. The businesses providing tourist goods and services:

Business people see tourism as an opportunity to make a profit by supplying goods and services that the tourist market demands.

3. The government of the host community or area:

Politicians view tourism as a wealth factor in the economy of their jurisdictions. Their perspective is related to the incomes their citizens can earn from this business. Politicians also consider the foreign exchange receipts from international tourism as well as the tax receipts collected from tourist expenditures, either directly or indirectly.

4. The host community:

Local people usually see tourism as cultural and employment factor. Of importance to this group, for example, is the effect of the interaction between large numbers of international visitors and residents. This effect may be beneficial or harmful or both.

Tourism:

Thus, tourism may be defined as the sum of the phenomena and relationships arising from the interaction of tourists, business suppliers, host governments, and host communities in the process of attracting and hosting these tourists and other visitors. Tourism is a composite of activities, services, and industries that delivers a travel experience: transportation, accommodations, eating and drinking establishments, shops, entertainment, activity facilities, and other hospitality services available for individuals or groups that are traveling away from home. It encompasses all providers of visitor and visitor-related services. Tourism is the entire world industry of travel, hotels, transportations, and all other components, including promotion that serves the needs and wants of travelers.

Finally, tourism is the sum total of tourist expenditures within the border of a nation or a political subdivision or a transportation-centered economic area of contiguous states or nations. This economic concept also considers the income multiplier of these tourist expenditures. One has only to consider the multidimensional aspects of tourism and its interactions with other activities to understand why it is difficult to come up with a meaningful definition that will be universally accepted. Each of the many definitions that have arisen is aimed at fitting a special situation and solving an immediate problem, and the lack of uniform definitions has hampered study of tourism as a discipline. Development of a field depends on

1. Uniform definitions
2. Description
3. Analysis
4. Prediction and
5. Control

Modern tourism is a discipline that has only recently attracted the attention of scholars from many fields. The majority of studies has been conducted for special purposes and have used narrow operational definitions to suit particular needs of researchers or government officials; these studies have not encompassed a systems approach. Consequently, many definitions of "tourism" and "the tourist" are based on distance traveled, the length of time spent, and the purposes of the trip. This makes it difficult to gather statistical information that scholars can use to develop a database, describe the tourism phenomenon, and do analyses. The problem is not trivial.

It has been tackled by a number of august bodies over the years, including the League of Nations, the United Nations, the World Tourism

Organization (WTO), the Organization for Economic Cooperation and Development (OECD), the National Tourism Resources Review Commission, and the U.S. Senate's National Tourism Policy Study. The following review of various definitions illustrates the problems of arriving at a consensus. We examine the concept of the movement of people and the terminology and definitions applied by the World Tourism Organization and those of the United States, Canada, the United Kingdom, and Australia. Later, a comprehensive classification of travelers is provided that endeavors to reflect a consensus of current thought and practice.

World Tourism Organization:

The International Conference on Travel and Tourism Statistics convened by the World Tourism Organization (WTO) in Ottawa, Canada, in 1991 reviewed, updated, and expanded on the work of earlier international groups. The Ottawa Conference made some fundamental recommendations on definitions of Tourism, travelers, and tourists. The United Nations Statistical Commission adopted WTO's recommendations on tourism statistics on March 4, 1993.

Tourism:

WTO has taken the concept of tourism beyond a stereotypical image of "holiday-making." The officially accepted definition is: "Tourism comprises the activities of persons traveling to and staying in places outside their usual environment for not more than one consecutive year for leisure, business and other purposes." The term usual environment is intended to exclude trips within the area of usual residence and frequent and regular trips between the domicile and the workplace and other community trips of a routine character.

Main Characteristics of Tourism identified from the Definition:

1. Tourism arises from a movement of people to, and their stay in, various destinations.

2. There are two elements in all tourism: the journey to the destination and the stay including activities at the destination.

3. The journey and the stay take place outside the usual place of resident and work, so that tourism gives rise to activities, which are distinct from those of the resident and the working population of the places, through which th tourist travels and in which they stay.

4. The movement to destinations is of temporary, short term character, with the intention of returning to the usual environment within a few days, weeks or months.

5. Destinations are visited for purposes other than taking up permanent resident or employment remunerated from within the places visited.

Different Definitions of Tourist:

The 19th Century Dictionary defines 'tourist' as a "person who travels for pleasure of traveling, out of curiosity, and because he has nothing better to do." The term 'tourist', the Oxford Dictionary tells us, was used as early as the year 1800. According to the Dictionnare Universal, the 'tourist' is a person who makes a journey for the sake of curiosity, for the fun of traveling, or just to tell others that he has traveled. The term 'tourist' in the sense of a pleasure tour is, however, of recent origin. In the words of Jose Ignacio De Arrilliga, "tourism in its first period was considered as a sport or rather as a synthesis of automobiles, touring, cycling camping, excursions and yachting. In the early nineteenth century, the term 'tourist' assumed a meaning of 'one who makes a tour or tours', especially one who does this for recreation or who travels for pleasure, object of interest, scenery or the like.

Definition by League of Nations:

All the above definitions of the terms 'tourist' are of general nature and, therefore, could not serve the purpose of measurement. It was, however, the League of Nations which did a pioneering work in defining the term for the purposes of statistical measurements. Realizing the importance of collecting tourist statistics and of securing international compatibility, the Committee of Statistical Experts of the League of Nations in the year 1937 established the definition of the term 'tourist'. The League of Nations with the concurrence of member countries defined the term 'foreign tourist' as: "Any person visiting a country, other than that in which he usually resides, for a period of at least 24 hours"

The following persons are considered as tourists as per the above definition:

(i) Persons traveling for pleasure, domestic reasons or for health, etc.

(ii) Persons traveling to meetings, or in a representative capacity of any kind (scientific, administrative diplomatic, religious, athletic, etc.)

(iii) Persons traveling for business purposes.

(iv) Persons arriving in the course of a sea cruise, even when they stay for less than 24 hours. (The latter should be reckoned as a separate group, disregarding if necessary their usual place of residence.)

The following category of persons are not considered as tourists:

(i) Persons arriving, with or without a contract of work, to take up an occupation or engage in any business activity in the country.

(ii) Persons coming to establish a residence in the country.

(iii) Students and young persons in boarding establishments or schools.

(iv) Residents in a frontier zone and persons domiciled in one country and working in an adjoining country.

(v) Travellers passing through a country without stopping, even if the journey takes more than 24 hours.

The above definition was confirmed by the United Nations in the year 1945 and it was as stated that the 'tourist' was a person who stayed in a foreign country for more than 24 hours and less than 6 months for any non-immigrant purpose. The definition was adopted by many countries for the compilation of travel statistics.

United Nations-Rome Conference:

In 1963, the United Nations Conference on International Travel and Tourism held in Rome considered a definition and recommended that it be studied by the United Nations Statistical Commission. A revised definition was prepared and adopted. the conference considered an overall definition of the term 'Visitor', which for statistical purposes describes:

Any person visiting a country other than that in which he has his usual place of residence, for any reasons other than following and occupation remunerated from within the country visited.

This definition covers:

(i) Tourists, i.e., temporary visitors staying at least twenty four hours at the destination visited and the purpose of whose journey can be classified under one of the following headings:

(a) Leisure (recreation, holiday, health, study, religion, and sport);

(b) Business, family, mission, meeting.

(ii) Excursionists, i.e., temporary visitors staying less than twenty-for hours at the destination visited (including travelers on cruises).

The above definition excludes travelers who, in the legal sense, do not enter the country (e.g., air travelers who do not leave an airport's transit area). The Expert Statistical Group on International Travel Statistics convened by the United Nations Statistical Commission recommended in 1967 that countries use the definition of 'visitor' proposed by the United Nations Conference on International Travel and Tourism in Rome in 1963. The Group considered that it would be desirable to distinguish within the definition of visitor a separate class of visitors, who might be described as 'day visitors' or 'excursionists' defined as consisting of visitors on day excursions and other border-crosses for purposes other than employment, cruise passengers, and visitors in transit who do not stay overnight in accommodation provided within the country. The special characteristic of this category of visitors distinguishing it from the main class of visitor, is that there is no overnight stay. In 1968 the Commission approved the Rome definition.

The various definitions discussed above have gradually received general acceptance. According to recent studies. Published by the World Tourism Organization, nearly 75 percent of the countries world over use these definitions in collection of international travel statistics.

Main Characteristics of Tourists identified from the above Definition are mentioned below:

1. He takes up his journey of his own free will.

2. He takes up the journey primarily in search of enjoyment.

3. The money spent on the visit is the money derived from home, not money earned from the places of visit.

4. He finally returns to his point of origin.

Definitions of tourist adopted by different countries:

India:

The definition of 'foreign tourist' adopted by the Government of India's Tourist Department as per the recommendations of the United Nations Conference on International Travel and Tourism, Rome, 1963 is as follows:

"A foreign tourist is a person visiting India on a foreign passport, of whose journey can be classified under one of the following headings"

1. Leisure (recreation, holiday, health, study, religion and sport.)

2. Business, family, mission, meeting.

The following category of persons are, however not regarded as foreign Tourists:

1. Persons arriving with or without a contract, to take up and occupation or engage in activities remunerated from within the country;

2. Persons coming to establish residence in the country;

3. Excursionist i.e., temporary visitor staying less than twenty four hours in the country (including travelers on the cruises).

The following are not included in statistics:

1. Nationals of Pakistan and Bangladesh;

2. Nationals of Nepal entering India through land routes along Indo-Nepal border;

3. All foreigners entering India from Bhutan by land

Definition of a domestic tourist in India:

Domestic Tourist- A per son who travels within the country to a place other than his usual place of residence and stays at hotels or other accommodation establishment run on commercial bases or in dharamshalas or stays with friends and relative and uses sightseeing facilities, or goes on a pilgrimage for a duration of not less than 24 hours or one night and not more than 6 months at a time for any of the following purposes:

- Pleasure (holiday, leisure, sports and so on)
- Pilgrimage, Religious and Social functions.
- Study and Health.

The following are not regarded as domestic tourists:

- Persons arriving with or without a contract to take up an occupation or engage in activities remunerated from within the state center.

- Persons visiting their home town or native place on leave or a short visit for meeting relations and friends, attending social and religious functions and staying in their own houses or with relatives and friends and not using any sightseeing facilities.

Foreigners resident in Indian:

Here we observe that as per the India definition, a traveler must hold a foreign passport to be included in the category of an International Visitor; this implies that Indians settled abroad and holding Indian Passports will not be counted as International Visitors when they come to India for recreation, business or other such purposes. However, nonetheless they are counted as Domestic Visitors and so here we see that coategorisation is based on nationality rather than place of residence. But as per WTO definition they should have been included in the list of International Visitors. From this we can clearly see the difference in the Indian definition and the one given by WTO.

United States:

The Western Council for Travel Research in 1963 employed the term visitor and defined a visit as occurring every time a visitor entered an area under study. The definition of tourist used by the National Tourism Resources Review Commission in 1973 was: "a tourist is one who travels away from home for a distance of at least 50 miles (one way) for business, pleasure, personal affairs, or any other purpose except to commute to work, whether he stays overnight or returns the same day." The National Travel Survey of the U.S. Travel Data Center in 1994 reports on all round-trips with a one-way route mileage of 100 miles or more, and since 1994 on all trips involving one or more nights away from home, regardless of distance. Trips are included regardless of purpose, excluding only crews, students, military personnel on active duty, and commuters.

Canada:

In a series of quarterly household sample surveys known as the Canadian Travel Survey which began in 1978, trips qualifying for inclusion are similar to those covered in the National Travel Survey in the United States. The main difference is that in the Canadian survey, the lower limit for the one-way distance is 50 miles (80 kilometers) rather than 100 miles. The 50-mile figure was a compromise to satisfy concerns regarding the accuracy of recall for shorter trips and the possibility of the inclusion of trips completed entirely within the boundaries of a large metropolitan area such as Toronto. The determination of which length of trip to include in surveys of domestic travel has varied according to the purpose of the survey methodology employed. Whereas there is general agreement that commuting journeys and one-way trips should be excluded, qualifying distances vary. The province of Ontario favors 25 miles. In Canada's international travel surveys the primary groups of travelers identified are nonresident travelers, resident travelers, and other travelers. Both nonresident and resident travelers include both same-day and business travelers. Commuters are included and are not distinguished from other same-day business travelers. Other travelers consist of immigrants, former residents, military personnel, and crews.

United Kingdom:

The National Tourist Boards of England, Scotland, and Northern Ireland sponsor a continuous survey of internal tourism, the United Kingdom Tourism Survey (UKTS). It measures all trips away from home lasting one night or more, taken by residents for holidays, visits to friends and relatives (non holiday), or for business, conferences, and most other purposes. In its findings the UKTS distinguishes between short (1 to 3 nights) and long (4+nights)-duration holiday trips. The International Passenger Survey collects information on both overseas visitors to the United Kingdom and travel abroad by U.K. residents. It distinguishes five different types of visits: holiday independent, holiday inclusive, business, visits to friends and relatives, and miscellaneous.

Australia:

The Australian Bureau of Industry Economics in 1979 placed length of stay and distance travelled constraints in its definition of tourist as follows: "A person visiting a location at least 40 km from his usual place of residence, for a period of at least 24 hours and not exceeding twelve months."

In supporting the use of the WTO definitions, the Australian Bureau of Statistics notes that the term "'usual environment' is somewhat vague." It states that "visits to tourist attractions by local residents should not be included" and that visits to second homes should be included only "where they are clearly for temporary recreational purposes."

Comprehensive Classification of Travelers:

Traveler Terminology of International Tourism

Underlying the foregoing conceptualization of tourism is the overall concept of traveler.

Traveler is defined as "any person on a trip between two or more countries or between two or more localities within his/her country of usual residence."

Travelers may be included in tourism statistics or may not be. All types of travelers engaged in tourism are described as visitors, a term that constitutes the basic concept of the entire system of tourism statistics.

Visitors are persons who travel to a country other than the one in which they generally reside for a period not exceeding 12 months, whose main purpose is other than the exercise of an activity remunerated from within the place visited. Visitors are subdivided into two categories:

1. Tourists, i.e., temporary visitors staying at least twenty four hours in the country visited and the purpose of whose journey can be classified under one of the following headings:

(a) Leisure (recreation, holiday, health, study, religion, and sport);

(b) Business, family, mission, meeting.

2. Excursionists, i.e., temporary visitors staying less than twenty-for hours in the country visited (including travellers on cruises).

The above definition excludes travellers who, in the legal sense, do not enter the country (e.g., air travelers who do not leave an airport's transit area – Transit Visitor).

The drawback of definition of a Visitor as per WTO is that it does not talk about visits made within the country. For these purposes a distinction is drawn between a Domestic and International Visitor

Domestic Visitor:

A person who travels within the country he is residing in, outside the place of his usual environment for a period not exceeding 12 months.

International Visitor:

A person who travels to a country other than the one in which he has a usual residence for a period not exceeding 12 months.

Cruise Passenger:

He is a visitor who arrives in the country aboard cruise ships and who does not spend a night in an accommodation establishment in the country.

The broad class of travelers categorized as migrants, both international and domestic, is also commonly excluded from tourism or travel research. They are excluded on the grounds that their movement is not temporary, although they use the same facilities as other travelers, albeit in one direction, and frequently require temporary accommodation on reaching their destination. The real significance of migration to travel and tourism, however, is not in the one-way trip in itself, but in the long-run implications of a transplanted demand for travel and the creation of new travel destinations for separated friends and relatives.

Notes:

(1) Visitors who spend at least one night in the country visited.

(2) Foreign air or ship crews docked or in lay over and who use the accommodation establishments of the country visited.

(3) Visitors who do not spend at least one night in the country visited although they may visit the country during one day or more and return to their ship or train to sleep.

(4) Normally included in excursionists. Separate classification of these visitors is nevertheless recommended.

(5) Visitors who come and leave the same day.

(6) Crews who are not residents of the country visited and who stay in the country for the day.

(7) When they travel from their country of origin to the duty station and vice-versa (including household servants and dependents accompanying or joining them).

(8) Who do not leave the transit area of the airport or the port? In certain countries, transit may involve a stay of one day or more. In this case, they should be included in the visitor statistics.

(9) Main purposes of visit as defined by the Rome Conference (1963).

Other groups of travelers are commonly excluded from travel and tourism studies because their travel is not affected by travel promotion, although they tend to compete for the same types of facilities and services. Students and temporary workers traveling purely for reasons of education or temporary employment are two leading examples. Another frequently excluded group consists of crews, although they can be regarded as special subsets of tourists and excursionist.

Differences between Travel and Tourism:

Though the words Travel and Tourism are synonymized and used interchangeably but Tourism is a wider concept and encompasses a lot more than travel alone. Travel implies journeys undertaken from one place to another for any purpose including journeys to work and as a part of employment, as a part of leisure and to take up residence; whereas Tourism includes the journey to a destination and also the stay at a destination outside one's usual place of residence and the activities undertaken for leisure and recreation. All tourism includes some travel, but not all travel is tourism. A person may often travel for a wide variety of purposes of which tourism is only one. However if properly handled, a part of the travel for non-tourism purposes can be motivated into travel for tourism as an additional purpose. For example a person on a journey as a part of employment to a place with one or more tourist attractions like a spot of scenic beauty or historical significance, a pilgrimage, a lake, etc. can be induced to spare some time and money for a short visit and or stay for tourism purposes alone. In this sense every traveler is a 'potential' tourist and is upto the mangers of the industry to tap this 'potential' and convert the traveler into an 'actual' tourist.

Summary:

In this lesson we have seen how travel and tourism has changed over time and acquired new dimensions with the development of various facilities and infrastructure. The rapid growth in the movement of people, both domestically and internationally, has brought about an industry of vast proportions and diversity. Also, it is universal-found in all countries of the world, but in greatly varied qualities and proportions. The economic importance and future prospects are also worthy of careful study. These considerations lead to the ways in which the study of tourism can be under taken. There are a number of basic approaches to the study of tourism, and in this book we include all of them in the various chapters. By the time you complete the block you will know a great deal about the social and economic implications of tourism, and you will have developed a keen interest in our world and fascinating panorama of places, peoples, cultures, beauty, and learning that travel provides in such abundance.

CHAPTER II

TOURISM INFRASTRUCTURES

Introduction:

In this unit you will understand the meaning and importance of touristic infrastructure and superstructure in growth and development of tourism at a destination. You will also come to know the role played by public and private sector in development of infrastructure and superstructure.

The second half of the unit explains the various basis of classification of tourism. To understand the phenomenon of tourism better, it has been classified into various types and forms of Tourism.

Need for development of Infrastructure:

The term 'tourist' infrastructure denotes to all those built in services which are essential for modern social life and economic development. It includes all the transport facilities such as roads, railways, and airports, water supplies and sewerages systems, supplies of energy such as electricity and gas and communication facilities. These services are commonly supplied by the public authorities.

Touristic infrastructure means the development of the accommodation sector, transport system, touristic sports, travel agencies, tour operators, the entertainment industry, arts and crafts, the souvenir industry and so on. Basically, infrastructure includes all forms of construction on and below ground required by any inhabited area in intensive communication with the outside world and as a basis for extensive human activity within.

Economists frequently put stress on the development of the touristic infrastructure as it is the pre-requisite for its accelerated economic growth. And that is why it is observed that high level of capital investment in building infrastructure is a characteristic of all the developing countries. The existing infrastructure in India does not cope with the need of serving the touristic economy. In this connection provision of hotels and other supplementary accommodation facilities can be regarded as the key-note to promote tourism in India.

Touristic infrastructure is an essential feature of the developing economy for its rapid growth and development. Tourism is one of the important factors for eradication of unemployment, earning foreign exchange and it also plays a vital role in the regional development of nation.

In the rural areas where anticipated returns on public and private investment of the development of nation. In the rural areas where anticipated returns on public and private investment of the development of the touristic activity by itself in reality may turn out to be nil, if the employment is not realistically planned and done in stages. Therefore, on must be cautious in planning the provision of touristic infrastructure in these areas. The economic exploitation of these areas by tourists generally depends on the natural and economic resources of vast regions more difficult to access, frequently involving problems of connection infrastructural work, the supply of consumer's goods and skilled labour etc.

The influx of tourists have accentuated the need for touristic infrastructure. The discovery and development of the new tourist resorts involve increase in the movement of people, goods and services to the under developed regions. The construction of hotels, production of goods and services etc. largely depend on and is determined by available touristic infrastructure.

The discrepancy between the existing infrastructure and the growing requirement of the economy reveal the importance of building tourist infrastructure. The development of tourism may entail a more complete utilization of the system of infrastructure and of services and in turn improve the productivity of related investment.

The building up of touristic infrastructure is aimed at extending inter-regional economic ties which promote and accelerate the formation of domestic market. Expansion of transport system increases the ties of the countryside with the tourist spots and promotes the disintegration of the natural economy. The territory is an asset which must be exploited for the benefit of the entire economy. The importance of the transport facilities has a great impact on the socio-economic conditions of a developing economy. It is observed that weakness of transport links between various tourist places in the exterior is a feature of the developing economy which is also one of the factors responsible for their mounting economic difficulties.

There is a need to open new tourist spots, important from the point of view of domestic as well as foreign tourists, with a simultaneous transport construction. Shortage of capital and difficulties of planning in condition of economic backwardness has been on the way of building suitable infrastructure for the development of tourism. In addition to this, it is also observed that the existing capacities of the infrastructure because the demand for means of transport is subjected to big seasonal fluctuations. It is noticed that large hotels and transport facilities are utilized for shorter periods and the rest of period they are partly used.

Thus there is a question of efficient use of existing infrastructure. Since the maintenance of the whole infrastructure in condition of tropical climate, monsoons, and short temperature fluctuation is expensive, its use to optimums capacity is very acute in building new infrastructure. It is realized that while exploitation of land water resources for agricultural development constitutes the important bas for the regional development of the nation, touristic riches of the country offer an additional element of considerable significance for the economic development of the region. India faces a lot of problems in building the necessary touristic infrastructure which plays a crucial role in accelerating economic development. The state should exert all-pervading pressures on their entire economy to make good hotels, transports, power electricity and all other services needed for this propose. An increase in the production of the electric power meets the basic requirements of the economy and above all promotes the development of the industry. As the industry develops, the demand for electric power rises.

The development of tourism requires such factors like financial resources and technical personnel for large scale exploration and evaluation of the tourist areas. This will certainly determine the possibility of modern tourism. Lack of technical personnel's has also been one of the greatest bottlenecks in smooth running of this highly specialized industry. There are already for regional technical institutes at Delhi, Mumbai, Kolkata and Chennai and number of Food Craft Centers are also run, which are training young men and women to take assignment mainly in the accommodation sector.

There is a growing need for personnel in the field of tourism management. Tourism education has largely been neglected, but the proper and efficient functioning of tourist industry requires a complete knowledge about the latest techniques developed in the field. In the frame work of planning, the integrated economic development in the regions, it is of utmost importance to accord priority to the construction of a regionally adequate infrastructure along with the measures of land and water resources development of the regions. There is also urgent need for a detailed research relating to the different aspects of tourist industry, in order to lay a sound base for its future development.

Touristic Infrastructure:

An integrated package of infrastructural facilities water power, road, air transportation, tourist attractions etc. as give in figure 2.1, is the basic urgent requirement for India to achieve its goal. Boosting tourist traffic in this country and others in the region depended largely on the extent to which these minimum facilities are provided to the tourists. The place of tourism in national planning varies according to the priority accorded to it. Many countries regard it as luxury industry and accord it a low priority in their national plans. The plans of nation are based on the priorities, infrastructure, inputs available and the importance of balanced socio economic development. The successful setting up of the tourist industry is dependent basically upon the growth and development of the general economic infrastructure of the nation.

The place of tourism in national planning varies according to the priority accorded to it. Many countries regard it as luxury industry and accord it a low priority in their national plans. The plans of nation are based on the priorities, infrastructure, inputs available and the importance of balanced socio economic development. The successful setting up of the tourist industry is dependent basically upon the growth and development of the general economic infrastructure of the nation.

The infrastructure requirements may be divided into the following groups:
- Those which provide lines of access and communication with the outside world.
- Those which enable the movement of people at the destination.
- Those which supply essential services of lighting, heating power, water, drainage and sewage disposal for the development.

Tourist may reach a particular destination by road, rail or water or by air or by a combination of these modes of transportation. To provide the necessary infrastructure may accordingly call for the construction of the roads, railway lines, harbors, airport runways. These all are required to carry the required volume of traffic to and from the tourist areas. There is also a need for telecommunication and other means of communication. The access work has to be extended to provide means of communication and movement within the area. In addition, network of utility services extending over the whole area of development has to provide for the public conveniences and night lighting etc.

The underground and service installations described above are of paramount importance to successful tourism. Construction of these require considerable period of time. It is best to build roads of adequate dimension initially instead of small inadequate road which later have to be torn up and replaced with better and more adequate facilities. Great care should be taken in the construction of roads. They should be hard, all weather surfaced, be properly graded and drained. They should be safe and built to international standard. Service installations such as road side facilities, road side parks, road side picnic facilities, rest park which include toilet facilities, scenic turnouts, auto repair and service facilities are all needed for tourism.

The airport runway should be built to international standard. The runways may be used for the new super-jets and there may not be heavy expenditure on modifications in future. Roadside parks, picnic tables, rest areas, scenic turnouts and similar road side park type facilities should be regularly maintained to keep the park in a neat orderly condition.

Service stations should be providing in sufficient quantity. The attendants at these stations should be courteous, hospitable and friendly. They must have the knowledge of tourist stations in their immediate vicinity and advise the tourists concerning accommodation, shopping and entertainment in their community.

Infrastructure:

- WATER SUPPLY SYSTEM
- SEWAGE DISPOSAL SYSTEMS
- NATURAL OR ARTIFICIAL GAS LINES.
- ELECTRIC CONNECTION SYSTEMS
- DRAINAGE SYSTEMS
- HIGHWAYS
- ROAD DRIVE
- PARKING LOTS
- PARKS
- NIGHT LIGHTING
- AIRPORT RUNWAYS
- PARKING AREAS.
- ACCESS DRIVES
- FACILITIES AT AIRPORT
- MARINE & DOCK FACILITIES
- BUS AND TRAIN STATIONS FACILITIES
- RAILWAY LINES
- OTIIER TOURISM INSTALLATIONS

Touristic Superstructure:

The super structural services are also needed for tourism development. It includes access facilities for transport (airport terminals, rail and coach stations) hotels, motel and other accommodation units, café, bars and sport recreational facilities and entertainment. Most of the super-structural facilities are provided by private companies or individual entrepreneurs central state and local governments also give financial and other aids for these facilities.

Touristic Superstructure:

- Accommodation
- Entertainment
- Restaurant
- Shopping

Touristic superstructure comprises all the individual facilities within a tourist area and consists of passenger traffic terminals, accommodation, hotel motel, catering and entertainment and shopping etc. These are mostly costly of all the elements as they involve the construction of building. Most of these facilities are provide by individual developers and operators. These are planned individually or may be components of an overall plan. Passenger traffic terminals, airport building and terminal, port facilities, railway, bus and coach terminals etc. are usually planned in conjunction with the related infrastructure. The capacity of a destination is determined by the capacity of its accommodation units. There is a need to establish an optimum, accommodation capacity which is economically viable for the operators and in turn for the economic prosperity of the community.

Other facilities like catering, entertainment and shops does not represent much of the planning problems. These are readily provided by commercial entrepreneurs. The nature and Varity of these facilities matters much and goes to the root of the nature of the tourist destination. In almost all the tourist planning, these facilities are being regulated. Special care should be taken of the architectural design of building. The hotel building should be distinctively designed in accordance with the local environment. The tourists immerse themselves in an environment totally different from that which they are accustomed to in their everyday life. Air-conditioning, central heating, and plumbing and other modern comfort amenities must also be used in the building of the hotel.

Accommodations are of great importance for successful tourism. They are fundamental to tourism. The hotel must provide the various types of physical facilities, prices ranges locations and services offered which meet the expectations, wants and needs of the travelers. The demand for accommodations varies according to the social class, price that the guests are willing to pay, level of prices and similar other consideration. Suitable accommodation should be available for all segments of the market. In planning accommodations, the point to be noted are the nature of the environment, the destination itself, the expected markets, the mode of transportation the type activities engaged in at the destination etc. Before any investment in hotels and similar lodging facility is made, the traveling and vacation habits of the prospective guests should be carefully studied.

Construction of large luxury hotels and development of holiday resorts could come into the picture as of part of a comprehensive approach. Shortage of hotel accommodation has been one of the inhibiting factors in the development of tourism in India, and whatever accommodation is available is concentrated in the certain metropolitan cities and hill stations. There are many tourist attractions. Where are no suitable accommodation facilities? We require both primary and secondary type of accommodation.

Role of Maintenance of Infrastructure and Superstructure:

All the states have started taking part in almost all the sphere which is related to the welfare of the public. Tourism is no exception to this. The state creates services which are indirectly useful to tourism. It encourages and supports the private sector and creates a few pilot schemes. The importance of tourism in the national economy is gaining a place in almost all the countries of the world. It is an expanding industry. Expansion of tourism increases the level of employment by creating new jobs. Construction of new building is one of the parts of tourism activities which constitutes a capital investment and provides work for a number of people. There is a market for certain products produced in the country and with the application of multiplier effect and accelerated effect, almost all the section of the society are benefited.

Thus tourism is a public utility infrastructure. The public authorities have an important role in the creation of necessary infrastructure for tourism. Tourism infrastructure consists of all the units that exist for handling tourist traffic. Tourist demand causes the creation of transport and communication facilities, urbanism, irrigation, etc., resulting in a general economic improvement of benefit to all the inhabitants.

Intervention by public authorities to support and promote national tourism, has assumed a completely new appearance over the last few years. State intervention takes the form of setting up bodies for controlling tourism activities by giving financial support to private organizations operating in the sector for setting up advertising agencies abroad, for creating tourism study centers and for the development of research and survey in order to gain a better knowledge of internal and external markets.

Tourism infrastructure is usually understood to include:

• Supply of network and mains: This includes water, electricity, gas, telecommunications, sewers, garbage etc.

• Basic public utilities and services: This is the administration of religious places, health, education, culture, commerce, police etc.

The infrastructure ensures the operation of facilities essential to modern life like health, communication, supplies, administration safety etc. To meet the needs of tourist, it is not enough to see that they reach their destination comfortably and quickly and are suitably housed and fed. They make trip for a particular purpose. Such facilities therefore, should be afford able to them. Along with transport and accommodations there is a whole range of supplementary units for the utilization of tourist resources. Some events i.e. international games, exhibitions, conferences lead to the construction of several permanent structure. After the event is over, the buildings remain and are used for other purposes.

A country wishing to receive tourists must give them the best of reception by making available the necessary public services. Roads are needed for travel. Car park, beaches, health services, security, services, port post and telephone facilities are very much needed. At any place the tourists may be in the need of al these facilities. These services should be provided in such a way that tourists do not feel any inconvenience and the quality should be of at least of that standard which the tourists enjoy in their own country.

Some of the infrastructure helping tourism may not have been created for purely tourist purpose, but their smooth running will help for the reputation of the country in the field of tourism. Water, gas and electricity services should be provided. There must be postal connections and places must have medical facilities. For example, clinics should be established at winter resorts, children's nurseries and game rooms have to be built. The economic activity of a country benefits from the existence of correct infrastructure. This is particularly for the countries which are at developing stage.

In addition to the above, the state also provides specialized tourist equipment at the resorts e.g. equipment at ski-resorts, small pleasure ports and air field in the tourist areas. These installation are beyond the scope of private enterprise as the initial investment is much higher as compared to the returns. The setting up of a museum, restaurants, work of art and safeguarding the countryside can only be financed by public funds.

Thus we find that the state takes number of activities which are a must for tourism development in a country. Some of these activities are social responsibilities and some of them are beyond the scope of private sector.

The extent of the state's role in tourism varies according to the conditions and circumstances peculiar to each country. The Politic economic-constitutional system, socio-economic development degree of tourism development etc. vary from nation to nation. In general, in almost all the centrally planned economies, the state is the sole initiator, executor and administrator of all tourism programmes.

Types of Tourism:

Tourism is an economic product meeting the demand of the human beings and as such its market is created according to fluctuation of supply and demand. The majority of the demand of tourism enumerate the motives which can prompt a person to make a journey for tourist region. These motives are varied and do exercise a decisive influence on the destination of the journey. Thus the diversity of touristic motivations generate the various types of tourism. The types of tourism can be categorized under the various heading.

On the Basic of Origin and Destiny:

Tourism is not limited within the boundaries of a nation. Tourists may travel to a foreign country or within their own borders. The following types of tourism are found in the tourist flow patterns within a national boundary:

• **Inbound Tourism:**

In this category are included the tourists received by a certain country from other countries, the later being the origin country of the tourist:

• **Outbound Tourism:**

There are many persons of a country who go abroad. Outgoing tourism comprises of tourists normally residing in the country and going abroad.

• **Domestic Tourism:**

The national inhabitants of a country travel occasionally to other places within their national territories. The movement of tourist within the country of nationality is known as domestic tourism.

On The Basis Of Movement Pattern:

The tourists stay in a place for a long time or they travel continuously and spend little time in various tourist places. On the basis of how the tourists spend their time, the following distinctions can be made.

• Residential Tourism:

Residential tourism comprises of those tourists who have a holiday period of over on month and spend it in one specific tourist place. These tosurist choose the quieter and peaceful places with a mild climate. Residential tourism usually takes place in the peak season i.e. the highest point of the total demand.

• Seasonal Tourism:

Seasonal tourism comprises of those tourists who have a holiday period of not more than one month. These tourists also remain in one specific place for not more than month. The main point of difference in the residential and seasonal tourism is the time factor.

• Roving Tourism.

There are certain categories of tourists who travel throughout their holiday period. They travel from places to places and never spend more than 5 nights anywhere. They are continuously on the move. Their purpose of travel is different from those of residential and seasonal tourists. They are most wide spread in spring and autumn:

On The Basis The Seasonal Character Of Tourism:

There are various factors influencing the mass tourist's flows during a particular season. Some of the incentives for travel for a sporting nature depend on natural conditions and the seasons - hunting, fishing, winter sports etc. There are also religious festivals-fairs, art and music festivals, trade fairs exhibitions which attract the tourists during a particular season. The following types of tourism belong to this category:

• Winter Tourism:

In most of the European countries, this tourism takes place in the month of December to March. Winter tourism have two prime incentive-the search for snow and search for sunshine.

• Summer Tourism:

Summer tourism take place during the summer months. The main incentives for this type of tourism are sun-shine and bathing, preferably in the sea. In he European countries, it is a very varied type of mass tourism. It has low average quality than that of other seasons.

• Circumstantial Tourism:

It is a localized tourism as it is attracted by traditional festivals of a religious artistic, sportive, folklorist nature.

On the Basis of the Incentives

There are various incentives which generate the tourist flow patterns. Therefore, tourism may be classified as follows:

• Recreational Tourism

Tourists who wish to devote their holidays to rest, to recuperate their physical and psychic and who wish to refresh themselves when tired are included in the categories of recreational tourism. There's is the longest stay in tourist resorts which generate relaxation to them - by the sea, in the hills, in the rest centers which ensure for them the sought after comfort. Their main preference is the climatic resorts. The tourists having intellectual incentives, want to see new things, know new people, their history, art and local customs and their natural surroundings are also included recreational tourism.

• Pleasure Tourism or Leisure Tourism:

It includes those tourists who leave on holiday for a change of climate out of curiosity, to relax, to see something new, enjoy good scenery, unfamiliar folk lore, and the quiet and noisy modern tourist centers. Some tourist of this category fined pleasure in traveling from the fact of constantly changing places and surroundings. The constant expansion of industrialization and automation, the anonymity and hectic pace of life, and the growing lack of leisure in a frequently irksome routine job lead men today to look to leisure activities and travel as escape from the pressures and strains they are subjected to. These tourists look for peace and quietness in their surroundings.

• Sporting Tourism:

Like sport itself, tourism is a mass phenomenon of this century. Like sports too, it is only natural in its potential neither good nor evil in essence and can be positive in its effects only if it is subjected to wise planning and guidance. This tourism is motivated by the wish to practice sports. Water and winter sports, hunting and fishing are in good demand. In this case there are big sports football, hockey, boxing championship etc. which attract the country not only the sportsmen concerned, but also thousands of followers and other interested people.

There are also sporting tourism of the devotees. There are winter sports, natural, mountain climbing, trekking, hiking, sailing, golf, hunting, fishing, sports, canoeing, water skiing, skating, under sea fishing, dancing, beach games, mini-golf, hydro-cycling, and the various indoor amusements which offer fun and diversion. Countries which are well placed to develop sports have a good scope for tourist flow. They can get good benefits from the sporting tourism. For the elite sportsmen, tourism in one of the strongest motivating forces. "Citius, Altuis, Vor Tius" is all very well, but more enjoyable in Tokyo than in Birmingham or Belgrade. The thought that a high performance will qualify one for world travel is perhaps the major motivation for the top flight athlete.

India is place for existing sports. Polo is played at the important clubs in the principal cities of India. Skiing in Himalayas, golf courses, yacht clubs, trekking, sun bathing water sports are some of the specialties in the field of sports.

• Business or Technical Tourism:

According to some theoreticians, sociologists and economists a business journey cannot be regarded as tourist journey because it lacks the voluntary element'. According to them, business journeys are professional journeys and do not leave to the person concerned either the choice of destination or time of his journey and thus the fundamental idea of liberty of the individual in tourism is absent. On the other side, all the definition of tourism include business journeys under tourism. Business tourism implies not only the professional journey of industrialist but also all other journeys to fairs and exhibitions or of technical achievements which awaken or rather generate interest among people who have nothing in common with the profession in question. The inclusion of business journey into tourism is also due to the fact that businessmen behave not only as consumers but often during their free time, as real tourists by profiting from the attractions offered by the country.

On the Basis of the Socio-Economic Aspects of Demand:

Tourism can again be classified on the basis of the economic aspect of demand:-

• Self-financing Tourism:

It includes the tourists who finance their own tour to satisfy demand. All the incoming, outgoing and domestic tourism belong to this category. Self-financing tourism is profitable both for the private tourist enterprise and for the national economy.

• Juvenile Tourism:

This classification of tourism is based on the informative and educative objective of tourists.

• Social Tourism:

Social tourism is found in sector of the population whose income level does not permit to meet their demands. Social tourism is made feasible with the help of and through all sorts of facilities provided by the state and by some of the private enterprises. It is observed that the benefit of social tourism goes to the national population as most of the tourism to this category belong to domestic tourism and very few to outgoing tourism.

According to Range:

Tourism may also be classified according to its ranges:-

• Domestic Tourism:

In this case people travel outside their normal domicile to other areas within the country. People find it easy to travel domestically because there are no language, currency and documentation barrier.

• International Tourism:

It is a kind of tourism wherein people travel to a country other than in which they normally live and which forms separate national unit within its own political and economic system. Due to the different currencies internal tourism has repercussions on the balance of payments as each country has to balance its transactions with the rest of the world. There are also obstacles put by the authorities for crossing the national frontiers, with the result, there is need for documentation – passports visa and other conditions of entry and movement. This all regulates the flow of the tourists. Now a days, due to the improvement in the language skills, currency and customs and the growing free movement of people between developing countries, the distinction between domestic and international tourism is diminishing.

On the Basis of Purpose of Visit:

Tourism can also be classified on the basis of purpose of visit of the tourists:-

• Holiday Tourism

There is a now a significant demand recorded by the tourist industry for active holidays, both national and international. In some pursuits i.e. climbing and skiing, the element of risk is uppermost. Old resorts based their attractions on holidays and sports. In holiday camps, a great majority of people showed a desire for a physical recreation and there was strong correlation between good behaviour and sports participation. It is seen that optional vacation planning improved attitudes towards physical activities, both during holiday and on returning home. People have a great interest in hobbies holidays. Family walks and common vacations, as well as camping and many of the family tourist recreations are valuable.

- **Business Tourism**
- **Common Interest Tourism:**

It includes tourists with other specific purposes for their journeys and some-times sub-divided further into:

- Visit to friends and relatives.
- Study tourism
- Religious tourism and
- Miscellaneous purpose tourism

On the Basis of Sociological Aspects:
Some other terms have been often applied more or less discriminately to tourism, in particular, mass, popular and social tourism, to which it is desirable to attach more precious meaning at the outset.

- **Mass Tourism:**

When large numbers of people participate in tourism, it is called as mass tourism. It is essentially a quantitative motive and is based n the proportion of population participating in tourism or on the volume of tourist activity.

- **Popular Tourism:**

It is qualitative motion and by its nature it may give rise to mass tourism. It denotes activities meeting with a wide acceptance by people, because of their attractiveness and availability. The acceptance by people may be as it meets their needs or tastes and is availabil9ity at a low price.

- **Social Tourism:**

Social tourism is the type of tourism produced by those who could not be able to meet the cost without social interventions i.e. without the assistance of an association to which the individual belongs, or by the states

Problems in the Development of Social Tourism:
The worker throughout the world are being allowed paid holidays either by law or by collective agreement. Large number of workers are obliged to spend their holidays at home partly because of lack of means for tourist expenses and partly because of lack of means for tourist expenses and partly because of lack of information, transport difficulties and shortage of suitable accommodation. All those problems can easily be solved through

organized social tourism. The financial difficulties can be overcome through subsides and saving schemes, experience and information can be solved through package deals with carriers and accommodation problem can be solved through contracts with resorts. Thus organized social tourism can bring tourism within the reach of many who would otherwise be unable to travel.

The problem of finance can be dealt with by the use of saving fund. The trade union can take an active part in the saving schemes. The members of these unions can contribute and in holiday time they may be allowed to withdraw a little larger than deposits. The saving fund scheme is very useful in Belgium, France and Australia. There can be some holiday funds which can be organized jointly by some unions and employers, with the participation of transport and hotels and transport enterprises and the state or local authorities. In France, works committees subside travel and run holiday homes for the workers, partly by organizing contributions. In Netherlands, some employers grant holiday bonus of upto 2% of the annual wage, in addition to normal holiday pay.

In the United Kingdom, holiday bonuses are also granted to the workers. The amount is fixed in proportion to length of services. In Belgium, workers are paid a "holiday wages" which under the law must be double the normal wages, and employer some time grants cash benefits for travel. In Russia, the trade unions pay the whole or most of the lodging expenses in workers rest homes. In Poland the state pays part of expenses of travel and accommodation. In New Zealand, the state employees are benefited from price reduction hotels. Another form of financial assistance is the provision facilities such as holiday centers or through state subsidy or tax allowance. In France, nonprofit making associations for population education, sports, culture and tourism are exempted from the turnover tax and entertainment tax. The state gives assistance in the form of equipment for camps and for youth organizations. In East Germany, the authorities finance the investment of all services. In Norway, state loans are awarded either interest free, or at reduced rate for the development of holiday centers.

In the case of transport difficulties, transport companies often cooperate in special reduced fare schemes. Chartered flight can help a lot in reducing a travel cost to the individuals. In USA some carriers operate credit schemes as "Travel now pay later". In Federal Republic of Germany, 33% for group of 25 or more and even greater reductions for students, school children or youth organizations are provided for railway travel. In Belgium cheap rail tickets are issued to the workers and their families during the holiday season on presentation of a social security card or certificate from the employer. In Hungry 50% reduction is offered to all person entitled to holidays with pay. In Czechoslovakia, a free rail ticket is attached to the workers holiday form.

The problem of accommodation is another difficulty for the development of social tourism. Hotels being beyond the reach of low income groups. From the point of view of social tourism, supplementary accommodation is very important. Holiday centers for workers have been established by a number of trade unions and employers. In Argentina, a number of trade unions and employers. In Argentina, a number of holiday centers have been established in beauty spots at sea-side consisting of special boatels, bungalows, and chalets. These are provided with some other recreational facilities. In Switzerland, there are number of holiday centers for social tourism. There is a famous health resorts Leysin-with the progress of medicine, it was meant that it would gradually diminish but with the cooperation of certain organization, the resort was adopted to attract a new type of tourists. Small golf courses, a swimming pool, tennis court and arrangements of schemes were establishment and sanatoria and hotels were converted to meet the new demand. Caravan camps and hotels are popular with young tourists. Camping has the advantage of being one of the least expensive forms of holiday. Financial aid is given to camps by the state in France and other countries. In Greece, camps are operated by some large industrial firms for the benefit of their employees. In most of the countries, these camps are run by camping clubs and youth movement.

As regards the lack of information, the public authorities, trade unions and the national tourist organization and other bodies must give attention for supplying the information's of the special attraction of different resorts. In USA, there are information offices in large cities. These offices issue publication advising workers for spending their holiday. In Canada bulletins are issued to the trade union offices and other organizations.

"We have been greatly impressed by the importance attached to social tourism in the concept of the developing economy of our country. The object of social tourism is not only to provide holidays to people of the lower income groups who normally are unable to afford them, but to fit them into schemes of the newly developed ideas of paid holidays for workers, assistance in the youth travel movement as well as to the movement of pilgrims throughout our land. Our objective is the welfare state. The welfare state depends for its existence upon the willing cooperation of the working classes and the peasantry who form 98% of the population of our country. The welfare state has to function for their benefit and would have no meaning if it did not. One of the objectives of the welfare state must necessarily be of paid holidays to workers and subsidized travel for the youth of our country. It is one of the essential items and is a kind of education for the young people to be able to see their country, meet the people of cultural interest as well as of industrial importance.

It is only thus that the lack of understanding of each other's needs, of the different people that live in this country, can be put to an end. Further such social tourism world create deep interest and enthusiasm for the great industrial revolution, we are witnessing. Planned economy has to be brought home gradually to large masses of our people by affording them an opportunity of seeing our industrial plans in action. So visit to Nangal Bhakra, to the steel plants, to Sindri Chittaranjan. Bangalore and other centers must necessarily be arranged on a confessional basis for those wanting to see the sites and acquaint themselves with the spot of the great industrial revolution."

In 1958, the Standard and Rate Structure Committee recommended that"

• The system of paid holidays for workers should be introduced in every hotel establishment and extended elsewhere. This must be a compulsory provision.

• Subsidized tours on every large basis should be organized by the railways, for the student community and young people generally;

• Subsidized tours should be organized on a large scale for pilgrims to travel from their homes to the places of pilgrimage throughout India.

Other countries earmark large sum of money for this particular purpose of oracle tourism.

Cultural Tourism:

Cultural Tourism covers all those aspect of travel where by people learn about each other's ways of life and thought. Personal and international contact have always been an important way of spreading ideas about other cultures. Tourism is an important means of promoting cultural relations and international cooperation. Development of cultural factors within a nation can be viewed as means of enhancing resources for tourism. The whole way in which a country represents itself to tourists can be considered its cultural factors. The food drinks, hospitality manufactured and craft product and other aspects of a nation's life, appeal to travelers and visitors. The success of tourism depends not only on better transportation and hotels, but also on adding a particular national flavor in keeping with traditional ways of life and in projecting a favorable image of the benefits of such goods and services.

Cultural tourism is characterized by a service of motivation such as the desire to learn and to study in a center famous for its high standards of living and teaching, to study the habits of the institutions and the life of foreign people to visit historical monuments (traces of past civilization) the great modern achievement, the art galleries, the great religion centers, to participate in art festivals and celebrations, to take part in and assist in music theater, dance, folklore festivals etc.

India is large and popular country with a great past and great tradition. It can boast of some four thousand years of civilized life. It is oldest living civilization whose traditions arise directly from its past. For these reasons, for any foreigners a visit to India must have profound cultural impact, and in this first and broad sense, all forms of tourism in India involved, at least an aspect of culture-contact and is therefore potentially cultural tourism", Theatres, libraries, museums and other national institutional are a great asset in attracting the interested visitors. Museum and monuments are among the expected features in tourism itinerary. Cultural tourism will constitute one of the important features of the plan and it is proposed to evolve master plans of the areas surrounding some of the selected archaeological centers with the object of preserving their environment and natural setting. It is suggested to acquire the services of experts in cultural tourism under the aegis of UNESCO and UNDP to assist in the preparation of these plans.

The following group of monuments are included in the proposal:
• Cave temples of Elephanta, Ajanta and Ellora;
• Buddhist Centres at Sarnath, Gaya, Nalanda, Rajgir, Kushinagar, Sravasti and Sanchi;
• Bijapur, Aihole Badami, Pattadkal and Hampi; and
• Khajuraho, Bhubaneshwar, Puri and Konark;

Cultural tourism will constitute one of the important features of the five year plans and it is proposed to evolve master plans of the areas surrounding some of the selected archaeological centers with the object of preserving their environmental and natural setting. Some years ago India acquired the services of Dr. F.R. Allchein in cultural tourism under the aegis of UNESCO to assist in the preparation of these plans. The cave temples of

Elephanta. Ajanta and Ellora, Buddhists centers at Sarnath, Gaya, Nalanda, Rajgir, Kushinagar rasvati and Sanchi, Bijapur, Aihole, Badami, Pattadkal Hampi, Khajuraho, Bhubaneswar, Puri and Konarak are being taken under the plan.

Conference Tourism:

Conference tourism is gaining more and more importance. There are a number of international conferences, conventions meetings of the statutory bodies, of international organisation and an innumerable conferences, assemblies and national symposiums, which are held every year within different countries. Local, state, national and international conventions are continually being held. Yearly meetings are held by national association, union groups, fraternities and societies, educational associations, professional groups, and meetings sometimes out number hundreds and thousands of participants. These participants stay several days in the economic aspect of conferences. They have to prepare appropriate premises and to build conference halls with all the necessary modern equipment to ensure their satisfactory operation.

The tourists visit India with varied aims. They visit India with the purpose to get into the heart of a country, eat the traditional food, drink the local beverages and live as near to the natives as possible. Many of them prefer to survey strange lands from familiar surroundings. India has facilities for all types of tourists. It is a colorful and picturesque nation. Its monuments testify to one of the oldest and richest civilizations. The forests, mountains, valleys, plains or desert walls, all are of great interest to the naturalist the botanist and the lovers of nature.

Religious Tourism:

Man undertook journeys to places which he considered sacred or where he thought his deity resided. And so began the practice of going on pilgrimages which has remained in vague throughout the ages with of course local variation and periodic adjustments. The practice of religious expeditions to sacred places took deep roots among the Egyptians, the Jews and the Greeks. It attained its zenith under Islam, the prophet proclaimed it to be the duty of every Muslim, at least once in his life, to visit Mecca, Mohammed's birth place.

Christian pilgrimages arose from devotion to the memory of the Christ. The devotees made it a point to visit places which were invested with memories of their Lord's earthly life. Two of the most sacred places to which the Christians visit are Beruthelem and Jerusalem. As the number of pilgrims swelled so increased the number of places to which they would like to visit.

While pilgrim resort were falling in the east, their counter parts began to emerge in the west. The stating point in west is found in the veneration of religions martyrs and the care of their tombs. Pilgrims were also drawn to the graves of saints and seers, convinced as they were of their divine success and blessings. Those who were known for the performance of miracles also attracted devotees and believers from far off places. Africa has the largest the number of tombs of martyrs. Rome got the pride of place among the holy cities of the world as it has got the famous tombs of St. Peter and St. Paul.

Another motive for pilgrimage is the object of securing relics from holy places. It has been highly desirable in many parts to acquire some object which has enjoyed at least a mere connection with the hollowed corpse. The religious people take little wax dropped from a sanctified paper, a catholic devotee bent off the toe of mummified body of a saint in Goa. Some pilgrims carry away as a memento a little dust from the graves of saint and martyrs. There are pilgrims who take 'parsad' from the religious temples. Many people go on a pilgrimage in order to ask for forgiveness of their sins. It may be called as expiatory pilgrimage. There are also pilgrimages undertaken to thank the deity for fulfilling the devotee's wishes. Thus we find that the journey for religious purposes has always been considered an act of obedience to the supposed will of God or the deity concerned.

India is one of the oldest country of pilgrimages. People have come to this sub-continent in all ages and from all parts of the world in quest of religion, knowledge and spiritual satisfaction. Religious minded tourists have a deep interest in India's monumental heritage. There is no place in our country which is not held sacred for one reason or another. Its rivers and lakes, mountains, sea beaches, towns and temples, are all attraction for domestic and foreign travelers. India has been the birth place of many religions-Hinduism, Buddhism and Jainism and today Muslims, Christians, Sikhs and Zoroastrians live and worship peacefully in the secular state of ours.

Pilgrims naturally form the over whelming bulk in this group. We can sub-divide them into:

• The regular visitors and tourists of Indian domicile in various parts of the world, people who are anxious to discover the cultural centers of the religions of their forefathers;

• The growing number of Buddhists from Japan, Thailand, Ceylon etc. Who visit the great centers associated with Buddha.

• The Americans and Europeans who are interested in some aspect of Hinduism, Buddhism, Islamism and Sikhism.

The Hindus, Muslims, Christians, Sikhs, Jains and Buddhists and the followers of other faiths and religions have their holy places which they must visit at least once in a life time. Thus we find that the pilgrim's traffic is the biggest part of tourist trade. It is very common that the travellers fits a visit to holy site or a tourist resort into his business trips. This should ensure a steady stream of visitors to India from other countries.

The government has some time back highlighted the importance of the development of religious tourism. We have neglected to make the most of the holy places attractive which are of interest to tourist. There is a considerable scope for promoting tourists from South-East Asian countries by offering different package tours of places of Buddhist interest. Such tours could cover Bodhgaya, where the Buddha attained enlightment, Sarnath, where in the quietness of the Deer Park, the Budha preached his first sermon, Sanchi with its great Stupa, and Rajgir in Bihar. Important Buddhist sites like Ajanta and Ellora and the ancient universities of Nalanda create great interest among tourists.

There could be a wider tour of India, in which the visitors might see magnificent religious places Christian churches in Orissa, richly carved temples of southern India, huge mosques at Delhi and Agra and beautiful Golden Temple at Amritsar, and the array of shrines, temples and palaces of Banaras. For religious tours to be successful, the guide must be hand-picked, knowing something of the tenets of different religious answering knowledgeably.

Forms of Tourism:

There are various forms of tourism. The different forms are based on he duration, the number in the party and the economic effects of tourism. These varied forms can be categorized as follows:

According to the number in Party:

This distinction is based on how the individual elements of the trip are bought by the tourists:

Individual Tourism:

FIT- Free Individual Traveler-When 1 to 10 people move for tour it is included in FIT. They may purchase a tailor made tour-made as per their requirement or package tour (ready-made tour).

Group Tourism

When more than 15 people are traveling for tourism purpose it is group tourism GIT (Group Inclusive Tour) they usually go for ready-made package tours.

According to Arrangements:

• Independent:

Accommodation and transport arranged separately by tourist. Individual tourism is the case, when a person or group of persons leave on journey for which they themselves establish the destination and programmes and which can at any time be freely altered. The tourist move about individually or as a member of the group, irrespective of the way the travel and the stay is arranged. Transportation, accommodation and other elements are arranged separately either by the tourist himself directly with the carrier, hotel or other suppliers or through a travel agent. The individual or the family themselves take care of ensuring such provision or services as they might need. This is known as independent travel.

• Inclusive or Package Tours:

Organized collective tourism (organized tourism) or inclusive tour is where the tourist buys a trip, for which he is unable to distinguish the prepaid cost of his fare from the cost of accommodation and other element. It is also known as a package tour. The tourist may move about as an individual or as a member of group, according to the particular arrangements entered into. Thus, in this form of tourism, a travel agency offers to anyone interested, against payment of an inclusive sum, participation in a journey to a destination and following a programme and time table fixed in advance for an entire group. The participants do not have to concern themselves with anything, all the provisions and services being assured by the organizer.

According to Duration:

• Long Haul Tourism:

It implies a journey of long duration, say, several weeks or months for the tourist himself. In view of the extreme mobility of modern tourism, principally motorized, a long journey as a general rule means a visit to several countries, which results in the journeys of short stay in each tourist places. The journeys or stay at destination, should be at least 24 hours. It is also known as trip or visit.

• Short Haul Tourism:

It covers brief journey s of a week or ten days. When numerous, their economic importance is considerable for the nation. Sociologically, this type of tourism suits a clientele who are unable to avail long holidays.

• Excursion Tourism:

It does not involve any overnight stay. These are usually described as day trips or day visits, both domestically and internationally. Excursion tourism has been reintroduced into the WTO definition of tourism. It is thus a journey not exceeding 24 hours and without accommodation having to be provided. Excursion tourism is important in the areas where the favorable rate of exchange allows interesting purchase to be made at the time of journey.

According to Means of Transportation Used:

• Pedestrain Tourism (hikers

• Road Tourism (Motor coach.

• Motorised tourism. (Motor car)

• Rail Tourism

• Maritime Tourism (cruises).

• Air Tourism.

On the Basis of Effect on Balance of Payment:

This is related to foreign tourist arrivals which brings foreign exchange into a country and thus have a favorable effect on our balance of payment.

• Receptive Tourism:

This is related to foreign tourist arrivals which brings foreign exchange (money) into the country and thus have a favorable effect on our balance of payment.

• Passive Tourism:

It is travel residents of a country going abroad. They take out currency and thus there is a negative effect on the balance of payment.

Quantitative Tourism:

• Mass Tourism:

When large volume of tourist participate in tourism, it is called mass tourism.

Qualitative Tourism:

• Popular Tourism:

Any tourism which is popular and have positive impacts is termed as popular tourism. Eco-Tourism which is eco-friendly and does not deteriorate the natural environment can be termed as popular tourism.

• Social Tourism:

When people of limited means participate into tourism or measures are taken to encourage them to participate or to make it possible, it is known as social tourism.

Summary:

Infrastructure includes all forms of construction on and below ground required by any inhabited area for communicating with the outside world and as a basis for extensive human activity within e.g. roads, water supply, electricity supply, sewerage disposable etc. Economics frequently put stress on the development of the touristic infrastructure, as it is the pre-requisite for its accelerated economic growth. Most of the infrastructural facilities are provided by public sector. Superstructure includes all forms of construction of building above the ground. It includes access facilities for transport-airport terminals, railway stations and bus stations, hotels, motels and other accommodation units, café, bars and sports recreational facilities. For better understanding of tourism phenomenon different forms and types of tourism have been identified like inbound tourism, Outbound Tourism, Domestic Tourism, Seasonal Tourism, Roving Tourism, Recreational Tourism, Social Tourism etc.

CHAPTER III

COMPONENTS OF TOURISM

Introduction:

Tourism has developed into a truly worldwide activity that knows no political, ideological, geographical, or cultural boundaries. Tourism is an amalgamation of many things into a composite whole. In this unit you will study the Characteristics of Tourism, the basic travel motivators and factors influencing the growth of Tourism.

In the second half of the unit you will study the major components and elements of Tourism. If any one of the component or element is missing the unified whole phenomenon of Tourism is affected.

Services And Tourism:

Service and tourism go hand in hand. However, as we begin our study of tourism, it is important to know that these activities make a significant economic impact on almost every nation in the world! Services are growing at a faster rate than all agricultural and manufacturing business combined. In fact, tourism related businesses are the leading producers of new jobs worldwide.

Tourism has developed into a truly worldwide activity that knows no political, ideological, geographical, or cultural boundaries. For a long time tourism was disparate and fragmented, but with maturity it has become gained a professional identity. It has formed lobbying groups such as the World Travel and Tourism Council, which includes airlines, hotel chains, and travel agents among its members and concentrates on making tourism of an economic value to the host countries. The future prospects for tourism are brighter than ever as people continue to travel for work or pleasure. "Given its historical performance as luxury good during expansions and a necessity during recession, travel and tourism future economic prospects look quite bright".

The growth and popularity of tourism activities has not been accidental. Tourism has become more than just another industry; it has developed into an important part of the economic foundation of many countries. The positive benefits of tourism activities in periods of economic stagnation or decline have not gone unnoticed. Tourism activities have historically demonstrated a general upward trend in numbers of participants and revenues. Even during times of recession, travel and tourism expenditures continue to rise.

Tourism is an economic activity where tourist is a consumer. Tourism is concerned with the consumption of people. Thus tourism involves consumption and expenditure of tourist at a place other than where he reside. The aim of the leisure traveller is not earning income at a destination but spending income at a destination. The effect of tourism expenditure is the same as the effect of resident population's expenditure. Only in international tourism, foreign exchange earnings are important for the tourist receiving country.

Characteristics of Tourism:

Tourist product is the total of services and products consumed by the tourist. International transportation is an integral part of the tourist product.

Tourism, at management level is the composition of economic activities that are geared to satisfy the needs of the travelers. Due to existence of many different products, services involved in tourism, one cannot specify and define a distinct tourism industry. But rather there are industries, sectors and services catering for the needs of the travelers.

There are few characteristics of tourism differentiating it from other economic activities. These are:

• **Tourism is an invisible export activity:**

Tourism is recorded in the statistics as 'invisibles'. Tourists consume what they consume at their countries with emphasis on recreation and leisure services and goods

• **Products and services are complementary:**

The demand in tourism is not for a specific product but rather for a bundle of services and consumption commodities. The services which comprise the final tourist product are different from each other and at first look they seem to be independent of each other. That is why destinations assume they can control the tourism demand and the prices of the tourist products they offer to international markets. Different tourist services are complementary and closely related to each other forming a final tourist product for the tourist. Accommodation at a destination depends on the existence and availability of suitable transportation to and from the destination. Catering is mostly dependent on accommodation.

In the cultural tourism market the tourist products of different countries may complement each other such as religious and archaeological tours to

Turkey, Egypt, Israel and Greece.

- **There is no distinct industry solely producing for tourism:**

There is no such production activity to be called as tourism industry or sector. (The use of tourism industry term is preferred than tourism sector in line with the internationally accepted usage). Services, commodities and products produced for tourism and offered to tourists have distinct characteristics. Production, sale and consumption in tourism take place concurrently.

- **Tourism products are perishable:**

Tourism service and tourist product cannot be stored for future and it should be consumed when it is available or otherwise it is lost forever. There is no inventory of the product. Like, a bed in a hotel or seat in an aircraft that is not sold at a certain date is lost forever. Hence the tourism products are perishable.

- **Direction of transaction is reverse:**

In tourism there is an exchange of goods and services between the tourist generating centers and destinations. The direction of flow in tourism is reverse of the trade good. In tourism the consumers are shipped to the location where the services, commodities and good are located.

- **Intermediaries in consumption:**

The demands of the tourists and their consumption of tourist products and services are realized through intermediaries. The products can be consumed with the help of intermediaries. Examples of intermediaries, at firm level are tour operators and travel agencies; at personnel level are guides and hotel or restaurant staff in service.

- **Tourist product is fragmented:**

The tourist product is defined as a package tour. The product components of a package tour are: International transportation, Destination / Ground-Land services, Local transport / Transfers, Accommodation, Catering, Recreation, Guiding, Thus it affects many sectors of the economy.

- **Travel in an experience:**

Travel is an experience, there is no tangible product in tourism. The tourist buys an intangible service that could not be tested before the actual consumption starts. It is an image-dream that is sold and experience to be lived. Image and experience necessitate the involvement of intermediaries in consumption process; either firms or individuals. It is vital that an intermediary helps the tourist to experience the image and consumption. The only tangible assets in tourism are souvenirs.

• Demand is volatile / unstable and Seasonal:

Tourism is an unstable export. It is affected by, Economic and political conditions – war, strike, political crisis etc. and to the behavior of tour operators and travel agencies; Preferences of tourists; Natural disasters, epidemics etc. Tourism demand is concentrated in summer months both in mass tourism and in cultural tourism. Seasonal concentration is linked to the use of natural tourism resources of a country and is severe in the Mediterranean destinations. Seasonality is also observed at some countries in winter such as Austria, Switzerland. Indian Destinations have lean season and peak season depending upon the favorable climatic conditions at the destination. Peak season means more tourist coming in some specific months and lean season means less number of tourist coming in some specific months.

• Enterprises in tourism industry:

Tourism is mostly composed of too many small and medium sized enterprise. There are few giant firms, conglomerates in the industry which affect the tourism industry structure. They dominate the international tourism industry and international tourism market. Just a very few number of enterprises are capable of catering to all the needs of all tourists. Mostly the industry is composed of many small and medium sized enterprises.

Basic Travel Motivators:

Travel motivations vary. Travel motivations are heterogeneous. Travellers travel for many different reasons. These motivations can be influenced by irrational subjective factors as well. Travel service suppliers try to serve the needs of a very heterogeneous travel demand and try to produce products for a wide appeal.

Various attempts have been made to study as to why people wish to travel or become tourists. McIntosh has stated that basic travel motivators may be grouped into the following four broad categories:

(i) Physical motivators, which are related to physical relaxation and rest, sporting activities and specific medical treatment; all are connected with the individual's bodily health and well-being.

(ii) Interpersonal motivators, which are related to a desire to visit relatives, friends, or to meet new people, or simply to escape from the routine of everyday life.

(iii) Status and prestige motivators, which are identified with the needs of personal esteem and personal development, these are related to travel for business or professional interests, for the purpose of education or the pursuit of hobbies.

Factors Influencing the Growth of Tourism

Socio-economic factors like income, mobility, age, education and cost are crucial in the evolution of demand. Together with leisure these are responsible for determining the growth of international tourism. The most comprehensive list of factors influencing the growth of tourism however comes from Louis Erdi (1970) of the Swiss Federal University. The list includes:

(i) Greater affluence and more leisure for an increasing number of people, particularly in the developed countries.

(ii) The emancipation of the young, and the relatively higher wages they possess (when they have no family responsibilities), enabling them to travel.

(iii) Transport facilities especially air, very much better and cheaper, and there is a high rate of car ownership.

(iv) An enormous growth in international business, necessitating travel.

(iv) Package tours allow people, not used to making their own arrangements, to travel with an easy mind, and are of good value because of bulk buying of transport and hotel accommodation.

(v) Relief from adverse climatic conditions in the home country may be found abroad.

(vi) Travel has become a status symbol.

(vii) Conferences and business meetings are proliferating.

(ix) Better education has interested a large section of the public in cultural tourism.

(x) World exhibitions and trade fairs have become very popular.

(xi) Publicity has become more and more aggressive, whetting the appetite of even the most unwilling to travel.

(xii) Ideological pressure groups (political, cultural, scientific, etc.) hold more and more annual conventions, etc.

Components of Tourism:

The tourist industry can be described as shown in Figure 3.1 Accommodations include all forms of lodging, even camping and caravanning, and all types of food and beverage services. Shopping encompasses any form of retail purchase, such as souvenirs, arts and crafts, clothing, groceries, and others. Activities comprise services such as entertainment, sports, sightseeing, local tours, cultural events, festivals, and gambling. Transportation includes all forms by land, air, or water.

The entire tourism industry rests on a base of natural resources, which must be wholesome and attractive, preferable possessing unusual natural beauty and appeal to vacationers. These natural resources must be adequate in dimension to avoid crowding, and they should be free from such hazards as pollution, dangerous or poisonous plants, animals, or insects. Similarly, development of tourism should be on sites free from natural disasters, such as floods, droughts, or earthquakes.

Thus there are four major components of Tourism. Namely

- Accommodation
- Transportation
- Attractions (Natural, Built and Cultural Resources)
- Support Services (Services enabling shopping and other activities)

Strictly speaking, tourism is typically not defined as an industry. Even though there is no Standard Industrial Classification (SIC) code for tourism, it is a major economic activity. There is a market for a demand for travel, lodging food, shops, entertainment and other tourism services. This demand has created the need for tour operators, travel agents airlines, cruise ships, buses, accommodations, food and beverage facilities, and other Tourists Suppliers and Activities The best tourism products will not sell themselves, but must be marketed through vigorous efforts. Those providing the products are the principal marketers. But travel agents, tour companies, associations, and other intermediaries are important lines in the marketing and distribution system. Goods and services that supply tourist needs. This economic activity is the tourist industry, or more properly, simply tourism. Tourism is fragmented industry with many parts and varied activities. As a young industry, it has not yet achieved the cohesiveness necessary for all components to work together for the common good. Each segment makes its own contributions to the total tourism picture, yet the segments are interrelated and depend on each other.

For example, the success of a Colorado ski resort depends on transportation to bring skiers to the slopes, housing to accommodate them restaurant to feed them, and other services (medical facilities, après-ski lounges, and retail shops) to take care of their needs. Most of the enterprises affiliated with skiing are small. Although they are operated as independent businesses, they do in fact depend on each other and serve as small parts of the total picture. This dependence calls for cooperative effort and similar policies; however the fact that the business often compete in the each other for the consumers dollars make cooperation difficult. Many of them are fiercely independent, dominated by their own self-interest. As tourism grows and matures, the industry will become more united and speak with a single voice on major issues. Firms will become larger and the weak links in tourism chain of services will be eliminated. Thus the future of tourism promises to be bright, dynamic and exciting

Peter's inventory of tourist attractions:

1. Cultural: Sites and areas of archaeological interest; Historical buildings and monuments;

Places of historical significance; Museums; Modern culture; Political and Educational Institutions; Religious institutions.

2. Traditions: National festivals Arts and handicrafts; Music; Folklore Native life and customs.

3. Scenic: National parks; Wildlife, Flora and Fauna; Beach resorts; Mountain resorts.

4. Entertainment: Participation and viewing sports Amusement and recreation parks; Zone

and oceonariums; Cinemas and theatres; Night life; Cuisine.

5. Other attractions: Climate; Health resorts or spas; Unique Attractions not available elsewhere.

According to Robinson, the attractions of tourism are, to a very large extent, geographical in their character. Location and accessibility (whether a place has a coastal or inland position, and the ease with which a given place can be reached) are important. Physical space may be thought of as a component for there are those who seek the wilderness and solitude. Scenery or landscape is a compound of landforms, water and the vegetation and has a relation to the amount of sunshine, temperature and precipitation (snow as well as rain. Animal life may be an important attraction, firstly, in relation, to bird watching or viewing them in their natural habitat and, secondly, for sporting. Landscape in the form of their settlements, historical monuments, variety of cultural features, ways of life, folklore, artistic expression, etc. Provide valuable attractions to many.

Elements of Tourism:

The four basic components of tourism, namely, transport, attraction, accommodation and support services are very important components. However, in addition to basic components, there are certain elements or ingredients which are also crucial to tourism. These elements are the fundamental attractions of tourism. These include:

(a) Pleasing weather

(b) Scenic attractions

(c) Historical and cultural factors

(d) Accessibility

(e) Amenities

Pleasing Weather:

One of the most important and crucial attractions of any tourist place is fine weather with warm sunshine. For holidaying, good weather is a particularly important ingredient since it plays an important role in making a holiday a pleasant or an unpleasant experience. Millions of tourists from countries with extremes of weather visit sea beaches in search of fine weather and sunshine. Sunshine and clear sea breeze at the beaches have attracted many since a very long time. In fact, development of spas and resorts along the sea coasts in many countries were a result of travelers' urge to enjoy good weather and sunshine. In Europe, countries like France, Italy and Spain. Italy has built Sardinia along the Adriatic and Mediterranean coasts taking advantage of brilliant sunshine.

Many of the Mexican resorts, resorts of Pacific and California, Florida, and Hawaiian Islands in the United States are yet other example of what good weather can do. All these areas in fact capitalizing on good weather have become important tourist spots. Areas with attractive winter climates, winter warmth and sunshine are also important centers of tourist attraction. Many areas have become important winter holiday resorts attracting a large number of tourists. Around these winter resorts, a variety of winter sport facilities have been installed to cater to the increasing needs of tourists. In countries with tropical climates, many upland cool areas have been developed as hill station resorts. Climate then is of particular significance to tourism as areas with good climatic conditions can be potential tourist areas.

Scenic Attractions:

Scenic attractions like good weather are very important factors in tourism. Scenery or the landscape consisting of mountains, lakes, waterfalls, glaciers, forests, deserts, etc. are strong forces attracting people to visit them. Breathtaking mountain scenery and the coast scenery exert a strong fascination for the tourist. The magnificent mountain ranges provide an atmosphere of peace and tranquility. Tourists visiting the northern slopes of the Alps in Switzerland and Austria and the southern slopes in Italy and also the Himalayan mountain slopes of India and Nepal for the first time cannot but be charmed by their physical magnificence. Great natural wonders such as the Grand Canyon in the United States, the Giants Causeway of Northern Ireland, the Niagara Falls, the Geysers of Iceland, the glaciers of Alps, the forests of Africa, the mighty rivers, the lakes and the deserts are a source of great interest to many tourists and have become the basis of an expanding tourist industry.

Historical and Cultural Factors:

Characters of historical and cultural interest exert a powerful attraction for many. Since many centuries these have had a profound influence on the traveler. Large numbers of tourists are attracted every year by the great drawing power of Stratford-on- Avon in England because of its association with Shakespeare, or the city of Agra in India because of its famous Taj Mahal or Pisa in Italy because of its famous leaning tower. Thousands of Americans and Canadians visit Europe because of its long historical heritage; besides, many view Europe as their original homeland and have a sentimental attachment to it. Any foreign visitor to England must visit London not because it is the largest city in the country and the capital, but because of its historical associations and traditions and its many cultural attractions. In a similar way the visitor in France includes Paris in his itinerary as he does Rome and Moscow in a visit to Italy and the Russia respectively. Many countries which are developing tourist industries are using the legacy of their historical past as their major tourist attractions. In India, the world-famous caves of Ajanta and Ellora are an example. These caves are India's oldest and most beautiful testimony of religious architecture and painting, and are man-made caves hewn out of rocky mountains conceived and executed some 2000 ago.

Accessibility:

Accessibility is a very crucial factor as it is a means by which a tourist can reach the area where attractions are located. Tourist attractions of whatever type would be of little importance if their locations are inaccessible by the normal means of transport. It the tourist attractions are located at places where no transport can reach or where there are inadequate transport facilities, these become of little value. The tourist attractions which are located near to the tourist generating markets and are linked by a network of efficient roads and can be easily reached by air receive the maximum number of tourists. The distance factor also plays an important role in determining a tourist choice of a destination. Longer distances cost much in the way of expenses on travel as compared to short distances. An example can be that of India. 3.9 million Tourist arrivals for a country of the size of India may look rather unimpressive. However, if one looks at certain factors like the countries distance from the Europe, Canada, Japan and Australia, one may conclude that the long distance is rather one of the factors responsible for low arrivals. It costs a visitor from these countries quite a substantial amount. Europe and North America continue to be the main generating and receiving areas for international tourism, accounting for as much as 70 per cent and 20 per cent respectively of international tourist arrivals. The intra-regional tourism (tourism between countries of the same region) has an appreciable influence on the distribution of world arrivals. Of the total international tourist movements within Europe and North America, at least 80 per cent are intra-regional. In the Americas the United States and Canada alone account for nearly 50 per cent of all international tourist traffic in the regions, where intra-regional international tourist movements are therefore also predominant. In Europe, intra-regional tourism accounts for over 80 per cent of international tourist movements. Easy accessibility thus is a key factor for the growth and development for tourist movements.

Amenities:

Facilities are a necessary aid to the tourist center. For a seaside resort, facilities like swimming, boating, yachting, surf-riding, and such other facilities like dancing, recreation and amusements are important for every tourist center. Amenities can be of two types: natural, e.g., beaches, sea bathing, possibilities of fishing, opportunities for climbing, trekking, viewing, etc. and man-made e.g., various types of entertainments and facilities which cater for the special needs of the tourists. Excellent sandy beaches, sheltered in sunshine having palm and coconut trees and offering good bathing form very good tourist attractions. Certain other natural amenities such as spacious sheltered water for the purpose of sailing, or the opportunities for fishing and shooting are also very important.

Accommodation:

Accommodation is very basic to any tourist destination. The demand for accommodation away from one's home is met by variety of facilities. The term is loosely used to cover food and lodging. The types of accommodation have undergone considerable changes since the last 25 years. There has been a decline in the use of boarding houses and small private hotels. The larger hotels are managing more or less to keep their share of holiday trade, especially in big metropolitan areas and popular tourist areas. Elsewhere, particularly in more traditional holiday resorts and in some seaside resorts in Europe, these are having a lean time. In recent years some changes have been reflected in the type of accommodation and there has been a growing demand for more informal types of accommodation. New types of accommodation, particularly holiday villages, apartment houses, camping and caravan sites and tourist villages etc. have become very popular in recent years.

Accommodation may in itself be an important tourist attraction. In fact, a large number to tourists visit a particular tourist region or a town simply because there is a first class luxury hotel or a resort which provides excellent services and facilities. Some countries like Switzerland, Holland, Austria, France and Belgium have gained reputation for providing excellent accommodation with good cuisine. Many hotel have gained reputation for their excellent food, services and facilities. The French Government for instance, paved the way for tourist development of Corsica by launching a big hotel building programme.

Geographical Components:

H. Robinson, in his book A Geography of Tourism published in the year 1979 has brought out a list components of tourism which have been termed as geographical components of tourism. These are brought out in the following table:

Geographical Components of Tourism:

1. Accessibility and location

2. Space

3. Scenery

(a) Landforms. e.g., mountains, canyons, coral reefs, cliffs, etc.

(b) water. e.g, rivers, lakes, waterfalls, geysers, glaciers, the sea.

(c) Vegetation. e.g., forests, grasslands, moors, deserts, etc.

4. Climate: Sunshine, clouds, temperature conditions, rain and snow.

5. Animal life

(a) Wildlife, e.g., birds game reservations, zoos.

(b) Hunting and fishing

6. Settlement features:

(a) Towns, cities, villages

(b) Historical remains and monuments

(c) Archaeological remains.

7. Culture: ways of life, traditions, folklore, arts and crafts etc.

Benefits and Costs of Tourism:

Tourism brings both economic and noneconomic benefits and costs to host communities. The benefits occurring to the traveler, such as the contribution of pleasure travel to rest and relaxation, the educational benefit, the understanding of other people and cultures, and the physical and mental well-being of the traveler.

There is no question that tourism delivers benefits, but tourism is not perfect. There are costs and benefits, and they do not accrue equally. Many of the social costs incurred are difficult or impossible to measure. Books such as The Golden Hordes, Tourism: Blessing or Blight, and The Holiday Makers point out some of the unpleasant aspects of tourism.

Improperly planned and developed tourism can create problems. The demands of tourism may come into conflict with the needs and wishes of local residents. Thoughtless development, inappropriate development, over development, or unfinished development can easily damage the environment.

Tourism has been blamed for polluting beaches; raising the price of labor, land goods, and so on; spoiling the countryside; contaminating the values of native people; crowding; congestion; noise; litter; crime; loss of privacy; creating social tensions; environmental deterioration; lack of control over destination's future and low-paid seasonal employment. These problems are common to many forms of development and in many cases represent dissatisfaction with change for the status quo or over development. They emphasize the need for a coordinated overall economic development plan of which tourism will be one part.

We must accept that tourism is neither a blessing nor a blight, neither Poison nor panacea. Tourism can bring great benefits but it can also bring social problems. The world has experience in how to increase the benefits of tourism, and at least some experience in how to lesson social problems. What has to be done is to balance the benefits and costs to come up with the best cost/benefit result.

Tourism students and executives must have a clear understanding of both the positive and negative impacts of tourism on the quality of life of a nation, a province or state or a community. What are the positive aspects? The negative aspects? We need a balance sheet.

First we look at the plus side of the ledger.

• Provides employment opportunities, both skilled and unskilled, because it is a labor intensive industry.

• Generates a supply of needed foreign exchange

• Increases incomes

• Creates increased gross national product

• Can be built on existing infrastructure

• Develops an infrastructure that will also help stimulate local commerce and industry

• Can be developed with local products and resources

• Helps to diversify the economy

• Tends to be one of the most compatible economic development activities available to an area, complementing other economic activities.

• Spreads development

• Has a high multiplier impact

• Increases governmental revenues

• Broadens educational and cultural horizons and improves fallings of self-worth

• Improves the quality of life related to a higher level of income and improved standards of living.

• Reinforces preservation of heritage and tradition

• Justifies environmental protection and improvement

• Visitor interest in local culture provides employment for artists, musicians, and other performing artists, enhancing the cultural heritage.

• Provides tourist and recreational facilities that may be used by a local population

• Breaks down language barriers, socio-cultural barriers, class barriers, racial barriers, political barriers, and religious barriers.

• Creates a favorable worldwide image for a destination

• Promotes a global community

• Promotes international understanding and peace

On the minus side of the ledger we find a number of problems that can be created by tourism, especially by its over development.

• Develops excess demand for resources

• Creates the difficulties of seasonality

• Causes inflation

• Can result in unbalanced economic development

• Creates social problems

• Degrades the natural physical environment and creates pollution

• Degrades the cultural environment

• Increases the incidence of crime, prostitution, and gambling

• Increases vulnerability to economic and political changes

- Threatens family structure
- Commercializes culture, religion and the arts
- Creates misunderstanding
- Creates conflicts in the host society
- Contributes to disease, economic fluctuation and transportation problems

Like all change, tourism exacts a price. However, it is here it is huge and it needs to be planned and managed.

Summary:

In this unit we have examined the subject of tourism, its characteristics and basic travel motivations. The rapid growth in the movement of people, both domestically and internationally, has brought about an industry of vast proportions and diversity. Also it is universal found in all countries of the world, but in greatly varied qualities and proportions.

There are four major components of Tourism Accommodation, Transportation, Attracation and Support services. In addition to these components there are certain elements like pleasing weather, scenic attraction, historical and cultural factors, accessibility and amenities which are also crucial to tourism.

CHAPTER IV

PRINCIPLES AND PRACTICES OF TOURISM

Introduction:

International tourism is world's largest export earner and an important factor in the balance of payments of most nations. Intercultural awareness and personal friendships fostered through tourism are a powerful force for improving international understanding and contribution to peace among all the nations of the world.

In this chapter you will study the model of tourism, how intermediaries help in providing the services and facilities from tourism supplies to the tourist. You will also go through the milestones in development of Tourism, five periods of tourism, Tourism challenges and opportunities and trends in tourism and travel.

Role of WTO in Promoting Sustainable Tourism:

Tourism is a dynamic, evolving, consumer-driven force and is the world's largest industry if all it interrelated components are placed under one umbrella; travel; lodging; conventions, expositions, meetings, events restaurants, managed services and recreation.

The leading international organization in the field of travel and tourism, the World Tourism Organization [WTO], is vested by the United Nations with a central and decisive role in promoting the development of responsible sustainable, and universally accessible tourism, with the aim of contributing to economic development, international understanding, peace, prosperity, and universal respect for, and observance of, human rights and fundamental freedoms. In pursuing this aim, the organization pays particular attention to the interests of the developing countries in the field of tourism.

Acting as an umbrella organization for world tourism, WTO plays a catalytic role in promoting technology transfers and international cooperation, stimulating and developing public-private sector partnerships, and encouraging the implementation of the Global Code of Ethics for Tourism, with a view to ensuring that member countries, tourist destinations, and businesses maximize the positive economic, social and cultural effects of tourism and fully reap its benefits, while at the same time they minimize its negative social and environmental impacts.

Through tourism, WTO aims at stimulating economic growth and job creation, providing incentives for protecting the environment and cultural heritage, and promoting peace, prosperity and respect for human right.

Membership includes 143 countries, 7 territories, and some 350 affiliate members representing the private sector educational institutions, tourism associations, and local tourism authorities. Unfortunately the United States is not a member, but may soon be.

The WTO and the World Travel and Tourism Council declare the travel and tourism industry to have the following characteristics.

- A 24-hour-a-day, 7-day-week a year economic driver.
- Accounts for 10.2 percent of world GDP
- Employer of 200 million people or 7.8 percent of the global work force
- Travel and tourism will support creation of more than 505 million jobs per year during the 2000s.
- Leading Producer of tax revenues

Tourism for Prosperity and Peace:

At the start of the new millennium, tourism is firmly established as the number one industry in many countries and the fastest growing economic sector in terms of foreign exchange earnings and job creation. International tourism is the world largest export earner and an important factor in the balance of payments of most nations.

Tourism has become one of the world most important sources of employment. It stimulates enormous investment in infrastructure, most of which helps to improve the living conditions of local people as well as tourists. It provides governments with substantial tax revenues. Most new tourism jobs and business are created in the developing countries helping to equalize economic opportunities and keep rural residents from moving to overcrowded cities.

Intercultural awareness and personal friendships fostered through tourism are a powerful force for improving international understanding and contributing to peace among all the nations of the world.

The World Tourism Organization encourages governments, in partnership with the private sector, local authorities and nongovernmental organizations to play a vital role in tourism. WTO helps countries throughout the world to maximize the positive impacts of tourism while minimizing its possible negative consequences on the environment and societies.

Tourism the world largest industry offers the greatest global employment prospects. This trend is caused by the following factors:

1. The opening of borders; despite security concerns, we can travel to more countries now than 10 years ago. The U.S. has a visa waiver program with 28 European countries.

2. An increase in disposable income and vacations.

3. Cheaper and more exclusive flights

4. An increase in the number of people with more time and money.

5. More people with the urge to travel.

According to the World Travel and Tourism Council the industry business leader's forum-tourism and travel generate, directly and indirectly, 10.2 percent of global gross domestic product [GDP], investment, and employment. The industry is forecast to grow strongly in real terms during the next 10 years.

Long-Term Prospects Tourism Vision:

Travel is likely to increase in the coming years, which will have a significant impact on tourism. Some of the reason for the anticipated increases are as follows:

Longer Life Span. The average person now has a life expectation of about seventy-five years. In fact, in just a few years, some baby boomers will be taking early retirement.

Flexible Working Hours. Today, many people work four to ten hour a day and have longer weekends. Of course, many others especially in the hospitality and tourism industries work on weekends and have leisure time during the week.

Early Retirement. Increasingly, people are being given the opportunity to retire at fifty-five. This early retirement is generally granted to employees with thirty years of service to their company or government agency.

Greater Ease of Travel. Today, it is easier to travel on holidays and weekends, for both business and leisure purposes. Each mode of travel affords increasing opportunities to take advantage of the additional leisure time.

Tendency to Take Shorter, More Frequent Trips. People now tend to take shorter but more frequent mini vacations, rather than taking all of their vacation time at one go. Europeans generally take much longer vacations than North Americans. For them, four weeks is the normal vacation benefit of new employees, and six weeks is typical after a few years' service.

Increase in the Standard of Living. More people in many developing countries have increased their income and wish to travel. China, with its new-found enterprise zones is producing hundreds of thousands of entrepreneurs who will soon be traveling to foreign countries. Millions of East European residents of the former Soviet Block countries now have the capability and the right to travel. In total, an additional three hundred million people will soon have passports.

Although the evolution of tourism in the lst few years has been irregular, WTO maintains its long-term forecast for the moment. The underlying structural trends of the forecast are believed not to have significantly change. Experience shows that in the short term, periods of faster growth [1995, 1996, 2000] alternate with periods of slow growth [2001 and 2002]. While the pace of growth till 2000 actually exceeded the Tourism 2020 Vision forecast, it is generally expected that the current slowdown will be compensated for in the mid- to long term.

WTO's Tourism 2020 Vision forecasts that international arrivals expected to reach over 1.56 billion by the year 2020. Of these 1.2 billion will be interregional and 0.4 billion will be long-haul travelers.

The fact that tourism is expected to grow rapidly presents both tremendous opportunities and challenges. The good news is the variety of exciting career prospects for today's hospitality and tourism graduates. Tourism, although mature industry is a young profession. Careful management of tourism and travel will be necessary to avoid repercussions and negativism toward the "pesky" tourist, which is already happening to some extent in Europe, where the sheer number of tourists overwhelms attractions and facilities.

There is an interdependency between the various segments of tourism, travel, lodging, foodservice, and recreation. Hotel guests need to travel to reach the hotel. They eat in nearby restaurants and visit attractions. Each segment is to an extent, dependent on another for business.

A Tourism Model:
As you study tourism model, notice its open nature and how each of the segments is related to the others Let's begin our study of tourism by looking at travelers {tourists}, who serve as the focal point for all tourism activities and form the center of model. Radiating from this focal point are three large bands containing several interdependent groups of tourism participants and organizations.

Individual tourists may deal directly with any of these tourism service suppliers, but they often rely on the professional services provided by tourism promoters shown in the first band of our model. Tourism promoters, such as travel agencies and tourist boards provide information and other marketing services. Moving to the next band of model, we see key tourism suppliers who provide transportation, accommodations, and other service required by travelers.

Tourism suppliers may provide these services independently, they may compete with each other, and at times they may work together. For example, airline, bus railroad, cruise ship, and car rental companies may compete individually for a traveler business. However they may also team up to provide cooperative packages such as fly-ride fly-cruise, and fly-drive alternatives. Or as airlines have discovered, they must establish strategic alliances with many other carriers to provide seamless travel across states, nations, and continents. Hotels and resorts may also compete against each other for the same traveler's patronage, yet cooperate with transportation providers to attract tourists to a specific location. Service providers representing all segments of the tourism industry may often work together to develop promotional packages designed to attract tourists or destinations.

How closely these individuals and organizations work together is ultimately influenced by the forces shaping the face of tourism activities. As our model shows, the tourism industry does not operate in vacuum. All of the participants, either individually or an s group, are constantly responding to a variety of social/cultural, political, environmental, economic, and technological forces. These forces may range from subtle changes, which are noticeable only after many years, to more dramatic hangs, which have immediate and visible impacts. Examples of these forces can be found all around us.

Gradual changes may be notice in destinations that were once fashion able but eventually faded in popularity, such as Niagara Falls in the Canadian/U.S. border and Brighton in England. Similar shifts can also be seen in transportation. Steamship passage across the north Atlantic was eclipsed by the faster and more efficient airplane, which opened new horizons for travelers. Immediate impacts can be seen in sudden shifts brought about by currency devaluations, wars, fuel shortages, and natural disasters. Rapid adoption of new technologies such as the Internet can have immediate and far-reaching impacts on tourism activities. A country that was once avoided may suddenly become a popular tourism destination because it is more affordable or accessible. Conversely, a once-popular destination may be avoided because of a recent natural disaster or political upheaval.

The number of travelers from nations also varies dramatically due to political and economic changes. Now that China has developed a sizeable middle class due to its economic growth, China now is the biggest Asian nation in terms of outbound travelers.

Let us look at how our model might work. Suppose you (a tourist) want to visit a sunny beach or a snow-covered mountain. You might begin planning your trip by surfing the websites of different airlines, condominiums, hotels, and/or resorts (tourism service suppliers) searching for possible flight schedules and accommodation options. You could simply call a travel agent (tourism promoter) who would search out the best alternatives to meet your option, would be taking a "virtual trip" to your desire destination by surfing offering on the Internet. Finally, you could contact local chambers of commerce or visitors bureaus to learn more about your preferred destinations.

Milestones in the Development of Tourism:

- Prerecorded History Travel begins to occur out of a sense of adventure and curiosity.
- 4850 B.C.-715 B.C. Egyptians travel to centralized government locations.
- 1760B.C.-1027 B.C. Shank dynasties establish trade routes to distant locations throughout the Far East.
- 1100 B.C.-800 B.C. Phoenicians develop large sailing fleets for trade and travel throughout their empire.
- 900 B.C.-200 B.C. Greeks develop common language and currency and traveler services emerge as city-states become destinations.
- 500 B.C.-A.D. 300 Romans improve roads, legal system, and inns to further travel for commerce, adventure, and pleasure.
- A.D. 300-A.D.900 Mayans establish trade and travel routes in parts of Central and North America.
- A.D. 1096-A.D. 1295 European travel on failed religious crusades to retake the Holy Lands from Muslim control introduced these military forces to new places and cultures.
- A.D. 1275-A.D. 1295 Marco Polo's travels throughout the Far East begin to heighten interest in travel and trade.

- 14th –16th centuries Trade routes develop as commercial activities grow and merchants venture into new territories.
- A.D. 1616-A.D. 1785 Grand Tour Era makes travel a status symbol for wealthy individuals seeking to experience cultures of the civilized world.
- 18th – 19th centuries. Industrial Revolution gives rise to technological advances, making travel and trade more efficient and expanding markets; increasing personal incomes make travel both a business necessity and leisure activity.
- 1841 Thomas Cook organizes first group tour in England
- 1903 Wright Brothers usher in era of flight with the first successful aircraft flight
- 1913 Westinghouse Corporation institutes paid vacations for its workers.
- 1914 Henry Ford begins mass production of the Model T
- 1919 First scheduled airline passenger flight debuts between London and Paris
- 1945 World War II ends and ushers in new era of property, giving rise to millions of people with the time, money, and interest to travel for pleasure.
- 1950 Diners Club introduces the first credit card.
- 1952 Jet passenger service inaugurated between London and Johannesburg, South Africa.
- 1978 Competition on routes and fares begins with signing of Airline Deregulation Act.
- 2001 September 11th terrorism attacks on the World Trade Center in New Your City and the Pentagon in Washington, D.C., heightened security measures for travel across the U.S.
- 2001 Transportation security Administration (TSA) created to ensure airline passenger safety as terrorism threats persist.
- 2002 Introduction of the EURO currency signaling liberalization of travel among member nations of the European Union.

The Five Periods of Tourism:

The historical development of tourism has been divided up into five distinct epochs (or periods), four of which parallel the advent of new means of transportation.

- Pre industrial revolution (prior to 1840)
- The railway age

- The jet aircraft age
- The cruise ship age

Pre industrial Revolution:

As early as 300 B.C., Ancient Egyptians sailed up and down the river Nile, carrying huge rocks with which to build pyramids as tombs for their leaders. The Phoenicians were among the first real travelers in any modern sense. In both the Mediterranean basin and the Orient, travel was motivated by trade. However, trade was not the only motivation for travel in these times; commerce and the search for more plentiful food supplies also stimulated travel.

The Roman Empire provided safe passage for travelers via a vast road system that stretched from Egypt to Britain. Wealthy Romans traveled to Egypt and Greece, to baths shrines, and seaside resorts. The Romans were as curious as modern-days tourists. They visited the attractions of their time, trekking to Greek temples and to places where Alexander the Great slept, Socrates lived, Ajax committed suicide, and Achilles was buried by an eruption of MT. Versifies, Yielded several restaurants, taverns, and inns that tourists visit even today.

Medieval travel was mostly confined to religious travel, particularly pilgrimages to various shrines: Muslims to Mecca and Christians to Jerusalem and Rome. The Crusades began in 1095 and lasted for the next two hundred years, stimulation a cultural exchange that was, in part responsible for the Renaissance. Across Europe, travel and trade flourished. With the increase in living standards came a heightened awareness of cultural pursuits. Later, aristocrats undertook Grand Tours of Europe, stopping at major cities for weeks or months at a time. It was considered a necessary part of "rounding out" a young lady's or gentleman's education. Fortunately, travel now has become possible for almost everyone.

The Railway Age:

Railroads played a major role in the United States, Canada, and several other countries. The pioneering spirit carried by the railroads opened up the great American West. Prior to the advent of rail travel, tourists had to journey by horse and carriage. By comparison, the railway was more efficient, less costly, and more comfortable. Resort communities came within the reach of a larger segment of the population in North America and Europe. The railroads brought changes in the lodging industry, as taverns along the turnpikes gave way to hotels near the railway stations.

The first railroad was build n the United States in 1830, but only 23 miles of rail were laid by the end of that year. In contrast, by 1860, there were 30,626 miles of track. In 1869, rail journey across America was made possible by the transcontinental connection, which enabled the journey across America was made possible by the transcontinental connection, which enabled the journey to be completed in six days. Before that, such a journey took several months by wagon or several weeks by clipper ships rounding Cape Horn, South America.

To ensure passenger comfort, railroads had excellent dining cars and sleeping berths. Railroads continued to extend their lines into the twentieth century until the Depression of the 1930s and World War II. With these events began a decline in railroad usage that was accelerated by the invention of the automobile. The freedom of the open road gave automobile travel a competitive advantage over train travel.

In order to prevent a complete collapse of the passenger rail system, the United States government created AMTRAK in 1971. AMTRAK is a semipublic organization; eight of the fifteen members of its board are selected by the President of the United States, three by the railroads, and four by preferred private stockholders. AMTRAK is subsidized by the United States Congress, in amounts ranging from $500 million to $800 million per year; this subsidy represents between 35 and 50 percent of its total revenue. AMTRAK has eliminated many unprofitable lines and improved overall efficiency and service quality. About half of AMTRAK's trains and passengers are in the heavily populated northeastern United States.

Despite these efforts, many passenger opt for the speed and sometimes price advantages of the airlines. To counter this, AMTRAK offers special prices on regional or transcontinental travel. Tour packages are also popular, particularly with retired people who prefer relaxing and watching the ever-changing scenery to driving.

Although rail travel has declined in the United States, railroads in Europe and Asia play far more important roles in passenger and freight transportation. Railroads are more cost-effective and more efficient means of transportation in densely populated areas. Europeans have developed trains that can travel up to 250 miles per hour. The French Tres Grande Vitesse (TGV, very high speed) runs between Paris and Marseilles in three hours. The channel tunnel [Chunnel] links England with France and enables both trains and automobiles to travel the 23 miles of the English Channel.

In Japan, the bullet train can go up to 250 miles per hour. Not all trains go quite that fast, but the ride is remarkable smooth a beverage glass can rest on a table and not spill. As with the United States, the Japanese and European rail systems are heavily subsidized by their respective governments. However, without such subsidies, the roads and the air would be more congested.

Many Americans visiting Europe take advantage of the Eurail pass. The Eurail pass, which must be purchased from travel agents outside of Europe, allows visitors to travel throughout Europe, with the exception of the United Kingdom. Visitors can get on and off the train at hundreds of cities and enjoy the local attractions.

Automobile Travel:

Automobiles evolved from steam engines in the late 1800s, when karl Benz and Gottlieb Daimler build a factory for internal combustion engines, which is now Mercedes Benz.

In 1891, the production of automobiles began in large numbers. Before long, Henry Ford produced his first vehicle and invented the techniques for making automobiles on an assembly line. By 1914, Henry Ford was producing one Model T Ford every twenty-four seconds. The assembly-line production continues today with the additional help of robots.

The United States has about 150 million autos registered. The country with the next largest amount is Japan, which has about 33 million registered.

The call of the great open road and the increased financial ability of more families to purchase automobiles led to a tremendous growth in travel and tourism Motel and restaurants sprang up along the highways. The automobile made places accessible to more people.

Air Travel:

The Wright brothers, who enjoyed the hobby of gliding, decided to fit an engine to one of their gliders with movable fins and wingtip controls. To find an engine light enough, they had to build their own. In 1903, they tested their 13-horsepower engine. On the first run it lifted the craft in the air for twelve seconds and covered a distance of 120 feet.

In 1909 an airplane crossed the English Channel, and by 1919 a scheduled passenger service began between London and Paris. Realizing that others were about to attempt to cross the Atlantic, Charle Lindbergh persuaded a group of investors in St. Louis to fund construction of a new airplane in San Diego. The "Spirit of St. Louis" was built in sixty days. With 450 gallons of gasoline on board (the tanks even blocked forward visibility), Lindbergh made the first solo crossing of the Atlantic Ocean in 1927. This history making twenty eight hour flight was major turning point in aviation history. This monumental achievement was catalyst for massive investment in the airline industry. The first scheduled air service in the United States began in 1915 between San Diego and Los Angeles. Later, in 1930the Douglas Company in California introduced the DC-2, which could carry fourteen passengers and fly at a speed of 213 miles per hour. The most famous airplane, the DC-3, came into service in 1936. To this day, well over two thousands of them are still flying.

In 1944, an international conference was held in Chicago to establish international air routes and services. American and European delegates disagreed about how much to restrict competition, the Americans pushed for unrestricted competition.

However, seventy airlines from forty nations ratified an important agreement of transportation rates and created the international Air Transportation Association (IATA). The IATA is the major trade association of the world's airlines. Through international agreements on financial, legal, technical, and traffic matters, the worldwide system of air travel became possible.

American and European representatives met again in Bermuda in 1946 to work out a compromise. The Bermuda agreement, by which countries exchanged benefits, was to later become a model for bilateral negotiations. The six freedoms of the air agreed upon in Bermuda were as follows:

- The right to fly across another nation's territory
- The right to land in another country for non-commercial purposes.
- The right to disembark passengers and cargo from the carrier's home country in a foreign country.
- The right to pick up passengers and cargo destined for the carrier's home country from a foreign country.
- The right of transport passengers and cargo from one foreign country to another foreign country.

The right of an airplane to carry traffic from a foreign country to the home nation of that airline and beyond to another foreign country. In 1954, the first Boeing 707 came into service. By 1958, Pan American Airways inaugurated transatlantic flight from New York to Paris. A Boeing 707 could carry 111 passengers over a range of about 6,000 miles at a cruising speed of

600 miles per hour. Also in 1958, Mc Donnell-Douglas introduced the DC-8 which boasted a similarly impressive performance.

Other aircraft were introduced to handle the medium and short range routes. The Boeing 727 was introduced in 1964. It became the workhorse of the U.S. domestic market, carrying 145 passengers at a cursing speed of 600 miles per hour. In 1968, the Boeing 737 established itself as the short range challenger to the McDonnell-Douglas DC-9. The Boeing 747, introduced in 1970 was the first of the wide-body aircraft. It could transport four to five hundred passenger at a cruising speeds of 600 miles per hour over distances of abut 7,000 miles.

A consortium of European countries developed the Airbus. The Airbus A 340 is designed for the long-distance market, and the Airbus A 320 is for the short distance market.

The Concorde was the first supersonic aircraft, developed at a cost of $3 billion by the British and French governments. However it has been a financial white elephant. The Concorde has cruising speed of 1,450 miles per hour, vastly reducing time needed to fly from London to New York. A 747 flight leaving at 11 a.m. London time will land at 1:40 p.m. New York time. On a Concorde, a flight leaving at 11:00 a.m. London time will land at 9:50 a.m. New York time. Air France operates the Concorde from Paris, Dakar, and Rio de Janeiro. British Airways (B.A.) operates Concords between London and Bahrain and from London to Washington, D.C., or New York.

Air transformation has further reduced the cost per mile of travel, enabling millions of people to become tourists. As result, hotels, restaurants, and attractions have grown to keep pace with demand. The speed of air transportation enables vacationers to take inter-continental trips. Europe and Asia are only hours away as are all the cities of North and Latin America.

Cruise Ships:

More than two hundred cruise lines offer a variety of wonderful vacations, from the "Love Boat" to freighters that carry only a few passengers. Travelers associate a certain romance to cruising to exotic locations and being pampered all day.

Being on a cruise ship is like being on a floating resort. Accommodations range from luxurious suites to cabins that are even smaller than most hotel rooms. Attractions and distractions range from early morning work-outs to fabulous meals, with night life consisting of dancing, cabarets, and possibly gambling. Day life might involve relaxation, visits to the beauty parlor, organized games, or simply reclining in a deck chair by the pool reading a novel. Nonstop entertainment includes language lessons, charm classes, port-of-call briefings, cooking dances, bridge, table tennis, shuffleboard, and more.

For example, the new Crown Princess is a "super Love Boat" weighing in at 70,000 tons and costing $200 million. This ship is longer than two football fields and fields and capable of carrying up to 1,596 passengers. The Crown Princes was designed by Italian architect Reizo Piano. Its exterior resembles a head of a dolphin, and it features the "Dome," a 13,000 square-foot entertainment complex forward on the top deck. The Dome boasts a casino with black jack, craps, roulette tables, and masses of slot machines as well as a dance floor, bar, and lounge with wrap-around windows.

Radisson Hotels International has entered the $4.6 billion cruise business with a dramatic catamaran a twin hulled ship designed to prevent most of the pitching and rolling that causes seasickness. The new ship, the Radisson Diamond, can carry up to 354 passengers. Completed in 1992 for about $125 million, its cost was about 10 to 15 percent higher than a comparable single-hull ship. With rates at about $600 per day, this ship has joined the top end of the cruise market.

The cruise market increased more than 500 percent between 1970 and 1990. However, only about 6 percent of Americans have been on a cruise. Rates vary from a starting point of $195 per person per day on Carnival Cruise Lines to $600 on the Radisson Diamond. Rates typically are quoted per diem (per day) and are cruise-only figures, based on double occupancy. No two ships are alike each has its own personality and character. The nationality of the ship's officers and staff contributes greatly to the ship's ambiance. For example, the ships under the Holland America flag have Dutch officers and Indonesian/Filipino crew, and those belonging to the Epirotiki flag have Greek officers and crew.

Casual ships cater to young couples, singles, and families with children. At the other end of the spectrum, ship's that appeal to the upscale crowd draw a mature clientele that prefers a more sedate atmosphere, low-key entertainment, and dressing for dinner.

About four million people took cruises in 1993. Many passengers are remarkably loyal to their particular vessel; as many as half of the passengers on cruise may be repeat guests.

Tourism's Challenges and Opportunities:

Meeting the needs of travelers by providing tourism-related goods and services has proven to be an attractive form of economic development. Attempts to encourage the development and growth of tourism activities are often desirable because tourism creates jobs and brings money into a community or country. However unplanned tourism growth can lead to problems.

Although tourism can create greater cultural understanding and enhance economic opportunities, it may also change social structure; may place increasing demands on transportation systems, public services, and utilities; and may lead to environmental degradation. Whether we are participants in or beneficiaries of (both positive and negative) tourism activities we are all in one way or another affected by tourism.

Pause for a moment and consider the following examples of how tourism might affect our lives and communities. For example, tourism could create coastal town seeking economic security. However, as that town grows into a more popular destination, it can become overcrowded and the original residents who sought increased tourism expenditures may be driven out because of increased housing costs, higher taxes, and/or changing business demands. Tourism can generate needed funds to improve the lives of an isolated native tribe in the rainforests of South America. Yet, it can also forever change the lives of these peoples as they are exposed to the cultures and habits of the tourists who come seeking what they consider to be the ultimate travel experience.

The further of tourism provides many challenges and opportunities as well as many unanswered questions:

- Can tourism growth and development continue without creating environmental problems?
- How will advances in technology change tourism experience and how will tourists and service providers deal with each other?
- Will the expansion of the use of technology by tourism suppliers lead to a "low-touch" service that is less appealing to guests?
- As tourism service activities continue to grow, will an adequate work force with the necessary skills be available?
- Will tourism change the social structure of countries and communities when they experience increased tourism activities?
- Will the threat of terrorism continue and spread around the globe, decreasing potential travelers' sense of security and thus decreasing the

level of international travel?

These are only a few of the questions that may arise as plans are made to respond to the demands of tourism growth. Information presented throughout this block will provide you with the fundamental knowledge necessary to begin forming your own opinions and possible answers to many of the questions and issues that you will face as decision-makers of tomorrow.

As you search for answers to the future of tourism, let your thoughts and actions be guided by ethical principles. Although most people can easily distinguish between right and wrong based on their own personal experiences, they are often faced with decisions where it is difficult to make these clear distinctions. In an effort to promote ethical behavior, organizations often publish codes of ethics to help guide individuals in their daily activities and decisions.

Even without the help of a code of ethics there are some very simple questions you can ask yourself about any situation or problem to identify ethical and unethical behavior:

- Will someone be hurt in this situation?
- Is anyone being coerced, manipulated, or deceived?
- Is there anything illegal about the situation?
- Does the situation feel wrong to you?
- Is someone else telling you that there is an ethical problem?
- Would you be ashamed to tell you best friend, your spouse, or your parents about your contemplated actions or your involvement?
- Do the outcomes, on balance, appear to be positive or negative?
- Do you or others have the right or duty to act in this situation?
- Is there a chance that you are denying or avoiding some serious aspect of the situation?

Finally and possibly the simplest, yet most thorough ethical guideline is the Golden **Rule:** Do unto other as you would have them do unto you.

Trends in Tourism and Travel:

- Eco tourism, sustainable tourism, and heritage tourism will continue to grow in importance.

- Governments will increasingly recognize the importance of tourism not only as an economic force, but also as a social-cultural force of increasing significance.
- More bilateral treaties are being signed, which will make it easier for tourists to obtain visas to visit other countries.
- The promotion and development of tourism is moving from the public sector [government] to the private sector [involved industry segments].
- Internet bookings will increase.
- Franchising of travel agencies and home-based travel agents will increase.
- Technology will continue to advance, allowing even more information to be available more quickly to more places around the world.
- Marketing partnership and corporate alliances will continue to increase.
- Employment prospects will continue to improve.
- Ticket less air travel will become commonplace.
- Travel and tourism bookings via the Internet are increasing rapidly.
- As an ever increasing number of tourists visit destinations, managing these destinations is becoming a challenge
- There will be an increase in number of "boutique" airlines.
- Low-cost no frills airlines, such as Jet Blue, ATA, Ted {as in United}, and of course Southwest, are gaining an increase market share at the expense of the six main U.S. airlines. In case of India low cost airlines are Spice Jet, Indigo, Air Deccan are having an increased market share.
- Increasing use of ticket less travel.
- Airlines will try to entice travelers to book their travel via their Web sites, rather than via Expedia and similar sites.
- Increased use of automatic airport check-ins.
- Continued expansion in the cruise industry.
- More alternative cruises.
- Increased concern for the health and safety of travel and tourism.
- An increase in nature tourism.

Summary:

Tourism is the fastest growing industry of the world and a powerful force for improving international understanding and contribution to peace among all the nations of the world. As shown in the tourism model, tourism is a multifaceted service industry that has a rich history and exciting future marked by many challenging opportunities. Our journey into the study of tourism began with a brief look back in history. History provides many important lessons that help explain the growth and significance of travel in world economies. In fact, the lessons to be learned from history can still be used to help serve the needs of travelers today and in future. Travel continues to be influenced by factors such as time, money, mobility, and a relative sense of safety.

CHAPTER V

GROWTH AND DEVELOPMENT OF TOURISM

Introduction:

Tourism has entered in this millennium with the prospect of continued expression and greater importance in the world economy, facing many challenges. The significance of tourism is recognized in both developed and developing and beneficial agent of both economic and social change. Indeed, tourism has stimulated employment and investment, modified land use and economic structure, and made a positive contribution of the balance of payment in many countries throughout the world.

This ever expanding spirit of travel has lived on down the ages. In recorded history, there have been instances whereby one is able to know that man has been traveling throughout the ages. From the very early historic period, travel has had a fascination for man. Much of the travel in the beginning was eagerly unconscious and rather a simple affair. This unit will give a detail of travel pattern through the ages.

Travel through the Ages:

During a million years, changes in climate, dwindling food supplies or hostile invaders alone have made the people leave their homes to seek refuge elsewhere. Perhaps, it was the invention of the wheel, about five thousand years ago, which made travel possible followed by the invention of money by the Sumerians (Babylonia) that led to the development of trade and the beginning of a new era. The Phoenicians were probably the first real travelers in the modern sense as they went from place to place as travelers and traders. Almost at the same time, trade and travel developed in India where the wheel and money were already known at the time of the Indus Valley civilization (3000-1500 BC). Traditions of travel in India are, perhaps, the oldest in the world, the motive being primarily religion or trade. The great sages of the past retired to the Himalayas in the North or to the dense jungles of the South to meditate or set up their Ashrams (hermitages), which really were schools or universities of learning.

As early as the third millennium B.C., Egypt was a popular place for people from the then known world. The Babylonian King Shulgi who ruled Egypt 4,000 years ago is said to have boasted that he protected roads, built gardens and rest houses for respectable travelers. The Bible describes these ideas in the following words: "Many shall run to and fro and knowledge shall be increased". The ancient Greeks traveled short distances in small boats. Jason and the legendary Argonauts built a large ship to search for the Golden Fleece undaunted by dangers described in Homer's Odyssey. Herodotus, in 5th century B.C., toured Phoenicia, Egypt, Cyrenaica, Greece and the Black Sea and recorded the history, customs, traditions and practices of the people living in these areas. Philosophers – Thales, Pythagoras and Plato – all traveled to Egypt. Aristotle visited Asia Minor before starting his peripatetic school for wandering students. Greeks traveled to spas, festivals, athletic meets and to consult the Oracle at Delphi and the Asclepiads at Epidaurus. They traveled by mules and carts and stayed at wayside inns. A character in one of the works of that time asks for "the eating houses and hostels where there are the fewest bugs."

Travel for Trade and Commerce:

Travel in the past, was not undertaken for the purposes of pleasure but was related to trade. Commerce and the activities associated with it. Travel for seeking fortunes was the strongest force behind moving out. Throughout the course of history, traders and merchants have traveled to far off places in order to trade with other nations. Even the travelers like Marco Polo and Christopher Columbus were primarily moving out in search of rich lands, which could provide them with additional resources. With the gradual opening of the trade routes, travel became easier as well as regulated. With time, the trade relations matured into cultural relations and helped in better understanding. This simultaneous emergence of cultural barter system was a favorable development towards increase in travel activity during this period.

Phoenicians were amongst the earliest travelers in the modern sense. These were also the people who were credited for the invention of money. The medium of money was increasingly being used in various business and commercial dealings. The payment for travel to different centers as well as accommodation could now be done with greater ease. The element of 'organization' of travel came into light due to this reason.

It is noteworthy that early travel in the east or the 'orient' as it is called was also largely based on commerce. Travels to countries like India and China, which are very old civilizations, enjoyed the reputation of being countries of fabulous wealth. This reputation picked up even more strength when the Europeans headed towards Indian shores for the very purpose of trade and commerce.

Travel for Seeking Knowledge:

In the subsequent periods, the urge to explore new lands and to seek new knowledge about distant places, was yet another motive. Homers' literacy work 'odyssey' records the travel undertaken by ancient Greek and Romans. There are many instances of great explorers like Magellan, Bartholomew Diaz and many others, who spent many formidable years of their lives in search of knowledge. Perhaps, these great explorers can be credited for being the pioneers of modern day travel.

Travel for Religious Purpose

During the middle ages, a significant dimension was taken by travel for religious purpose. It became a well-established custom or motivation in many parts of the world. A large number of pilgrims were traveling to the main shrines of Europe and elsewhere. The adoption and spread of Christianity led to numerous pilgrims to the holy land. Religion became the unifying force and pilgrimages strengthened religious bounds. It was a means of forgoing unity and understanding between people from widely different regions. In India as well, pilgrims traveled across the country for solace and salvation since time immemorial. Emperor Ashoka (3rd Century BC) the great traveled a great deal in his eagerness to spread the principles of Buddha. His entourage first traveled to Nepal starting from Patliputra and then ventured to Lumbini on to Kapilavastu, ending at Bodh Gaya, where Buddha got enlightenment. Harsha Vardhan (7th Cent. AD) was another such emperor greatly influenced by the Buddhist scriptures. During his time, dharamshalas, rest houses, monasteries and temples were built for the pilgrims.

Roman Empire and Pleasure Travel:

There is a close association of Pleasure travel with the Roman Empire. Romans probably were the first pleasure travelers. Travel received a great stimulus from the good communication system and security of Roman Empire. Romans developed a fine network of roads and developed new roads wherever they went. They recorded information giving knowledge about routes, the name of major roads, distances etc and published this in form of travel literature. Romans were able to travel over a hundred or more miles in a day using relays or horses. They journeyed to see famous temples, the monuments and the famous pyramids of Egypt. They also indulged in travel during holiday occasions, particularly the famous Olympics in Greece.

Another face of pleasure travel was the development of spas and seaside resorts during 16th and 17th Century AD. Medicinal baths (later named as spas) were very popular with the Romans. It was thought that the patients using the spas, would also require some diversions, so the resorts added facilities for pleasure and entertainment to their medical facilities. Entertainment and amusement like theatre, competitions, and festivals were often provided at the sites of spas. These spas become externally popular with travelers.

Development of seaside resorts is also linked with the growth the spas. Towards the latter half of eighteenth century, people started realizing the curative effects of sea water along with the lure of sun, sand and sea waters. By the year 1865, major seaside resorts spring up in Britain, France Italy and a few more countries of central Europe. Millions of people visited these seaside resorts every year.

Renaissance and the Grand Tour:

Yet another unimportant stage in history of travel was marked by renaissance. Italy was perhaps the most important country where Renaissance came as a huge wave. There was full scale development of urban system and network of roads. By the end of 15th century, Italy itself became the object of attention and gained the status of Europe's economic and cultural leader. But the political wars and disunity played an important part in the dissemination of the Renaissance and development of 'grand tour'. Italy however remained as the intellectual capital of Europe. A growing number of young noblemen were being sent abroad to complete education in France and Italy.

The development of grand tourism followed a shift in the focus of culture and of economic and political power. The wealthy and educated visited countries that had passed their peak of prestige but were still venerated for cultural and historical reasons. The Romans visited Greece and the Eastern Mediterranean; the English visited Italy. The Grand Tourists respected the learning, antiquities and social refinements of the world. The 18th century is considered as the Golden Age of the Grand tour, especially, the years between 1763 and 1793. During this period, a great many poets, authors and intellectuals wanted to broaden their knowledge and learn new arts and crafts. The grand tourists paved the way for popular tourism of the nineteenth and twentieth century's. A generally accepted itinerary was also laid down which involved a long stay in France and Venice, and then a return by way of Germany and the Low Countries via Switzerland. Of course, there were variations to this itinerary but this was the most popular tourist route.

Concept of Annual Holiday:

The introduction of annual Holiday in Europe was yet another important landmark which enabled many people to undertake travel in large numbers during the 18th century. This concept was the forerunner to the paid holiday which later on was responsible for an extraordinary growth of tourism during the 18th century. The term holiday refers to the 'Holy Days' associated with religious observances. A feature of ancient Rome, public holidays were among the most enjoyable events of the period. The most important and enjoyable public holidays was known as 'saturnalia' literally meaning the feast of Saturn. Also in Europe, certain days commemorating religious festivals and saint's day became holy days on which there was holiday from work.

In the year 1552, in England an act was passed during the region of Edward the VI, "for keeping of holidays and fasting days" subsequently, public and semi-official offices in England frequently closed on certain saint's day. There were, however, no general public holidays until the time of Industrial Revolution. The concept of modern annual paid holidays is very largely an outcome of the past industrial revolution. In the present day parlance the word 'Holiday' is used generally in a secular sense meaning a respite from the routine of daily workday life and a time for leisure, recreation and amusement. There is no second thought to the view that, these very developments paved the way for development of travel in the subsequent periods.

Travel in the Nineteenth Century:

The early part of the 19th century, witnessed a surge in technological development in England, and later in Europe and America. The technological advancement also had a profound effect on the transport sector which directly affects the movement of people. The introduction of newer means of transport, made traveling to distant places more practical and enjoyable.

Emergence of Railways:

Railways is the perhaps the most used mode of transport today. However, the first rail link between Liverpool and Manchester was started in the year 1830. The newly completed railway track in England featured special provisions for carrying people in addition to freight. The rail network in the beginning was responsible for carrying goods from industrial centers to the centers of trade and commerce, but it initiated the process of carrying passengers, which later on became a mass movement. It was for the first time that the seaside resorts were within the reach of many people who otherwise have not been able to reach these places. Initially, the newly formed companies in England were concentrating in meeting the demands of trade and commerce instead of on the passengers. Gradually, the railway companies started to concentrate on carrying more passengers leading to trend of short day trips. This trend, later paved the way for organized excursions for public at special fares.

Emergence of Organized Travel:

The year 1841, saw the birth of organized rail travel. Thomas Cook, a Baptist preacher of Derbyshire was inspired with the idea of engaging a special train to carry the friends of temperance society from Leicester to Southborough. A few weeks later, the idea culminated into collecting some 570 passengers, who made a journey at a specially reduced return fare of one shilling per passengers. Encouraged by this success, Thomas Cook arranged similar ventures by chartering trains to places, which were now becoming popular. Due to this concept, Cook later came to be known as the greatest travel organizers. In fact, he is considered as the 'Father of Modern Tourism'. In the year 1843, nearly 3000 school children were taken on a trip from Leicester to Derby. From the year 1843 to 1863, Cook conducted circular tours of Scotland with almost 5,000 travelers a season. The success story of the Liverpool and Manchester railway reached the neighboring countries in Europe. Railway tracks were laid in France, Austria and Switzerland. Across the Atlantic, the tracks were laid in America which ushered in the spurt of travel to and from places where the tracks were laid. It was estimated that in the year 1881, the railways carried over 600 million passengers over the lines operated by over one hundred odd companies. The element of competition also creped in as the companies tried to make travel as comfortable as possible.

Luxury in Rail Travel:

In the early 1870's further boost was given to travel by introducing comfort and pleasure in long distance journey. The first class railway travel was introduced by an American, G.M. Pullman, who developed the Pullman coaches with their luxury furnishings, and dining facilities. These coaches were manufactured in America and imported by some railway companies in England and other European countries.

The eastern countries were not for behind in catching up with this growth. It was on April 16, 1853 that the first train took off from Bombay to Thane, covering a distance of 33 kilometers. From this, small beginning, the railway system in India has grown into the World's second largest system under one management with the total length of network covering around 64,000 km.

Sea Transport:

While railways were responsible for encouraging inland travel, the steamship crossed the boundaries and made strides in intercontinental travel. Shipping made significant contribution to travel during the 19th century. A number of sailing ships were built in America and England. There was improved communication across the Atlantic with America which led to development of deep sea shipping. The history of the Canard steamship company in England demonstrates important features in the growth of North Atlantic shipping. Use of the ships in the cruising fashion for the charter and operation of cruises on a limited scale dates from the mid-19th century. The year 1869 brought about the possibility of a much-shortened route between the west and the east as a result of creation of Suez Canal which connected the Red Sea with the Mediterranean Sea.

Change in Pattern of Society:

The second half of the nineteenth century, witnessed the growth of travel as a result of development of industrialized societies such societies in Western Europe and North America greatly felt the urge to travel purely for the purpose of rest and relaxation. This trend certainly gave way to what came to be known as the tourism phenomena in the later part of the century and in 20th century. The concept of modern day tourism emerged very much from the development of industrialized societies of the West. In fact, the figures point to the direct relationship between the development of industrialized societies and expansion of tourism traffic. Various official statements, observations by travel writers and other literatures also pin-point to this relationship.

Due to the industrial revolution the very concept of society underwent a Sea change. There was change in both economic as well as social systems prevailing at that time. There was emergence of the working class and sudden concentration of populations creating unhealthy conditions in towns and cities. However, there was little relief from routine of putting long hours of work in difficult working conditions.

Gradually, the industrialization brought in better working conditions and increase in material wealth for a large number of workers. Now, even these workers could avail holidays for rest, relaxation and pleasure an urgent need was felt to develop more holidays. There was substantial increase in purchasing power and disposable income which led to growth of pleasure zones. Many tourist resorts were developed to cater to the increasing needs of people who could afford a holiday. In the later 19th century, the Italian Rivera also gained popularity along with the English and the French.

Travel in the 20th Century:

Pleasure travel continued to expand in the 20th century as well. The main features of modern tourism can be listed as:

- Changes in mental attitudes towards pleasure seeking.
- Recognized value to travel for education.
- Increase in material wealth.
- Social prestige associated with travel.
- Need to find relief from working routine.
- Improvement in passenger transport system.

Up to the first quarter of the 20th century, pleasure travel was essentially a luxury commodity meant for the privileged sections of the society having time as well as purchasing power. In view of this a number of associations related to travel and hospitality also formed which organized excursions, holiday's camps, family rest and holiday homes for the like mind people.

A temporary halt to tourist movement came during the quarter of 20th Century due to the abruption of the First World War. As such the war saw a considerable decline in tourist travel not only within Europe but also all over the world. But this decline was soon surpassed as the travel activity soon reached the pre-war peak levels. Early post-war period also brought prosperity coupled with large scale migration and increased demand for international travel. An increasingly importance role was played by the development of mass communication system like the television, radio and press. It paved the way of increasing travel by way of widening knowledge and interest of a large number of people about other countries. The post-war period also witnessed attitudinal changes which influenced the volume and value of tourism. It was responsible for breaking down international barriers, resulting in the fostering of an ideal, optimistic, peaceful internationalism – just the climate in which tourism is likely of flourishes the most. There was also a rise in standard of living of the working and middle class. Tourists began to appear in countries where tourism had been virtually unknown a few years earlier.

Motorized Road Transport:

The motorized private and public road transport and the improved road conditions led to a tremendous growth of travel. The ten years after the First World War saw the first great impetus in the invention of the private motor car and coach. The motor car revolutionaries the holiday habits of the Europeans and Americans. Further, there was provision of good motor roads which led to the development of both domestic and international tourism. It was in the last quarter of the nineteenth century, that increasing attention was paid to the desirability of holiday with pay so the concept of mass tourism emerged along with the introduction of holidays with pay. The introduction of annual paid holidays is very largely of English origin. By the year 1939, some 11 million people were covered by the Holidays with Pay Act. The concept of paid holidays led to:

- Great mobility of population
- Creation of new industries
- Broadening the horizons of people
- Growth of many towns of distinctive functions.

The international labor organization's convention on paid holidays was on innovation well ahead of time because only few European countries had the provision of paid holidays till then. Paid holidays are now established all over the world and act as an active stimulant for travel growth. However, this wave of prosperity and place was disturbed by economic destruction and political instability due to the Second World War during 1939 to 1945. But again rapid development was witnessed in the activity, both on domestic as well as international level. There was a threefold increase during 1955-65. Also, the year 1976 saw an increase of more than 90% over the year 1965 with 220 million international tourist arrivals in the World. But again this boom was intervened by the economic crisis of 1973-74. It was not a long slowdown.

Growth of Air Travel:

Another post-second World War phenomenon was the introduction of air transport for the masses. There was tremendous increase in speed, safety and comfort-provided by the new civil aircrafts due to which there was noticeable increase in long distance travel. In the year 1952, two-class travel was introduced and there was also an increase in the aircraft capacity, which meant improved economy.

But the mostly dramatic event was the advent of jet travel in 1958 which added the dimension of speed, comfort and efficiency. Air travel grew at a phenomenal rate after 1960. Continuous advancement is being made since then by adding the elements of sophistication and luxury. Further, the supersonic aircrafts like the Concorde have added glamour to this industry. Yet another development during this period was the concept of inclusive tours and charter flights. The main causes of rapid growth of tourism can be summed up as:

- Economics reasons
- Social factors
- Technological advancement

Statistical Overview of Global Tourism Industry:

An international tourist, according to WTO definition, is a person who spend more than 24 hours on holiday or business and for any other purpose in a country other than his own. Based on this definition, the number of international arrivals worldwide in 2004 was 762 million – compared to only 287 million in 1983. In 1950, there were only 25 million tourists. Twenty years later, the number reached 160 million. World tourist arrivals for the year 2005 crossed the 800 million mark and reached 808 million, whereas it was 842million for the year 2006 with a growth rate of 4.5%.

WTO's 'Tourism 2020 Vision', (Long-term forecast and assessment report), forecasts that international arrivals are expected to reach around 1,006 million by 2010 and to 1,561 million by the year 2020, if annual increases match the World Tourism Organization's (UNWTO) long term predictions of a 4% average annual growth rate.

According to UN WTO report the following regions will be generating maximum number of visitors in the years come:

- Europe : 717 million tourists
- East Asia and Pacific : 397 million tourists
- America : 282 million tourists

Some other important facts related with travels are:

- Tourism is the world's largest industry, with annual revenue approaching $500 billion.

- Leisure is estimated to account for 75% of all international travel.

- Domestic tourism is generally projected to be 4-5 times greater than International tourist arrivals.

- Tourism accounts for roughly 35% of export of services and over 8% of Exports of goods.

• About 12-13% of the global workforce is directly or indirectly employed in tourism and related establishments. (International Labor Organization)

• For 83% of countries in the world, tourism is one of the top five sources of foreign exchange.

Increasing leisure time and disposable income following real cost of air travel, newer marketing methods like the 'package tour' and opening up of new travel destinations, all these factors are enhancing tourism growth.

Infect, "International tourism has now entered in a more stable phase of sustained demand without big peaks and troughs. Although the rate of growth is slowing gradually, international tourism is firmly on track to grow at an average of 4% barring unexpected socio-economic and political events."

Summary:

Travel has existed since the beginning of time when primitive man set out, often traversing great distances, in search of food and shelter necessary for his survival. Throughout the course of history, people have traveled for purposes of trade, religious conviction, economic gain, war, migration and other equally compelling motivations. In the Roman era, wealthy aristocrats and high government officials also traveled for pleasure across the world. Seaside resorts located at Pompeii and Herculaneum in Italy afforded citizens the opportunity to escape to their vacation villas in order to avoid the summer heat of Rome. Travel, except during the Dark Ages, has continued to grow, and throughout recorded history, has played a vital role in the development of civilizations.

Tourism as we know it today is distinctly a twentieth-century phenomenon. Historians suggest that the advent of mass tourism began in England during the industrial revolution with the rise of the middle class and relatively inexpensive transportation. The creation of the commercial airline industry following the Second World War and the subsequent development of the jet aircraft in the 1950s signaled the rapid growth and expansion of international travel. This growth led to the development of a major new industry. In turn, international tourism became the concern of a number of world governments since it not only provided new employment opportunities, but it also produced a means of earning foreign exchange. Tourism today has grown significantly in both economic and social importance. The fastest growing economic sector of most industrialized countries over the past several years has been in the area of services. One of the largest segments of the service industry, although largely unrecognized as an entity in some of these countries, is travel and tourism. According to the World Travel and Tourism Council 'Travel and Tourism' is the largest industry in the world on virtually any economic measures including; gross output, value added, capital investment, employment and tax contribution.

CHAPTER VI

INDIAN TOURISM AFTER INDEPENDENCE

Introduction:

It was after world war 2nd, that India conceived the idea of tourism development. However Indian tourism industry is not growing with the required pace as it should be. But in the new millennium tourism is growing at a good pace. It is the economic significance that introduced its new marketing concepts like Incredible India campaign. In this unit you will study contribution of various committees and Plans for tourism. India is a land of myth and legend and enjoys rich heritage of culture and tradition. A large number of people undertook journeys throughout the length and breadth of the country in older times mainly for the purpose of religion, trade and commerce and satisfies the quest for knowledge. There are references to pleasure travel as well which was undertaken particularly in the middle ages. But tourism in its modern sense commenced only in the middle of the 20th century.

Worldwide also, the post-second World War period brought in a rapid development of tourism. There had been a remarkable increase in both domestic as well as international tourism. Like the countries of Europe, the beginning of Tourism in India can be said to have been also made by the railways with the publication of the first handbook of India in 1931. It gave significant information about attractions, accommodation and other travel related aspects and contained a large number of illustrations and photographs.

Formation of Tourism Development Committees:

The Sargent Committee 1945:

It was in the year 1945, that a committee under the Chairmanship of Sir John Sargent, the than Secretary, Department of Education, Govt. of India was appointed to advise the government on the development of tourism. The report was submitted to the government in May, 1947. Its key objective was to survey the potential for the development of Tourism in India by means of:

• Examining the scope for development of both foreign and domestic tourist traffic

• Suggest ways and means for motivating such traffic to various attractions

• Propose facilities like transport and accommodation at such places.

• Supply of informative and promotional literature.

The Sargent Committee came at the conclusion that it would be in the interest of India to encourage and develop both external and internal tourism. It recommended the setting up of a separate organization which could be entrusted with the following:

• Publicity

• Production of tourist literature

• Liaison with government departments, travel agencies and hotels

• Provision of guides and coordination with different agencies

It also suggested setting up of publicity offices in the major capitals of the world like London and New York.

As a result, a small tourist traffic branch started functioning under the Ministry of Shipping and Transport in the year 1949. Four tourist offices were also set up in the metros. However, a big development was made in the year 1957, by establishment of a separate Department of Tourism by the recommendations of the Estimate Committee of Parliament, Govt. of India. The twin objectives behind the setting up of this department were:

• Development of facilities at certain selected places visited largely by foreign tourists

• Facilities for home tourist at places of local and regional importance.

Adhoc Committee on Tourism (The Committee):

After a fairly rapid increase in tourist arrivals until 1959, tourist traffic to India slowed down in 1960 and 1961. There was a decline of 3.9% in 1962. So the government appointed an Adhoc Committee in March 1963 to "inquire into the causes of decline and to suggest ways and means of expanding tourist traffic". The specific tasks of the committee were:

• Assess the requirements of tourism in terms of hotels and transport and suggest necessary measures for speedy provision and improvement of these facilities.

• Examine the general conditions prevailing in the country from the view point of promoting tourist traffic and means of improving these conditions.

• Examine rules and procedures regarding frontier formalities.

• Recommended necessary re-organization of publicity programs.

• Suggest measures to protect leakages of foreign exchange.

This Committee was set up under the chairmanship of the Late L.K. Jha, the then Secretary, Department of Economic Affairs, Govt. of India, with the Late S.N. Chib, Director General of Tourism as Member Secretary, and 4 other members. It had informal discussions with a member of leaders in the fields of hotel, travel agency business, railways, civil aviation as well as representatives of some Embassies in New Delhi. The report was submitted to the Government of India in August 1963. It made a large number of recommendations and suggestions indicating the important being the following:

• Liberalization of formalities regarding visas, permits and licenses.

• Construction and improvement of airports and training to personnel at airports.

• Better transport facilities with respect to air transport, railways and surface transport.

• Provision of modestly priced accommodation, providing loans and subsides to this sector.

• Undertaking Publicity and promotion to create a better image of India by way of arranging familiarization (FAM) trips, opening of new tourist offices abroad and production of quality publicity material.

• Concentrated development of a few selected centers instead of spreading the limited resources over too wide field.

• Development of handicrafts and cultural activities, provision of Indian style entertainment like sound and light programme and popularization of Indian cuisine.

• Training facilities for personnel of hotels, travel agencies and tourist offices.

• Building up proper organizational set up by way of corporation, which will be responsible for all commercial activities.

This report was the first most significant step in evolution of Indian Tourism. Most of the recommendations were accepted by the Government. There public sector corporations were set up in 1965, which were later amalgamated into one corporation called India Tourism Development Corporation (ITDC) which came into operation from October 1, 1966.

Tourism Promotion in 5-Year Plans:

The planed period started in 1951 in India. The 5 year plans were formulated with the view of channelizing the utilization of resources and finances.

• **First Five Year Plan (1951)**

The tourist Division was functioning under the Ministry of Transport and its outlay included some provision for tourism activities. As such there was no allocation for tourism in this plan.

- **Second and Third Plans (1956-66)**

Tourist facilities were taken up in a planned manner at this time. An outlay of Rs. 336.38 lakh was allocated for development of infrastructure both at central and State sectors. Development was to start with the provision of basic requirements at importance places of tourist interest.

- **Fourth Five Year Plan (1969-74):**

Fourth five year plan was perhaps the most important chapter in tourism evolution of India as it was marked by three significant developments.

a. Abolition of Part-II schemes

b. Changed pattern of tourist traffic to India

c. Ministerial tenure of Dr. Karan Singh.

It was realised that potentially, India was unrivalled as a tourist destination, still the country received a minuscule percentage of arrivals worldwide. Dr. Karan Singh was conscious of this depressing record and was clear about his task – to activate the tremendous potentiality that India possessed to get an increasing share to growing tourist market.

He commissioned some basic studies which resulted in:

UNESCO Report on Cultural Tourism in India (1969)

The aim of this report was to define the various aspects of cultural tourism in the country and review them in light of current conditions. The monumental heritage was divided into 4 principal subject groups.

- Monuments of Indian Buddhism
- Hindu Monuments
- Indo-Islamic Monuments
- Monuments of European and British Association.

Further, the report gave a list of 66 'top priority' sites and 22 sites of 'second priority'. Recommendations were given regarding conservation, beautification and provision of facilities at these centers.

Report on Organization and Management Survey of Department of Tourism by IIPA (1970):

The report recommended that the organizational structure of Department of Tourism should combine the flexibility of commercial organization with the legal authority of government for regulating the tourist industry and ensuring co-operation of other central departments, state and local administration. It further recommended that the National

Tourism Organization be named after India Tourism Authority headed by one man – the chairman-cum-Chief Executive. The government did not accept the recommendations, but created a National Tourism Board under the chairmanship of Minister of Tourism and Civil Aviation.

UNDP Report on Tourism (1971):

The UNDP, team comprised of internationally renowned tourism professionals, recommended the following suggestions pertaining to:

• Imaginative Publicity and Promotion

• Strengthening the role of Travel agencies

• Promulgating effective measures for improvement in hotel and development of training programs.

• Streamlining of research and statistical methods.

UN Study on Beach Resorts in India (1974)

The main objectives of the UN study on Beach Resorts were related to the following:

• Development of the sea beaches of Kovalam, Goa and Mahabalipuram, and provide a basis on which their tourist potential may be developed;

• To establish priorities for investment and recommended a program consistence with social, cultural and economic ethos of the country;

• To project potential visitor demand and facilities required to serve this demand.

The above three areas were evaluated in respect of their features like:

• Quality of Beach

• Environmental Setting

• Climate

• Attractions and Activities

• Accessibility

• Infrastructure and availability of land

UN Report on Institute of Tourism (1974)

It stressed the importance and need of tourism training for the development of tourism in India and recommended the establishment of a National Institute of tourism Training, research and promotion. An important outcome of the Report was setting up of Indian Institute of Tourism and Travel Management (IITTM) in 1983 which would supposed to impart education and training in travel and tourism and general management through long-term and short-term courses. The need of IITTM was seriously felt in order to undertake intensive research and training programme due to the following reasons.

• There was a slightly change in the pattern of tourist arrivals to India because of introduction of reduced air fares and sudden demographic change of visitors.

• The development of winter sports project at Gulmarg and a beach resort at Kovalam gained momentum in 4th plan. Some other projects and schemes including developing Buddhist circuits, setting up of youth hostels, promotion of wild life tourism, provision of camping sites besides loan funds for hotel department and transport were also of immense significance. To boost overseas publicity, 'Operation Europe' in association with Air India was launched which was further extended to cover UK, USA and Canada. New tourist offices were opened in major cities of these countries.

Fifth Five Year Plan (1974-79):

The fifth plan witnessed an extension of tourism development that was started in the fourth plan. The central program included the integrated development of Kovalam, Gulmarg, Goa, Kullu and Manali besides the development of ten architectural complexes of tourist importance; provision of accommodation and transport facilities at selected wild life sanctuaries and making intensive publicity abroad. A couple of master plans also initiated for the selected tourism centres. Furthermore three sub-committees were appointed by the Central Co-coordinating Committee in association with National Institute of Design, Ahmedabad.

The following two major studies were commissioned in this plan :

• Cost-Benefit study of Tourism in India undertaken out by National Council of Applied Economic Research (NCAER), New Delhi

• The UNDP financial assistance provision of Alternative passenger transportation system for Gulmarg Project

Sixth Five Year Plan (1980-85):

The phase of integrated development adopted in the previous plans continued at this time and further emphasis was laid on:

• Integrated department of selected beach and mountain resorts

• Development of places of cultural, wild life and sports tourism.

• Provision for setting up of tourist villages and new youth hostels.

The two significant developments which marked the Sixth Plan role in tourism promotion most notable were:

Introduction of Concept of Travel Circuits

Travel circuits were defined as "predetermined routes along which the flow of tourist traffic could be channelized". The advantages of such circuits were:

a) Regionalizing the flow of tourist traffic leading to its wider dispersal

b) Enable a more realistic assessment of places where infrastructure was to be provided or augmented.

c) Encourage intensive development of facilities.

d) Ensure effective promotion of resultant tourism product abroad.

Two or three travel circuits were identified in each state and union territories. A list of sixty one travel circuits covering four hundred forty destinations were considered for development.

Tourism Policy (1982):

It was presented to both the Houses of Parliament on November 3rd, 1982 with the following objectives:

• To foster better understanding through travel.

• To preserve, retain and enrich the country's world view and life-style, its cultural expression and heritage in all their manifestations.

• To bring socio-economic benefits to the community.

• To give a direction and opportunity to the youth.

• To offer opportunities not only for employment, but also for taking up activities of nation building character.

The policy statement read that high priority would be accorded to the development of international tourism and increasing attention to foster regional tourism. The thrust areas of the tourism policy were:

• Providing cheap accommodation

• Development of cultural tourism

• Adoption of selective approach for determining investment priorities.

• Develop tourist traffic from neighboring countries and newer markets like west Asia and North African countries.

• Maintain a judicious balance between conservation and development.

Seventh Five Year Plan (1985-90):

The vast potential of tourism in the country was recognized by the Planning Commission in the Approach paper to the 7th Plan. The Commission agreed to accord tourism the status of an industry and laid emphasis on encouraging private sector investments in developing tourism. The industry status meant that tourism related business activities would be eligible to the same incentives and concessions as were available to other export industries. Subsequently, 15 states and 3 union territories declared tourism as an industry and four states declared hotels as an industry.

In this five year plan special emphasis was given on leisure and holidays tourism due to the emergence of travel circuit's concept. The main emphasis was on "vigorously promoting domestic tourism and moving towards diversification of overseas tourism to India. The allocation was Rs. 68.68 Crore as compared to Rs. 21 Crore in 6th Plan. In this plan period a National Committee on Tourism was set-up by the Planning Commission in 1986, with a view to formulate a long-term perspective plan for tourism sector. The committee was constituted by the Prof. Mohamud Yunus, Chairman of Trade Fair Authority of India with composed of 12 other eminent persons from tourism and related fields. The recommendations of the Report were:

• Tourism should be fully exploited for the economic development of the country.

• Since it was not feasible for the public sector to continue with large investments, private sector should initiate investment in the sector.

• The development strategy should be based on principles of:

a) Low-cost economy

b) Higher levels of productivity

c) Improvement in efficiency of infrastructure

d) Promoting competition

e) Selective approach instead of spread approach

• For balanced tourism development, following steps should be taken care of:

a) Development selected tourism circuits

b) Diversify tourism

c) Restore and develop National heritage projects

d) Explore new tourist generating markets

• Incentives for accommodation sector

• Professionalize the approach to marketing activities along with a national image building plan.

• A liberal policy for foreign airlines, charter flights, facilitation procedures and the like.

• Reorganization of structure of the Department of Tourism on the pattern of the Railway Board.

• Human Resource Development is of vital importance and Indian Institute of Tourism and Travel Management (IITTM) should be developed as an open body in Travel Trade educational development.

• Harmony between local and ecological conditions by assessing the tourism carrying capacity of each area.

The report was submitted by the Committee in 1988 and its recommendations were considered for implementation by all concerned organization.

Eighth Five Year Plan (1992-97):

In this plan period, it was observed that the future expansion of tourism should be achieved mainly through the private sector. The tourism infrastructure was to be provided privately and essential infrastructure should be created by public sector. The specific projects of Department of Tourism included the development of Buddhist circuit, construction of tourism complexes, provision of drinking water and public convenience and wayside facilities at tourist centers and development of beach and adventure tourism. In order to make integrated tourism development the National Action Plan was also introduced published in May 1992, which charted seven objectives as central concerns of the Ministry of Tourism:

• Socio-economic development of areas
• Increasing employment opportunities
• Development of domestic tourism for budget category
• Preserving national heritage and environment
• Development of International Tourism
• Diversification of tourism products
• Increase in India's share in world tourism.

The Eighth Plan aimed at to catch hold of the high spending tourists from Europe and USA. It also envisaged a 'master plan' to integrate area plans with development of tourism. Further, the strategy was thought to be, to devise suitable location-specific solutions, so as to reverse the process of degradation of natural resources and ensure sustainable development. Fourteen institutes of Hotel Management and Food craft Institutes were opened during this plan period. A major scheme related to setting up of culinary institutes was opened with foreign assistance and expertise. Another interesting development in this period was the adoption of liberalization, privatization and globalization policy (New economic policy) in year 1991. This gave a further impetus to enable foreign investment in tourism.

9th Five Year Plan (1997-2002):

During this plan period a total launched total outlay of Rs. 595 Crore was sanctioned for the execution of various early schemes the thrust areas for

tourism development were:
- Development of indigenous tourism (local culture)
- Development of natural, health and pilgrimage tourism
- Tourism promotion in North-East
- Enrichment of environment and eco system
- Development of national and international understanding
- Coordination with relevant agencies for synergized development of
- Tourism.

Tourism was recognized as a central input for economic development process and emphasis was laid on reviewing the tourism policy. A new tourism policy was formulated in year 1997. The action points of this policy were related to:
- Suvidha (facilities)
- Soochana (information)
- Security (safety)
- Conservation
- Product Development and Promotion
- Marketing
- Foreign Investment and Incentives
- Resources for Development
- International Cooperation
- Areas of special interest
- Economic and social benefits
- Professional excellence
- Private sector – public sector partnership

10th Five Year Plan (2002-2007):

There was considerable increase in the allocation of budget to Ministry of Tourism and the amount earmarked for tourism development was Rs. 2900 Crore. This plan has witnessed developments like bilateral air agreements, open sky policies; emergence of low cost airlines, frequent use of CRS both by customers and intermediaries. Special emphasis was given to promote India as a global tourism brand for which the 'Incredible India' campaign was launched which proved quite fruitful.

Tourism Information Offices:

One of the major steps undertaken during 1955-56 was the opening of tourist offices both in India and abroad. Steps were taken to establish Regional offices too at important ports of the tourist entry. Initially four tourist offices were opened in Delhi, Bombay, Calcutta and Madras. This was followed by the establishment of a chain of information offices all over the country. By the year 1955, nine such offices were opened. They supplied updated information on places of tourist interests to tourists on their arrival. However in view to attract more foreign tourists to India the Government decided to open a chain of tourist offices overseas. The first step in this direction was the establishment of Government of India Tourist Office at New York in the United States of America in December 1952. To arouse interest among Europeans to visit India, a tourist office was also opened in London in July 1955. Two more offices were opened, one in Paris in February 1956 and the other in Frankfurt in September of the same year. In order to generate tourist traffic from Australia and New Zealand, a tourist office was opened in Melbourne in September 1956. Also in 1956 an office was opened in Colombo on the occasion of 2500th anniversary of Gautham Buddha. The office in Colombo was responsible to generate Buddhist tourists from Sri Lanka.

Statistical Overview of Indian Tourism:

Let us now have a look at the Figures of Indian Tourism.

Modern tourism in India is increasing day by day. It is evident from the previous trends that Indian tourism overall growth is satisfactory. From 1950 where India had received 15000 foreign tourists it has gone to about 4.43 million tourists in 2006. This had made Indian tourism a big one. In addition to 4.43 million foreign tourists in India there is about 300 million domestic tourists also, which make India a tourist country. In India the average length of stay of tourists is quite high. It is about 27 days, which is quite higher than European countries.

The year 2004 has been a highly successful year for India's tourism. The foreign tourists crossed 3 million figure with arrival estimated at 3.37 million. The foreign exchange earnings also recorded an unprecedented growth of about 36% with receipts at US$ 4810 million. The growth of about 24% in foreign tourist arrivals during 2004 was achieved over and above a growth of about 14% witnessed in the year 2003. This was achieved despite the fact that the world over, there was a decline of about 1.5% in tourist arrivals in 2003, and only a growth of 10.7% in 2004. The year 2005 too had also recorded a great success in tourist arrivals.

For the third successive year, India witnessed a positive growth in foreign tourist arrivals, reaching a level of 3.92 million against 3.46 million during 2004. India achieved 13.2% growth rate in 2005. With this growth, the share of India in world tourism, which was hovering between .38% to

.39% for number of years was around 0.49%. Add to this year 2006 broke all the previous records and much awaited 4 million mark was achieved during this year. The earnings from tourism were Rs. 29603.56 Crore and India's share in global tourist finally crossed .50%. This has become possible due to the following reasons:

• Improve tourist infrastructure at important tourist destinations/circuits

• Focus attention on growth of hotel infrastructure, particularly of budget hotels

• Enhance the connectivity through augmentation of air seat capacity and improving road infrastructure to major tourist attractions

• Directly approach to potential tourism market through 'Incredible India' campaign

• Create world class collaterals

• Launch centralized electronic media campaigns

• Have greater focus in the emerging markets, particularly in the region of China, North East Asia and South East Asia

• Use internet and web connectivity

• Launch road shows in big source markets of Europe

The India tourism also continued to receive international acclaim when it won the 'Gold Award' of the Pacific Asia Travel Association (PATA) in the travel advertisement print category and 'Marketing Award' in 2004. The Ministry of Tourism also Won 2005 PATA Grand Award in the Heritage category for its 'Ajanta Ellora Conservation & Tourism Development Project' and the PATA Gold Award in the Print Media category for its 'Incredible – Taj'. Campaign

Summary:

Tourism industry and its growth in the 21st century is phenomenal. No doubt it took long time to promote Indian tourism resources. Vast geographical area, cultural diversity, religious centres, more than 1700 monuments, 26 World Heritage Sites, wildlife research, extreme weather conditions, unsurpassed cultural heritage site etc. are some of attraction from Indian tourism checklist. The tourist flow has not been, as much one would expect. Tourism is a highly complex phenomena and the magnitude of tourism is always on the increases To keep our performance anywhere near the track of world tourism, we have to formulate a policy of tourism by taking a far more comprehensive approach and evolve new strategies to tap the country's enormous tourism potential. We have to keep place with infrastructural changes and take necessary steps to make the stay of foreign tourists a memorable one.

CHAPTER VII

DIVERSIFICATION OF TOURISM

Introduction:

Tourism enters the new millennium with the prospect of continued expression and greater importance in the world economy, facing many challenges. The significance of tourism has been recognized in both developed and developing countries. There is a widespread optimism that tourism might be a powerful and beneficial agent of economic and social changes. Indeed, tourism has stimulated employment and investment, modified land use and economic structure, and made a positive contribution to the balance of payment in many countries throughout the world. Above all tourism is not only growing in numbers rather there has been noticed a considerable growth in the dimension of tourism as well. Tourism has gradually moved from the traditional resources towards the non-traditional resources. 'Diversification' is the buzz word in Tourism in the present scenario. Tourists' attention is shifting from established destinations such as sea beaches to emerging destinations. Tourism has become a multiple activity focused with integration of shopping and recreation, entertainment and education, culture and business. New travel patterns reflect changes in consumer behavior, economic strength of source markets, new destinations and political realignments. There is a new tourism 'wave' arising from developing Asian economies with less travel constraints. The trend of short breaks is also increasing. There is also a trend toward high yield and extended vacations that are purpose driven by education, wellness or other forms of motivation. Leisure destinations are not providing a greater menu of activities to accommodate the increasingly wide range of interests desired by the individual consumer and the family. Destinations and products have become weather independent whereas the markets have also become less weather dependent.

If we go through the annals of human behavior it seems that travel was one of the oldest human activities. It existed even before the recorded history, when the man was roaming in search of food and shelter during pre-historic period. From the very earliest historical period, travel has fascinated mankind in various ways. Much of travel in the beginning was largely unconscious and rather a simple affair. Travel in the distant past was not a thing of pleasure as is the case now. The travelers of the ancient period were merchants, pilgrims, scholars who went across the world out curiosity exploration and exciting experiences. Trade and commerce was however sole motivating factor in the ancient past, which made people travel to distant lands in order to seek fortunes. Travel got a big boost with the opening of the trade routes as the travelers from distant lands started moving about in large numbers and visited many places for the business purposes. Thus opening of new trade routes provided market places to merchants and these trade relations matured into cultural relations and better understanding of each other's way of life. Various arts, culture and customs exchanged and science, technology, religious faiths also experienced influence of each other.

Development of Tourism:

The importance of tourism industry can well understand as it promotes national integration, builds better international understanding besides generating a vast employment opportunities. The economy of many countries like Singapore, Thailand and France etc. is solely based on tourism. One of the major characteristics of modern society is the emergence of phenomenon of travel and tourism on mass scale. Almost all inventions and innovations in the world have in some way contributed to the increased ability of people to travel. Today, people talk of visiting capitals and exotic places around the world almost as an everyday happened stance. Our world has become a world where countries and communities are in contact with each other. Today, tourism is at its peak. It is more highly developed than it has even been.

People have always traveled, but with the periods creation of amenities and facilities on highway's. But before this people were concerned with the daily task of living; their idea of a trip was to their neighbor's farm, or to the local town market. The transition from a rural society to an industrial one brought with it the tourism phenomenon. In fact, one characteristic of industrial and post-industrial society is the onset of leisure time associated with travel.

The first major change in modern history came with the Industrial Revolution. Modern machines and techniques brought people into the cities. As we moved to an urban society, changes in religious organizations and in rural kinship system led to the formation of recreational groups. Leisure pursuits became a new aspect of our society. There was a change from the concept that "the idle mind is the devil's workshop" to the realization that leisure is a human right if not a God-given one.

The use of computers in recent years has resulted in what we may call a second industrial revolution. Computers have not only increased our ability to work quickly and produce more, they have given us even more leisure time and better incomes with which to pursue other interests. Although attitudes towards our work ethic and our free time are changing, most people still feel that they must work hard and play hard; that their leisure pursuits, which may be healthy and restful, should also keep them busy.

Traditional Tourism Resources:

Let us now have a look at the traditional resources that were mainly responsible for tourist movement in the past. These resources can be headed as:

Religious:

Religious tourism is as old as "human civilization" is. It was during the Buddhism era when people started travelling to the places, which were related to the life span of Gautam Buddha. The travel of people to Monasteries and education centers like Nalanda University give shape to religious tourism. Religious tourism has a different mode, each community, ethnic group at the ground level different form each other. They have their own way of worship and rituals.

Religious activities are undertaken by pilgrims of different faiths and beliefs including Hindus, Muslims, Christians, Sikhs, Buddhists, Jains, and Jews. They visited quite a large number of religious places in search of solace, salvation and renunciation. Some of the places which were familiar among pilgrims of Hindu and Buddhists become the notable centers of mass visitors of modern India.

Pleasure and holiday:

The Romans probably were the first pleasure travelers in the world. Travel became quite sophisticated by the time Christ was born. There are reasons to believe that pleasure travel also developed at the same time in China, India and Japan. The Romans used to travel up a hundred miles a day by using relays of horses, taken from rest posts five to six miles apart. They traveled to see the temples in the Mediterranean area and the Pyramids of Egypt. They also journeyed to medicinal baths, called "spas", and seaside resorts. The Roman Empire had an excellent network of roads. Plutarch spoke of "globe trotters, who spent the best part of their lives in inns and boats." Persons of means traveled in little (littiga) four-wheeled wagons or chariots. Others used carts or public coaches. Some Roman cargo ships carried a few passengers. Private vessels could be marvelously luxurious. The vessel that carried the beautiful queen Cleopatra to meet Mark Antony reportedly had billowing scarlet silk sails, silver tipped oars, decks draped with royal purple cloth. Holiday tourism was also on cards during ancient times but this was given a new shape in nineteenth century by Thomas Cook when he introduced the concept of 'Organized Tour".

Visiting friends and relatives:

This was one of the older concepts of tourism, in which people visit from one place to other, to meet their friends and relatives, reasons may be to attend some special ceremonies etc.

Sun, sand and sea:

Travel in the past was mainly dependent on going to beach or seaside resorts or hill stations. Such resorts provided rest and relaxation to tourist from the daily chores of life. Such resorts also provided entertainment and recreational facilities like health clubs, carious, other sport, games for children etc. Hence, they combined different activities at one place for providing a wholesome time to families.

Aboriginal sites:

People in the past used to visit places especially concerned with their origin.

Quest to visit learning centre:

In ancient and medieval period people used to take trips to famous learning centres like Ashrams, institutions and centers disseminating knowledge and information for the betterment of human being.

Non Traditional Resources:

However, with the passage of time, a paradigm shift has been noticed from traditional to non-traditional tourism resources resulting in diversification of the tourism products. During the past decade, particularly in the new millennium, a number of dimensions have been added to the tourism product.

1. Alternative forms of tourism:
• Medical Tourism
• Health tourism
• Ecotourism
• Ethnic Tourism
• Rural/ Farm/ Village Tourism
• Golf Tourism
• Theme Parks Tourism

- Spiritual Tourism
- Adventure Tourism
- Camping Tourism

Paradigm Shift in Tourism Industry:

The following are major factors for paradigm shift in tourism industry:

• **Diversification in Travel Pattern:** There is evident change in old and modern travel pattern. Earlier there was flow of tourists from east to west, now it is North-South flow. People now taking trips to within their region, which lead to end in the Atlantic dominance. This paradigm shift suggests the Asia-Pacific dominance. There is also a shift in duration of tour from long tour to short stay; reasons may be lack of time and development in transportation facilities. Now travel is considered as a free trade.

• **Diversification in Destinations:** The travel has now changed from established tourism destinations to unexplored travel destinations. Emergence of China, African countries and India in global tourism map are the best examples of this shift in destination choice.

• **Diversification in Industry Nature:** The nature of tourism industry has changed a lot. Earlier countries were concerned with number of visitors but now they are thinking of economic and social benefits of tourism. Earlier there was a lot of competition among countries but now they are opting for intelligent cooperation. Product was the major dominating factor in old tourism, which is now based on customer orientation.

• **Diversification in Products:** Earlier travel was limited to natural environment and people were interested in single activity and biggest constraint on tourism was seasonality. Now the product has changed to artificial environment and people are opting for multiple activity based tours. Modern tourism is now has taken shape of all seasons tourism.

• **Diversification in Developer Control:** The developers control over tourism has also changed with time. There was the time of political lobbying, which now changed to approvals via referendum. These days' developers are giving more importance to jobs and small businesses rather than just going for more and more economic impacts of tourism. We have changed our focus from environment protection to environment improvement. Earlier tourist arrival was considered as cultural intrusion, where as it is now considered as a major force for heritage protection.

• **New Concern of Promoters:** Present concern is now on developing franchise opportunities, meeting investors' needs through economic simulation. Tourism is now on top priority list of states' budget and other related stakeholders.

• **Change in Consumer Attitude:** Tourist has also changed a lot. He is now a value conscious traveler, who is traveling for self-improvement through vivid experiences.

• **Shift in observing technologies:** The observing technologies have also changed from simple print media to interactive media and maps has been replaced by GIS and GPS technology.

• **Pragmatic Marketing Style:** This is one of the best thing happened to tourism. Now targeted customers are considered as data base rather than socio-economic groups. The place of one way communication has been taken by relationships through customer management techniques.

Factors for Diversification of Tourism Industry:

The major factors for tourism industry expansion can be listed as:

• Increased urbanization

• Desire to escape from daily routine

• Growth of information and technology

• Growth of transport facility leading to greater mobility and accessibility

• Increased disposable incomes

• Change in age-wise composition of tourist with the dominance of 18-50 age groups.

• Change in family set-up like late marriages, Prevalence of DINKs (Double Income No Kids), and emergence of nuclear families etc.

It would not be wrong to say that, the above listed factors and the diversification process of tourism are complementary to each other. On one hand, the demand for newer forms of tourism arise because of the above factors and readiness of people to experiment and on the other hand, the initiators, (developers) want to offer something unique and novel to the prospective travelers. Therefore, in the present scenario, a prospective traveler has a variety of options for fun and recreation.

Summary:

Travel has existed since the beginning of time when primitive man set out, often traversing great distances, in search of food and shelter which provided him clothe, food and other necessary help for his survival. Throughout the course of history, people have traveled for purposes of trade, religious conviction, economic gain, war, migration and other equally compelling motivations. In the Roman era, wealthy aristocrats and high government officials traveled for pleasure and recreation across Europe and

Asia. Seaside resorts located at Pompeii and Herculaneum afforded citizens the opportunity to escape to their vacation villas in order to avoid the summer heat of Rome. Travel, except during the Dark Ages, has continued to grow, and throughout recorded history, has played a vital role in the development of civilizations.

Tourism as we know it today is distinctly a twentieth-century phenomenon. Historians suggest that the advent of mass tourism began in England during the industrial revolution with the rise of the middle class and relatively inexpensive transportation. The creation of the commercial airline industry following the Second World War and the subsequent development of the jet aircraft in the 1950s signaled the rapid growth and expansion of international travel. This growth led to the development of tourism industry. Today tourism became the concern of a number of countries since it generates not only provided new employment opportunities, but it also produces foreign exchange. Tourism today has grown significantly in both economic and social front.

The fastest growing economic sector of most industrialized countries over the past several years has been in the area of services. One of the largest segments of the service industry, although largely unrecognized as an entity in some of these countries, is travel and tourism. Changing life styles of the people and the opening up of the economy has contributed to the growth of tourism industry. With the advent of globalization travel barriers have been broken and there is flow of free trade. Tourists' attention is shifting from established destinations such as European countries to emerging destinations as Asia-Pacific countries. Tourism has become a multiple focused with integration of shopping and recreation, entertainment and education. New travel patterns reflect changes in consumer behavior, economic strength of source markets, new destinations and political realignments. In modern tourism industry there is diversification from traditional tourism resources (Sun, sand, sea, religion, leisure, holiday etc.) to non-traditional resources like alternative tourism forms and business tourism.

CHAPTER VIII

ALTERNATIVE TOURISM

Introduction:

Something has surely happened in the world of tourism recently. There are opinions stating that the era of traditional package holidays or "mass tourism" has come to an end. The newer tourism forms can be seen as representing totally new concepts and approaches for modern tourism practices. This unit has the purpose of understanding what 'Alternative Tourism' is. To understand this concept we should explore what tourism is and begin classifying in some way the diverse types of tourism. The diverse tourism types are created from the experiences that tourists want to experience; such are the cases of the nature tourism, cultural tourism, and adventure tourism. Each type of tourism is a way to give a denomination to a new market niche for a different experience. Such is the case of the two big types of tourism:

(1) Mass Tourism, and

(2) Alternative Tourism.

Mass Tourism:

Mass tourism is a concept that is very commonly used for such tourism where tourism products and services are consumed by tourists on mass scale. The basic characteristics of mass tourism are:

• The sheer numbers involved mean that the tourism products have to be offered under condition of mass production.

• There is a growing level of expenditure on consumer goods associated with tourism.

• A few producers dominate particular markets.

• Producers take the lead in developing new tourism attractions.

• By and large, mass tourism products are little differentiating.

Mass tourism refers to the participation of a large numbers of people in tourism. In this sense the term is used in contrast to the limited participation of people in some specialist forms of tourist activity. Mass tourism is essentially a quantitative notion, based on the proportion of the population participating in tourism or on the volume of tourist activities. The driving forces behind mass tourism are said to be the desire to get away from daily routine and in search of pleasure commonly known for the four

Ss: 'sun, sea, sand and sex'.

Mass tourism is responsible for the unprecedented growth of tourism industry in modern days. One cannot just deny the economic benefits generated by tourism in the form of income generation by tourist expenditure, employment creation, foreign exchange earnings, tax receipts, social benefits, tourism multiplier, transaction multiplier and many more. Notwithstanding the good effects of tourism in economy one cannot overlook the adverse consequences of mass tourism development.

Alternative Tourism:

Mass tourism is seen as desirable the more traditional form of tourism development where short-term, free market principles dominate and the maximization income is paramount. Mass tourism has caused problems, because it has. There has, quite justifiable, been a need to identify an alternative approach to tourism development that lessens the negative consequences of the mass tourism approach. Thus the alternative tourism perspective has become as popular paradigm.

Under the alternative tourism concept we can find a series of classifications and types of tourism. What characterized the concept of 'Alternative' is the existence of small or medium company, created by families or friends, where the possibility of more contact with the communities is and where most of the times there is a respect for environment. The various alternative tourism forms can be explained as follows:

Medical Tourism and Health Tourism:

The very concept of health tourism goes back the time of The Ramayana and Mahabharata. In modern era financially well off people determined to stay well and stress free and this segment is an expanding and profitable market according to Mary Tabachi of Cornell University's School of Hotel Administration "Health Tourism is any kind of travel to make yourself, or a member of your family, healthier". Health tourism today focuses mainly on two areas:

- **Pampering and**
- **Wellness**

Pampering involves offering people an experience that makes them feel good-services such as massages, herbal wraps and exfoliating scrubs. Wellness involves helping healthy people prevent problems so they stay well, both physically and mentally. Sometimes this means offering diagnostic testing to identify potential problems. More often, guests who have self-identified concerns are taught how to relieve stress, change eating habits, reduce the likelihood of sports injuries or improve their sex lives.

Health Tourism has a promising future in the land of Kerala where the first plastic surgery was performed by Sushruta about 2000 years ago. Kerala is a heaven for health seekers as it offers authentic ayurvedic treatments. In-fact, it has pioneered health and medical tourism in India. The state has made concerted efforts to promote it in a big way, which has resulted in a substantial increase in visitor arrivals into the state. Kerala and ayurveda have virtually become synonymous with each other. The bias towards health tourism in Kerala is so strong that Kerala Ayurveda centres have been established at multiple locations in various metro cities. Kerala participates in various trade shows and expos wherein the advantages of this traditional form of medicine are showcased. The states equable climate, natural abundance of herbs and medicinal plants, and the cool monsoon season are best suited for ayurveda's curative and restorative packages. On the world level, Thailand is famous for spa treatments. Another facet of Health Tourism in India is the popularization of Yoga the world over. Yoga has gained all the more importance because of exponents like Swami Ramdev and B.K.S. Iyengar. One can practice Yoga for all sorts of seasons:

- To remain fit
- To stay healthy/ recover your health
- To balance nervous system
- To calm your busy mind
- To live in a meaningful way

It is believed that Yoga helps one in finding the very source of happiness, beyond pleasure and pain. It leads to 'self-realization' and seeks to recover one's full potential. This highlighted importance of Yoga, which has also been recognized and accepted by international celebrities like Halle Berry, Prince Charles and others, is a matter of pride for the Indians. Every year in the month of March, International Yoga Festival is held on the banks of River Ganga at Rishikesh which attracts people from far and wide. In fact, Rishikesh is called the 'Yoga Capital' of the world as it attracts those who are in search of mental peace in the midst of humdrum of modern life. There are many ashrams in Rishikesh offering courses on meditation, Yoga and Hindu philosophy. Another luxury resort in the Himalayas is the Ananda Spa, which lists in the top 5 spas of the world.

Although health and medical tourism are used interchangeably many a times, but there is a marked difference between the two medical tourism essentially deals with the surgical part of curing. Talking particularly about India, it has come a long way as the facilities in India are of international standards at a much cheaper rate, which is encouraging patients from neighboring countries including Middle East, UK and even USA for specialized treatments. India's healthcare industry is worth $23 billion (4% of GDP). The industry is expected to grow by around 13% per year for the next four years.

A cost of medical procedures seems out of control in the west, patients are becoming medical tourists to India. Surgeries in India cost one-fifth of what they cost in USA. Given the availability of top of the live facilities related to hospital and diagnostic, this has become a virtual growth sector.

According to CII, India has a potential of attracting 1 million health tourists per annum, which could contribute $ 5 billion to the economy. Recently enacted fiscal and non-fiscal incentives by the government are set to further stimulate development of health sector. The various surgeries offered by multi-specialty hospitals in India are:

- Bone Marrow transplant
- Cosmetic surgery
- Gynecology and obstetrics
- Joint replacement surgery
- Neurosurgery
- Osteoporosis
- Refractive surgery
- Vascular surgery
- Cardiac care

Due to considerable difference in cost of treatments, some clinics such as Kaya skin clinic have seen a 200% increase in overseas clients in the past six months (cosmetic surgery). Not far behind is the concept of Dento Tourism Increasing number of tourist are curing their teeth while touring India. Here, the focus is mainly on 45-60 age group, because it is at this age that dental problems begin and the patients also have enough savings to spend on travel and leisure as well.

Ecotourism:

Ecotourism is the most fascinating and most recent form of nature tourism. It encompasses activities which make a destination integrated, environment friendly sustainable and useful for visitors and local inhabitants. It is not a nature-based tourism attraction where visitors go and enjoy nature and its surroundings. But it takes place in nature's solitude and visitors and destination operators attempt to envisage appropriate methods and measures to give direct and indirect benefits, both to hosts and guests, in a mutually accepted manner. While mass tourists are more interested in the traditional sun, sand and sea, driving, shopping, night life etc., experiences which ranked as most important to eco-tourists are the following:

- Less crowded destinations
- Remote wilderness
- Learning about wildlife and nature
- Learning about natives and their cultures
- Community benefits
- Viewing plants and animals
- Physical challenge

Ecotourism, in other words, incorporates both a strong commitment to nature and a sense of responsibility. Fortunately, the sense of responsibility that ecotourism has adopted in the last decade has become a growing force for responsible tourism and conservation. It is about a quality experience rather than necessarily a pristine environment.

Ecotourism is not only the fastest growing sector of the tourism industry, it has also been accepted as a hopeful new approach to preserving fragile land and threatened wild areas and provide opportunities for community-based projects. However, eco-tourists too, differ greatly in several aspects like:

- Destination traveled
- Length of stay
- Desired level of physical effort and comfort
- Importance of nature in trip motivation
- Level of learning desired
- Amount of spending
- Desired activities
- Personal demographics

Ecotourism – Resources

The following nature of attractions and the major ecotourism resources in India:

- Biosphere Reserves
- Mangroves
- Corals and Coral reefs
- Deserts
- Mountain and Forests
- Flora and Fauna
- Wetlands

India as such has not achieved significant position in ecotourism operation. There is very few tourism attractions, where all activities related to tourism, including formulations, implementation and evaluation of programs are undertaken after consultation with the participation of local people. Only some places in Kerala, Tamil Nadu and Rajasthan have considerably cashed this concept. Globally, a number of countries including Brazil, Kenya, Nepal and Australia have achieved significant positions in ecotourism management. India, introduced eco-tourism policy for the first time in 1997 and framed operational guidelines for all players of destination management. Ecotourism is certainly a boom, if planned and organized properly at all scales and levels. Efforts are to be made to encourage local people's cooperation and their suggestions should be incorporated.

Golf Tourism:

Golf has been chosen as a thrust area for tourism development. A golf tourist likes to play at different courses. With golf courses in Asia and Europe becoming prohibitively expensive, India's cheaper alternatives, can lure an estimated 60 million golf enthusiasts from worldwide. The abundance of signature courses in the country becomes a definite advantage. Then there are a host of other attractions such as club houses and different sports facilities around the course to keep the families occupied.

What makes golf particularly attractive is that it is an all-season passion. It can especially be beneficial to states like Himachal and Uttarakhand which are trying to get out of the problem of seasonality. The golfers venture out at least twice or thrice a year to test their skills on unknown terrain 70% of the gold courses in India belong to the Armed forces, however ITC classic, Jaypee greens, DLF, Sahara's Amby Valley are some of the top quality golf courses. Moreover, states like Goa and Kerala are ideal targets, with facilities of both airports and hotel infrastructure. Golf courses are sprouting all over India but are too scattered to be a cumulative attraction. High spending golfers look for a week of playing on a variety of courses. It all depends on how well the private and public sector hit it off, both on the course and off it. Over the course of 10 years, the number of people playing golf in Europe has increased by more than 87%. However, England has the largest number of golfers followed by Sweden and Germany.

Moreover, golf tourism caters to a lucrative market as

46% golfers are professionals / managers.

27% Blue collar workers

18% Office workers

9% Retirees

The main concerns related to golf tourism are:

• Water and Ecology

• Large Tract of Land

• Transfers within the Course

• Infrastructure

• Large Investment

Recently, the government moved fast and had a brochure outlining its policy to boost the sector, which it really can because India has some excellent stand-alone golf courses.

Spiritual Tourism:

It is basically a product of the older civilizations of the world, having a rich treasury of spirituality for e.g. India has always been a land of spiritualism because it is the birthplace of unimportant religious of the world. Hinduism, Buddhism and Jainism. It is also closely associated with some events and personalities of Christianity and Islam. It is the land of 'rishis' and 'munis' (saints). Even in the present day, many Indian spiritual leaders have and are inspiring people all over the world who are eager to find solace and move towards self-actualization. Some famous spiritual leaders (Gurus) of India are:

• Sri Sri Ravi Shankar (The Art of Living)

• Mata Amritananda

• Acharya Rajneesh (Osho)

• Chinmaya Mission

• ISKCON

A number of tourists, especially the ones from abroad are inspired by the wealth of spirituality in India and decide to settle at the centres of spiritualism. A number of foreigners are now settled in India and learning about Indian culture and the Indian ethos. Naturally, such people can motivate others to visit India. But the challenge is to promote this kind of tourism by requesting our spiritual leaders to stay in India as most of them have taken to foreign shores.

Adventure Tourism:

India's vast geographical diversity provides a wealth of outdoor adventure. Adventure tourism can be divided into 3 parts:

- **Land**
a) Mountaineering
b) Trekking
c) Skiing
d) Rock climbing
e) Jeep and camel safaris

- **In Water**
a) Rowing
b) White Water Rafting
c) Kayaking
d) Canoeing
e) Water Skiing
f) Yachting
g) Sailing
h) Scuba Diving
i) Snorkeling
j) Wind Surfing

- **Air**
a) Hang Gliding
b) Ballooning (hot Air)
c) Sky Diving
d) Para Gliding
e) Micro flight aircraft
f) Parachuting
g) Gliding and Soaring

- **Mixed Sports**
a) Bungee Jumping
b) Heli-skiing
c) Para – Sailing etc.

Most of these sports can be done by both the young and old except those which require strong physical effort. One needs to have the 'GO GET IT' attitude to indulge in adventure tourism and be ready for the unexpected. To develop adventure tourism, safe equipment and licensed operators are necessary.

Rural / Farm / Village Tourism:

It is closely related to the concept of ecotourism. Emphasis on introducing village tourism for those people who are willing to experience the ethos and culture in rural segments. It not only promotes rural heritage but also preserves the ecology. Another closely related concept is that of tribal tourism. Ethno or Tribal tourism can sustain the fragile ecology and culture of the area. Such tourism is developed in states like Chattisgarh – which boasts of forest cover next only to Amazon and houses a world famous aboriginal population and islands of Andaman & Nicobar. Mass tourism may have a serious backlash. So farm tourism, tourists are given a true insight into how things are carried out in village environment and they actually have a chance to participate in these activities. Rural tourism enterprises probably do not differ significantly from tourism enterprises in general. The Rural Tourism market is substantial, but it is also subject to strong growth. Its promotion is supported by the growth of short-break holiday market, by the demand for more activity based holidays, and by the growth in the numbers of more critical consumers reaching against mass tourism.

Theme Park Tourism:

Theme parks are settings in which all of the entertainments and facilities are designed around a particular subject or idea. To give them a tourist appeal these settings are given shape of an amusement park. The biggest theme/amusement park of world is Disney World Orlando (Florida USA), which attracts more than 40 million visitors annually. In the 1950s and 1960s Walt Disney Productions, Ltd. was one of the major producers of films for theaters and television. As the scope of his enterprises expanded, Disney retained as much artistic control as possible. The company was involved in the publication of books for children and the syndication of comic strips, most of them featuring such characters as Donald Duck and Pluto, the dog. In 1955 Walt Disney Productions, Ltd., opened a huge amusement park called Disneyland in Anaheim, California. Featuring historical reconstructions, and rides, it became a famous tourist attraction. Disney World opened near Orlando, Florida, in 1971.

The Lost World: Jurassic Park Part II, motion picture about an island populated with real dinosaurs. Released in 1997, this science-fiction adventure is the sequel to the box-office hit Jurassic Park (1993), in which a mad scientist built a dinosaur theme park on a remote island. Although those dinosaurs were destroyed, there are some left on another island. Dr. Sarah Harding (played by Julianne Moore) and Dr. Ian Malcolm (Jeff Goldblum) travel to the island to observe the dinosaurs and try to prevent Roland Tembo (Pete Postlethwaite) from rounding the beasts up and taking them to a theme park in the United States. The weather turns bad, the dinosaurs become violent, and one of the angry beasts makes his way to Los Angeles, California.

In the pattern of Singapore, a number of amusement and theme parks shall be set up around metro towns across the country and the world. Theme park tourism in Europe is also projected to rise at an 8.1% growth rate, increasing exchange earnings from $2.3 billion in 1999 to an estimated $ 3.4 billion in 2004. Attendance will increase from 107 million to 128 million, growing at a 3.6 % compound annual rate and augmented by the opening of several new parks in 2002. Boosted by an expanding economy, per capita spending will rise from $21.75 to a projected $ 26.25, growing at a rate of 3.8 percent.

In India theme park is a very new concept, pioneered by Appu Ghar in Delhi. In Esselworld at Mumbai the Water Kingdom amusement park is considered as the biggest water amusement park in India. Following this several such type of amusement are coming up in India viz. snake park, Dolphin Park (Chennai) and etc.

Acqua Park and fun city across the country. This theme park setting can be like developing a small museum in own house to a mega amusement centre.

Camping Tourism:

According to Cambridge Dictionary of American English, a camp is a place where people stay in tents or other temporary structure. It is a place in the countryside organized for people, to visit or live for a while to enjoy nature. Hedley S. Dimock lists the elements of organized camping:

The Characteristic elements that, blended together in the right proportion, constitute and organized camp include 1) person, 2) Outdoors living. 3) Living in Groups, 4) A camp community, 5) Leadership and conditions designed to satisfy personal needs and interests and to stimulate wholesome personal, social spiritual development.

The American Camping Association gives the following as a general definition of camping:

Organized Camping is an experience in-group living in a natural environment. It is a sustained experience under the supervision of trained leadership. Camping provides a creative, educational experience in cooperative group living in the outdoors. It utilizes the resources for the natural surroundings to contribute significantly to metal, physical, social, spiritual growth of individual campers

If we go back into early accounts of camps and camping, it is noticed that the natural activities inherent in the camp environmental constituted the camp program then gradually camping which should be simple, adventuresome living in the outdoors, had become a very complicated and high-powered enterprise. Camping tourism vary with the type and needs of campers in each camp in view of the interests, the needs, and the potentialities, which are inherent in the camp situation.

Following factors lead to growth of camping tourism worldwide

• Heritage and History, which has cast a romantic aura around outdoors living.

• To have a break from the daily routine.

• Camping in the school calendar.

• Increase in the income.

• Beautiful landscapes attract people to live there for some time.

Alternative Tourism–A New Approach for Tourism Promotion:

Alternative tourism forms have caused a change in the tourism industry and have made tourism a more responsible tourism. The travel has now changed from established tourism destinations to unexplored travel destinations. The attitude of tourism industry has changed a lot. Earlier countries were concerned with number of visitors but now they are thinking of economic and social benefits of tourism. Due to alternative tourism, tourism industry has taken shape of all-weather tourism. Tourist has also changed a lot. He is now a value conscious traveler, who is traveling for self-improvement through vivid experiences.

However, due to alternative tourism forms targeted customers are considered as data base rather than socio-economic groups. The place of one way communication has been taken by relationships through customer management techniques. With the promotion of alternative tourism the conventional ways of looking consumer behaviors are becoming outdated. The alternative tourism can be seen as a new marketing technique to attract tourists, who belong to responsible class and are more focused in getting experiences. Thus it can be said that alternative tourism can be termed as a new approach in tourism promotion because of its benefits to local community, more and more diversification of tourism, dispersal of tourism from traditional places, and making tourism an all season business deal.

Summary:

The traditional forms of tourism were not apt at satisfying the varied and diverse motivations that people have behind traveling. However, earlier, the people used to settle for the traditional 'sun, sand and sea' as they had little information about the unexplored opportunities and even the tour operations activities was not very organized. But with the advent of information Technology in virtually every field of our life and increased awareness level of the prospective travelers, the diversification of tourism is the answer to customer's needs. These diversified forms are a step further in maximizing the travel experience of a tourist. Mass tourism is not considered as more beneficial for local community whereas alternative tourism is termed as beneficial. Further it can act as a newer marketing concept, where opportunities for local community are present.

CHAPTER IX

NATURE AND CHARACTERISTICS OF TOURISM INDUSTRY

Introduction:

Travel is one of the oldest activities. It existed even before the recorded history, when the man was roaming in search of food and shelter. From the very earliest historical period, travel has fascinated mankind in various ways. Much of travel in the beginning was largely unconscious and rather a simple affair. Travel in the distant past was not a thing of pleasure as is the case now. The travelers of the past were merchants, pilgrims, scholars in search of ancient texts and even a curious wayfarer looking forward to new and exciting experiences. Trade and commerce was however sole motivating factor in the ancient past, which made people travel to distant lands in order to seek fortunes. Travel got a big boost with the opening of the trade routes as the travelers from distant lands started moving about in large numbers and visited many places for the business purposes. Thus opening of new trade routes provided market places to merchants and these trade relations matured into cultural relations and better understanding of each other's way of life. Various arts, culture and customs exchanged and science, technology, religious faith also experienced influence of each other.

Today we are living in an advanced economic era. The only country having a sound economic status can enjoy freedom by all ways. The concept of developed and developing nations is nothing but an economic criteria depending upon the living standards of these countries. To get financial sound status all countries are making their efforts, during sound financial position many countries have started nearly blind race of industrialization, which raised a big problem of environmental pollution. So the need of such industry felt which could earn maximum foreign exchanges being least pollutant. The quest ends with the promotion and development of tourism industry, which is the second largest industry of the world. The most significant characteristic of this industry is that it is least pollutant for which it is also called "Smokeless Industry". The importance of this industry can well understand as it promotes national integration, builds better international understanding besides generating a vast employment opportunities. In fact, the whole economy of many countries like Singapore, Thailand and France etc. is solely based on tourism.

One of the major characteristics of modern times is the phenomenon of travel and tourism. Almost all inventions and innovations in the world have in some way contributed to the increased ability of people to travel. Today, people talk of visiting capitals and exotic places around the world almost as an everyday happenstance. It is seldom one goes to a party or social function without hearing people talking about far off places they have visited or intend to visit soon. Our world has become a world where countries and communities are in contact with each other. One major avenue through which this contact is made is tourism. Today, tourism is at its peak. It is more highly developed than it has even been.

People have always travelled, but in the first few thousand years of human history only a select few could do so. Most people were concerned with the daily task of living; their idea of a trip was to their neighbor's farm, or to the local town market. The transition from a rural society to an industrial one brought with it the tourism phenomenon. In fact, one characteristic of industrial and post-industrial society is the onset of leisure time associated with travel.

The first major change in modern history came with the Industrial Revolution. Modern machines and techniques brought people into the cities. As we moved to an urban society, changes in religious organizations and in rural kinship system led to the formation of recreational groups. Leisure pursuits became a new aspect of our society. There was a change from the concept that "the idle mind is the devil's workshop" to the realization that leisure is a human right if not a God-given one. Still, old habits die hard, and whether conscious or unconscious, many people still think of idleness as wrong.

The use of computers in recent years has resulted in what we may call a second industrial revolution. Computers have not only increased our ability to work quickly and produce more, they have given us even more leisure time and better incomes with which to pursue other interests. Although attitudes towards our work ethic and our free time are changing, most people still feel that they must work hard and play hard; that their leisure pursuits, which may be healthy and restful, should also keep them busy.

General Concepts of Tourism:

Krippendorf explored the identification of leisure as one of the major influences of an industrial society. He indicated that man in an industrial society is concerned with three primary things: work, habitat, and leisure. The industrial society can be understood to have four subsystems that relate to these concerns:

(1) Its values

(2) Its economy

(3) Its government and

(4) Its environment or resources.

In turn, each of these parts of society can be analyzed further. Its values stress wealth and consumption. The economy can develop into super companies and a concentration of wealth. The environment can be treated as having either limited or infinite resources. Government's policies have direct influence on the lives of its people. According to Krippendorf's analysis, people travel so they can better endure their work and home life. Krippendorf documented a growing feeling among people that society is going through such profound changes that it will no longer be a society known for its work. He stated that the post-industrial society will be one that:

Should put the art and quality of life before the standard of living. Values such as freedom, participation, autonomy, and the desire for self-fulfillment are gaming priority in the hierarchy of needs. The professional careers, security, and salaries are losing importance. One begins to realize that man has an overabundance of money and possession, but that he does not have enough time. People are rediscovering the meaning of time. He concluded with the statement that, although the character of travel will change as society changes, tourism will contribute to the desire for a better life and help in building a better society. The study of tourism has become very complex. To understand it better, there is a need to consider the various points of view held by many participants in the field including tourists, businesses, governments of tourist generating countries (subsequently referred to as tourist governments), host governments, and the host communities.

Tourists: Tourists have a set of need and wants that travel fulfils. These needs and wants depending upon the tourist's time, money, cultural background, and social characteristics. The needs and characteristics of tourists help determine the destinations and activities chosen.

Business: The opportunity to provide services and products that meet the needs and desires of tourists, either to assist them in transportation or at the destination is a market function, referred to as the tourist industry.

The tourist industry is divided into its components of transportation, accommodations, shopping, and activities. All these components, from a duty-free stone in an international airport through festivals, super bowls, hotels, or rides in horse carriages are highly organized.

Tourist Governments: Economically and politically governments view tourism as a competitive export – money flows from their country or region to another. To some governments, particularly socialist nations, the flow of money is very important to their economy and stability, and must be carefully controlled.

Host Governments: Host governments enjoy the benefits of tourism – income, jobs, and tax revenues.

Host Communities: It is on the local community level that tourism has its greatest impact, both positive and negative. Tourists not only bring income, jobs, and cultural interaction, but they also bring environmental concerns.

While each of the five groups have differing complex viewpoints that require considerable effort to understand, their interaction increases the complexity of tourism, and together they make the world grow closer and more congenial.

The conceptual framework of tourism can be divided into 4 parts:
• Dynamic element
• Service element
• Functional element
• Consequential element

1. Dynamic Element – The Tourism Phenomenon:
The tourism phenomenon is an extraordinary occurrence, which developed historically from an activity of the privileged few to a mass cultural lifestyle, accepted as a basic need of our modern world. It is characterized by constant change, producing personal, social, and physical benefits, that holds great promise for human growth and development in society.

2. Service Element – The Tourism System:
The tourism system is an open-ended arrangement of components logically related or practically connected so as to enable people to use tourism resources. These components produce the results or opportunities that are a reflection of the characteristics and behaviour of tourists, otherwise called the demand component. On the other side is the supply component, which includes the destination environment and tourism

services. Connecting these two components of tourism is the linking component, which includes promotion, transportation/ tour operations, distribution channels, and pricing strategies.

3. Functional Element – Tourism Management:

Tourism management is the art of successfully accomplishing all the functions required fulfilling a goal, including, but not limited to, the major tasks required to operate and control the tourism system that includes tourists, hosts, business concerns, nonprofit organizations, and governments.

4. Consequential Element – Tourism Impacts:

The goal of the tourism system is to achieve outcomes that attain the best and most favorable balance of benefits and costs when all the tourism components are combined. Throughout the process the essential elements of hospitality needs to be preserved and maintained in a cultural authentic manner as possible. Hospitality is defined as the act, practice, or art of being friendly, kind, and socialites of guests, with appropriate concern for their health, comfort, security, and overall happiness. The exchange of cultural and human experience through tourism should be provided in the most harmonious manner, so that the needs of both the tourism and the host are met with equal care. When all involved in the tourism phenomenon "think globally and act locally in a responsible manner," this optimum goal is achieved.

Tourism: Definitions:

A variety of definitions exist for what we call tourism. Thus, it is important to know exactly what we are talking about when we say "tourism" for several reasons. The development of attractions and facilities required increasingly large amounts of money. A decision to build or not build depends upon numbers of potential users. Is there a large enough market to support such a project, be it a hotel, restaurant, or theme park? If we can arrive at a common definition of tourism, travel, and tourist then we are better able to use the number of data to determine whether or not to build, where to advertise, which destinations are growing or fading. In short, our business decisions will be better if they are made with a full understanding of what exactly we are talking about.

Tourism is not just one industry, although tourism gives rise to a variety of industries. Tourism is an activity engaged in by people who travel.

International Tourist:

1. League of Nations:

It is generally agreed that definitions of a tourist are unsatisfactory. According to the League of Nations in 1937, a "foreign tourist" is 'any person visiting a country, other than that in which he usually resides for a period of at least 24 hours'.

The following individuals are considered tourists: persons travelling for pleasure, for family reasons, for health, etc.; persons travelling for meetings, or in representative capacity of any kind (scientific, administrative, diplomatic, religious, athletic, etc); persons travelling for business reasons; persons arriving in the course of a sea cruise, even when they stay less than 24 hours (the latter should be regarded as a separate group, disregarding if necessary their usual place of residence).

The following individuals are not regarded as tourists: persons arriving, with or without a contract of work, to take up an occupation or engage in any business activity within that country; other persons arriving to establish a residence in that country; students and other persons in boarding establishments or schools; residents in a foreign zone and persons domiciled in one country and working in an adjoining country; travelers passing through a country without stopping, even if the journey takes more than 24 hours.

The definition of 'foreign tourist' was largely one of time-staying in the country for more than 24 hours. Exceptions were made for those on a sea cruise. The motivations for travel, to be included as a tourist, were rather liberal. As long as people were not arriving to take up work or not students they were called 'tourists' whether their purpose was business or pleasure.

2. IUOTO:

In 1950 the International Union of Official Travel Organizations (IUOTO), which later became the World Tourism Organizations suggested two changes to the above definition. The organization recommended that 'students and young persons in boarding establishments or schools' be regarded as tourists. It also suggested that excursionists and transit travelers not be defined as tourists. The IUOTO believed that the term 'excursionist' should be given to someone traveling for pleasure in a country in which he or she normally does not reside a period of less than 24 hours as long as the person was not there to work. A "transit traveler" could actually be in the country longer than 24 hours. According to the IUOTO this term referred to "any person travelling a country even for a period of more than 24 hours, without stopping, or a person travelling a country during a period of less than 24 hours, provided that the stops made are of short duration and for other than tourism purposes.

3. United Nation's Rome Conference:

In 1963 the United Nations Conference on International Travel and Tourism in Rome recommended a definition of the term "visitor" to include any person who visits a country other than the one in which he or she lives for any purpose other than one which involves pay from the country being visited. Specifically, conference members noted that visits could be for the following reasons:

(1) Leisure, recreation, holiday, sport, health, study, religion;

(2) Business, family, friends, mission, meeting.

4. United Nations Department of Economic and Social Affairs: In 1978 the Department of Economic and Social Affairs of the U.N. published guidelines that included a definition of the term "international visitor." The agency recognized that international visitors were those who visited a given country from abroad (what we might call inbound tourists) S and those who went abroad on visits from a given country (outbound tourists). It indicated that the maximum period a person could spend in a country and still be called a visitor would be one year.

Domestic Tourist:

World Tourism Organization: World Tourism Organization has also proposed a definition for "Domestic tourist" that is based on length of stay:

Any person residing within a country, irrespective of nationality, travelling to a place within this country other than his usual residence for a period of not less than 24 hours or one night for a purpose other than the exercise of a remunerated activity in the place visited. The motives for such travel may be: (1) leisure (recreation, holidays, health, studies, religion, sports); (2) business, family, mission, meeting.

A domestic excursionist is someone who meets the above definition but who does not stay overnight.

National Tourism Resources Review Commission: In 1973 the National Tourism Resources Review Commission published its landmark study of tourism in the United States. In it, the commission proposed that a domestic tourist was one who traveled away from home for at least 50 miles one way. The travel could be for any reason except commuting to work.The Canadian government specified that a tourist is one who travels at least 25 miles outside his or her community.

Definitions of Tourism:

Because of the complexity and importance of tourism in the world, there is a need to define it so as to better understand it. A definition would be the tourism is the sum of all the relationships arising from the interaction of tourists, businesses, tourist governments, and the host government and communities.

H. Robinson (1976) described a tourist as a person traveling for more than a day to any place other than where he normally lives. George Young (1973) utilizes a broader definition, saying that a tourist is someone who travels away from home.

W. Hunziker of defined tourism in 1942 as "the sum of the phenomena and relationships arising from the travel and stay of non-residents, in so far as they do not lead to permanent residence and are not connected with any earning activity." In (1975), the department of Hotel, Catering and Tourism Management at the University of Surrey in England, adopted a broader view; "Tourism denotes the temporary, short-term movement of people to destinations outside the places where they normally live and work and their activities during the stay at these destinations. Much of this movement is international in character and much of it is a leisure activity" (Hudman & Hawkins, 1989). A.J. Burkart and S. Medlik (1981) suggest both the journey and stay, outside the normal place of residence and work, if it is temporary, can be defined as tourism.

All the different definitions of tourism are evidence of how complex this subject is. In 1937, the League of Nations realized the importance of collecting tourism data. It suggested that tourists be considered as those people traveling for a period of twenty-four hours or more in a country other than the one in which they usually reside. The committee assigned to the task by the League of Nations regarded tourists as those traveling for pleasure, health and domestic reasons; those traveling to international meetings; those travelling for the purpose of business; and those arriving in a country by a sea cruise regardless of the length of stay, which was in many cases less than twenty-four hours.

People not regarded, as tourists are those entering a country to work, reside, or go to school. Also not considered tourists are people living near frontiers who work in an adjacent country, or travelers passing through a country without stopping. This was revised at a United Nations Conference on International Travel and Tourism in Rome in 1963 as follows: the term "visitor" describes any person visiting a country for any reason other than following an occupation enumerated within the country visited. Visitors were divided into two categories.

Tourists are temporally visitors staying over twenty-four hours in the country visited, whose journey is in one of the following categories; leisure, recreation, holiday, sport, health, study, religion, business, family, friends, mission, meetings.

• **Excursionists** include temporary visitors staying less than twenty-four hours in the country visited, including cruise passengers.

• This distinction between the two kinds of visitors is important, as excursionists require less planning for accommodations, but more with regard to transportation and shopping facilities.

In most cases the terms travel and tourism are used as synonyms, although some writers have tried to draw a fine line between the two. Douglas Frechtling former Director of the U.S. Travel Data Centre, uncomfortable with both terms, devised a definition for the term "traveller" as one who takes a trip of at least one hundred miles away from home and returns. The term tourism has become more popular for government agencies. Many states in the United States, the provinces and territories in Canada, as well as various countries, are using the term "tourism" in their agency titles. For example, there is the British Tourist Authority, the U.S. Travel and Tourism Administration, the Tourism Industry Association of Canada, and the World Tourism Organization (WTO). The everyday use of "tourist" is usually associated with some sort of pleasure trip, while "traveler" usually has a broader meaning to include trips for both pleasure and business.

All definitions have three common elements at either the domestic or international level. They are:

• Movement between two or more places (origin and destination);
• Purpose; and
• Time (temporary).

Most organizations have established a minimum mileage between two places to qualify as tourism. The explanations of the word tourist exclude certain types of trips. The U.S. Travel Data Centre excludes travel as part of an operation crew on some form of public transportation such as airplane or train, the journey to work, and student travel to and from school. In general, most measurements and definitions exclude migrant workers and other temporary workers, students, and immigrants.

The time element, referring to the length of time that a visitor is in an area, is divided into two categories: less than twenty-four hours and at least twenty-four hours. The basic concept is that tourists or travelers will return to their original residence having visited an area for the purposes defined as a trip.

Tourism Re-defined:

On 4 March 1993, the United Nations Statistical Commission adopted WTO's recommendations on tourism statistics. This endorsement represents a milestone for the tourism industry. Standard definitions and classifications provide decision makers with a common basis for accurately measuring the economic impact of tourism. Essentially, WTO has taken the concept of 'tourism' beyond a stereotype image of 'holiday making'. The officially accepted definition in the report is:

"Tourism comprises the activities of persons travelling to and staying in places outside their usual environment for not more than one consecutive year for leisure, business and other purposes".

The report distinguishes the following types of tourism:

• Domestic tourism, involving residents of a country visiting their own country.

• Inbound tourism, involving non residents visiting a country other than their own.

• Outbound tourism, involving residents of a country visiting other countries.

These three basic forms of tourism can in turn be combined to derive the following categories of tourism:

• Internal tourism, which comprised domestic tourism and inbound tourism,

• National tourism, which comprises domestic tourism and outbound tourism, and

• International tourism, which comprises inbound and outbound tourism.

Underlying the above conceptualization of tourism is the overall concept of 'Traveler' defined as "any person on a trip between two or more countries or between two or more localities within his/ her country of usual residence".All types of travellers engaged in tourism are described as 'visitors' – a term that constitutes the basic concept for the whole system of tourism statistics.

A 'Visitor' is defined as a person who travels to a country other than that in which he has his usual residence but outside his usual environment for a period not exceeding twelve months and whose main purpose of visit is other than the exercise of an activity remunerated from within the place visited. Visitors' are sub-divided into two categories:

• Same-day visitors: Visitors who do not spend the night in a collective or private accommodation in the country visited.

• Tourists: Visitors who stay for at least one night in a collective or private accommodation in the country visited.

Relationship between 'Leisure', 'Recreation', and 'Tourism:

The words 'Leisure', 'Recreation' and 'Tourism' are often used to express similar meanings. What exactly is the relationship between these words? Leisure is a measure of time left over after work, rest, sleep and household chores. Leisure is the time when an individual can do what he likes to refresh his/ her spirits. Recreation means a variety of activities, which a person could choose to refresh his/her spirit. It may include activities as diverse as a game of golf, watching television or travelling abroad. Tourism, therefore, is simply one of these activities, which a person could undertake to refresh his/her sprit. It places tourism firmly as a part of recreation activities spectrum of a person.

LEISURE TIME WORK TIME

Leisure: Free time available to a person after work, sleep and household chores.

Recreation: Activities engaged upon during leisure time

Recreation activities can be Home-based activities – watching TV, reading, gardening, etc. Daily leisure – going to cinemas, theatre, restaurants or calling on friends. Weekend leisure – day trips, picnics, visiting nearby tourist attractions, weekend trips, etc. Tourism – temporary movement from: home and work, place to a place where you do not normally reside and engaging in activities available there Business travel

Classification of Tourism:

Tourism can be classified into six distinct categories according to the purpose of travel.

• **Recreational:** Recreational or leisure tourism takes a person away from the humdrum of everyday life. In this case, people spend their leisure time at the hills, sea beaches, etc.

• **Cultural:** Cultural tourism satisfies the cultural and intellectual curiosity and involves visits to ancient monuments, places of historical or religious importance, etc.

• **Sports/ Adventure:** Trips taken by people with a view to playing golf, skiing in the mountains or hiking, fall within this category.

• **Health:** Under this category, people travel for medical treatment or visit places where there are curative possibilities, for example, hot springs, spas, yoga, etc.

• **Convention Tourism:** It is becoming an increasingly important component of travel. People travel within a country or overseas to attend conventions relating to their business, profession or interest.

• **Incentive Tourism:** Major companies offer Holiday trips as incentives to dealers and salesmen who achieve high targets in sales. This is a new and expanding phenomenon in tourism. These are in lieu of cash incentives or gifts. Today, incentive tourism is a 3 billion dollar business in the USA alone (Seth, 1997)

Elements of Tourism:

Tourism is an amalgamation of diverse elements all of which are essential for providing a memorable enriched experience to the final consumer i.e. the tourist. The 5 such basic components/elements are as follows:-

1. Accessibility:

The reach ability of a destination from the point of origin of a tourist is called accessibility. In other words, accessibility implies the connecting of one place to another through a mode of transport. It is a means by which a tourist can reach the area where attractions are located. If the tourist attractions are located at places where no means of transport can reach, or where there are inadequate transport facilities, the place becomes of little value. A place can be accessible by the use of an easy and convenient mode of transportation.

Broadly speaking, there are 4 modes of transportation:-

• Air

• Land

• Water

• Rail

These modes of transport can be used for both internal and external transportation.

External Transportation means moving from the point of origin to the final destination. e.g. A tourist leaves from Delhi to Singapore by air or moving from Delhi to Goa as a final destination by air, road or rail shall be called as External transportation.

Internal Transportation means traveling within a destination. e.g. Using any of the mode of transport for sightseeing at Singapore or Goa , transfers from airport to hotel and excursions.

2. Accommodation:

A provision for stay overnight provided to the tourists is known as accommodation. It includes all types of lodging units viz Hotels, Motels, resorts, guesthouses, camping sites etc.

3. Attractions:

Attractions of a particular destination make the prime reason for leisure travel for any tourist. Had there been no place of interest at a destination, tourists would never visit that place. Attractions can be natural or man-made. e.g. Dal lake in Srinagar is an example of Natural attraction whereas Taj Mahal in Agra is an example of a man-made attraction.

4. Activities:

Anything that a tourist indulges himself into, at the destination is called an activity. e.g. Boating, adventure sports, fishing, swimming etc. Activities rejuvenate a tourist and add spice to his overall experience.

5. Amenities:

Services/facilities which enable a visitor to enjoy various attractions/ activities at the destination and which draw him to that place and for the use of which he normally has to pay. Facilities are those elements in the tourist product, which are a necessary aid to the tourist centre. The facilities complement the attractions.

These include:
• Accommodation,
• Various types of entertainments
• Picnic sites & recreation
• Rafting or surfing equipment's, fishing net and rods, Spa, sauna, Jacuzzi in the hotel etc.

Conceptual Discussions:

Travel versus Tourism:

To a layman, the terms Travel and Tourism may appear to be synonymous, but in reality it is not so. Travel means going from one place to another, whereas tourism is travelling with some determined motive. Tourism is a core activity that involves other activities like travelling (transport), accommodation (hotels), and local sightseeing tours etc. "Every traveler is not a tourist but every tourist is a traveler". This statement shows that tourism comprises of all kind of travel whereas travel is just one part of the multifarious tourism Industry. Tourism comprises of all those industries which directly or indirectly help a tourist in fulfilling his demands at a destination. Therefore, travel of any form is it air, land or water, in simple words is a displacement or movement of a person from one place to another for business, leisure or holiday purpose. This displacement will get converted into tourism only when the tourist stays overnight at the destination travelled and thus adds to the economy of that place directly or indirectly.

For instance, if a person starts his journey from Chandigarh to visit Shimla and his mode of transport is surface, and then his entire journey from his point of origin (Chandigarh) would be considered as travel. However, tourism is a broader concept than travel. All the activities of that person right from the time he leaves his place of residence from Chandigarh to visit Shimla, his stay at the latter for more than 24 hours, the sightseeing he undertakes there and various other interrelated pursuits he indulges himself into, at the destination till the time he comes back to Chandigarh would be called as Tourism. Further, travel enhances boundaries, opens up the mind, and clears prejudices. Tourism provides employment benefits in backward areas, and helps make better roads, water, power and communication available to more people, raising standards of living.

Global Tourism Scenario:

Travel & Tourism is the world's largest industry and creator of jobs across national and regional economies. Tourism ranks in the top five export categories for 83 per cent of countries, notably in Europe, the Middle East and the Americas, and is the leading source of foreign exchange in at least one in three developing countries. Countries with the highest ratios of tourism receipts to GNP are typically small island nations. Although much of the gross tourism receipts (i.e. 50-70 per cent) "leak" out of these countries in order to pay for imported tourism inputs, the ratio of net receipts to GNP remains much higher than for larger countries. The fact remains that Tourism is not just one industry; it is many industries in one. Worldwide travel and tourism create a new job every 10 seconds. Out of every nine persons, one person earns a living from tourism, one out of every ten inhabitants of this planet is a tourist and thus, the predictions say that Travel is expected to grow 50 percent faster than any other sector of world employment.

WTTC (World Travel and Tourism Corporation) Research Shows that between 2001 and 2011:

• World Travel & Tourism is expected to generate US$ 6,201.5 billion of economic activity

• Total tourism demand shall be around US$ 10,678.5 billion by 2015.

• Travel & Tourism Demand is expected to grow by 5.4% in 2008 and by 4.6% per annum, in real terms, between 2008 and 2015.

• Global Gross Domestic Product will increase from 10.7 per cent to 11 per cent;

• Global employment contribution will increase from 207.1 million to 260.4 million or 9 per cent of total global employment;

• The global value of tourism related exports will increase from US$ 1,063.8 billion to US$ 2,538.3 billion or 12.8 per cent of global export value; and

• Global capital investment in tourism will increase from US$ 657.7 billion to US$ 1,434 billion or 9.3 per cent of global investment.

World Tourism Growth in 2007:

The year 2007 has started on a higher than expected note for global tourism. From January through April, international tourist arrivals worldwide rose by over 6% to 252 million, representing an additional 15 million arrivals as against the same period in 2006, according to the latest UNWTO World Tourism Barometer.

Asia and the Pacific (+9%) achieved the strongest growth, followed by Africa (+8%), the Middle East (+8%) and Europe (+6%). Although arrivals to the Americas (+4%), showed the slowest growth rate among the world regions during the first four months of 2007, this performance is nevertheless very positive as the region doubled the 2007 forecast growth (+2%).

Drivers of Tourism Growth:

Continuing world prosperity has clearly been a main driver. Emerging markets and developing economies in general, and especially those of Asia, maintained their extraordinary strength. Meanwhile, in continental Europe, and in Germany in particular, economic growth has picked up encouragingly. With increasing disposable income and factors such as the continued development of low cost airlines making travel available for larger shares of population, international tourism seems on track for another year of above average growth.

Regional Outcome:

Although Europe (+6%) is the world's most visited and most mature destination region, its arrivals growth rates in 2005 and 2006 were not far short of the worldwide average. And growth continued even more strongly through the first four months of 2007 supported by the sustained boom in the world economy – a boom in which Europe is now sharing more emphatically, with notably higher rates of GDP growth in the Euro zone.

Asia and the Pacific (+9%) stands out as the best performing region in the world in the first four months of 2007, confirming its role as one of the motors of international tourism expansion. The highest increase in arrivals was recorded by South Asia (+12%), while South-East Asia and North-East Asia (both at +9%) sustained the healthy growth of 2006. Only Oceania (+2%), bucked the strong growth trend.

The Americas (+4%) started 2007 by doubling last year's overall results. The region benefited from star performers Central America (+7%) and South America (+9%), and particularly of those of North America (+4%), already far ahead of last year's 1% growth. This trend was not, however, widespread. The Caribbean (-2%) has been the only sub-region in the world to record a decline over the first four months of 2007, reflecting the impact of decreased arrivals from the USA in many of its destinations.

Preliminary results for the first four months of 2007 point to a stronger than expected increase in international tourist arrivals in the Middle East (+8% as against +6% for 2006), as destinations such as Egypt (+14%) posted extraordinary growth rates. Nevertheless this trend might still vary as available data is still limited.

Africa's continued its strong growth (+8%), though at a slightly lower rate than in 2006 overall when it reached +10%. Short-term prospects for the continent look very bullish. Particularly in Sub-Saharan Africa there is growing optimism, with increasing emphasis on human resources and product development to help tourism better contribute to poverty alleviation.

Present Trends in Global and Indian Tourism Industry:

• With increased technology the coming years the world would witness the emergence of fast transportation system all around the world.

• The modern information technology has led to the creation of more demand for tourism.

• The market for budget hotels has continued to expand during the last decade.

• Special Interest Tourism is growing at a fast pace. Activities like Visiting Theme Parks, Adventure Tourism, and Casinos are attracting more and more tourists.

• In order to attract repeat visitors, hotel industry is extending special emphasis on personal attention to their customers.

• Short break are becoming an increasing feature of modern lifestyles as travellers opt to take many more trips of shorter length. Increased frequency of transportation and its network is making it easy for people to reach far away destinations much faster.

• One of the major changes that are occurring in world tourism market is increasing size of mature travellers. The Baby Boom generation (Babies born post World War –II) will retire and will lead to the development of Ethnic, cultural and heritage tourism. On the same pattern senior citizens are also taking more and more trips.

• Environmental Issues are becoming more important for lodging properties and more green hotels are coming up. In green hotels guests saves millions of gallons of water and prevent the release of tons of detergents.

• With environmentalism becoming more important to more people, the size of Eco tourist segment is increasing dramatically. A survey shows that 34 million Americans took a nature-based trip during their last vacation or plans to do so on an upcoming vacation.

• The early years of this millennium are marked by major social and economic shifts that have changed the way customer behave. Stimulated by increased knowledge, information and buying power, these shifts are creating aspirations or better life styles.

• One of the newest trends happening in global tourism is Single Holiday Tourists. As compared to Group Travel, people prefer to travel as single. Travel by Single Women travellers to India is increasing by 6 to 8 percent every year.

• With the increasing number of visitors to a common destination, managing visitors' requirements are becoming difficult for service organizations in the near future. Resulting in increased number of mergers, acquisitions, alliances and cooperative agreements.

• The participation of Non-Governmental Organizations in heritage conservation and preservation of heritage properties is increasing throughout world.

• To tap domestic as well international health tourism market, hotel properties will develop or convert their hotels into spa resorts on the Ayurvedic and other rejuvenating concepts.

• In India foreign hotel chains are thriving on the concept of franchising. All international players are scouting for properties in India.

• Internationally branded hotels are coming to India. The country has caught the fancy of leading international groups.

• Business travel constitutes about 12 percent of the share of the global travel industry sweepstakes. According to industry estimates, the Indian business travel industry will touch 1 billion marks by 2010.

• On the pattern of Singapore, a number of amusement and theme parks are coming up around metro towns across the India.

• To develop tourism, Golf has been chosen as a thrust area and Indian Department of Tourism is working with major courses to attract potential golf tourists.

Future of Tourism Industry:

Tourism is a trillion dollar industry worldwide and still growing. It employs more people than any other industrial sector and, in a world made smaller by a travel-conscious society, it makes a vital contribution to the economy of virtually every country on the globe. The future of tourism sector depends on protection of the earth's natural and cultural environments. Consequently, with proper planning, tourism can be an effective protector of the environment. WTO forecasts that international tourism will double by the year 2040, to nearly three billion arrivals a year. While this rapid growth will provide many opportunities for prosperity, it will also put a tremendous strain on tourism destinations: on beaches and mountain resorts; on small islands; on historic city centers; and on picturesque villages. It is in self-interest to actively prevent the deterioration of these resources.

WTO's Tourism 2020 Vision forecasts that international arrivals are expected to reach over 1.56 billion by the year 2020. Of these worldwide arrivals in 2020, 1.2 billion will be interregional and 0.4 billion will be long-haul travellers. The total tourist arrivals by region shows that by 2020 the top three receiving regions will be Europe (717 million tourists), East Asia and the Pacific (397 million) and the Americas (282 million), followed by Africa, the Middle East and South Asia.

East Asia and the Pacific, South Asia, the Middle East and Africa are forecasted to record growth at rates of over 5 percent per year, compared to the world average of 4.1 per cent. The more mature regions Europe and Americas are anticipated to show lower than average growth rates. Europe will maintain the highest share of world arrivals, although there will be a decline from 60 per cent in 1995 to 46 percent in 2020.

Summary:

The travel and tourism industry is fascinating with its aura of international glamour, excitement, and romance. Because it is global in scope, it must respond to many different social, political, economic, and legal environments. Travel is also a business, and as a business it demands from its personnel, certain skills and a sophisticated knowledge of the world. Like any business the travel and tourism industry must match its offering to prospective buyers. This economic activity of providing services to tourists includes a whole gamut of activities. Putting it other way round, Tourism means the practice of touring or traveling for pleasure or recreation and the guidance or management of tourists as a business. It is the sum total of the Activities of Persons traveling to and Staying in a Place outside their usual Environment for -- more than 24 hours and less than 01 consecutive Year for Leisure, Business and other Purposes is called tourism. Thus one can say that: "Tourism is a Dialogue between Imagination and Destination".

CHAPTER X

DYNAMIC AND STATIC NATURE OF TOURISM INDUSTRY

Introduction:

Tourism industry has been duly acknowledged as a prominent and sophisticated industry across the world in the present century. The phenomenon and scope of its direct and indirect participants are still unclear and needs to be defined. As tourist statistics of many countries do not adhere to the definition of tourism at the time of the data collection and estimation. It has resulted in creating a big doubt to include tourism as a discrete industry in their countries. There is no synergy between the definition of tourism and the data collection. This should not come as a surprise since tourism is not an industry to begin with rather it is an amalgam of diverse industries or sectors that directly or indirectly cater to the needs of the tourist. It is this diversity that has proved the biggest stumbling block in the tourism industry's battle over the past few years to legitimate itself in the eyes of the general public and governments (central, state and local). Factors such as the diversity and geographical spread of the tourism product, as well as the competing interests among tourism sectors are the main reasons for this constant struggle for recognition.

Tourism is a subjective experience and a combination of products and services - not a single product at all. It is a multi-faceted phenomenon. Tourism products, like all services, are intangible in nature. They cannot be seen, touched and felt or sampled before purchase. The selling of tourism is the selling of images. The tourism product is not a homogeneous product but they are heterogeneous in character. Moreover, services cannot be standardized. External factors can also affect the tourist experience. Tourism products are perishable. An unsold hotel room, an aircraft seat and a vacant Opera House concert seat is a loss of revenue forever. They cannot be stored for later use, as most of the tangible products. This leads to some of the major problems being confronted by the tourism operators: namely, demand fluctuation, seasonality, etc. Tourism is perhaps more vulnerable than any other industry in terms of seasonal fluctuations in demand. Demand fluctuation can be unseen, sometimes it happens due to natural disaster and man-made problems such riots, wars, strike, etc. Acts of God include adverse climate conditions and natural disasters. Acts of Man include strikes and international events (War on Iraq) and murders (murders of tourists in Bali Indonesia). Hence the prevalence of discounting in services can minimize the loss of the tourism industry.

The economic impacts of tourism are indeed remarkable. An ideal tourist destination with amazing attractions progresses at a rapid pace mainly owing to the economic implications. Many sorts of investments happen at the destination including Foreign Direct Investments (FDI). The destination planners and developers also take a keen interest in the tourist place owing to its revenue prospects. The investors are enticed to set up large, medium and small-scale enterprises. Projects like entertainment parks including amusement parks and theme parks, travel agencies and tour operators companies, event management firms, hotels including ventures like heritage hotels are established with due licenses, sanctions, subsidies, concessions, etc. The public private participation system is very much in vogue in many states and is considered to encourage private investment in tourism sector. The entrepreneurs are given government lands on lease for setting up projects on BOOT (Build Operate Own and Transfer) basis. It is a fact that the economics of tourism is a propelling force as far as both the public and private sector activities in a destination is concerned.

Dynamic and Static Nature of Tourism Industry:

Tourist Attraction:

A tourist attraction is a place of interest where tourists visit. Some examples include historical places, monuments, zoos, museums and art galleries, botanical gardens, buildings and structures (e.g., castles, libraries, former prisons, skyscrapers, bridges), national parks and forests, theme parks and carnivals, ethnic enclave communities, historic trains and cultural events. Many tourist attractions are also landmarks. Attractions can be discussed from two different angles. First, attractions may be either site or event based. Site attractions are permanent by nature while event attractions are temporary and are often mounted in order to increase the number of tourists to a particular destination. A destination should have always some dynamic augmentation to the core static attraction in order to draw more number of tourists and to sustain the tourist flow. Both static and dynamic nature of tourist attractions is mentioned here below.

• Static Nature: The structure and locations of attraction can be termed as a static aspect of tourism attraction. Spatial location and facilities there in at the attraction point are static since they don't change overtime. Attractions can be classified in a number of ways as given in figure-1.

• Cultural Attraction: Culture can be defined as a set of behaviors, arts, beliefs and institutions of a population that are passed down from generation to generation. Culture can be called as the way of life for an entire society. Tangible and intangible features of culture are codes of manners, dress, language, religion, rituals, norms of behavior such as law and morality, and systems of belief as well as the arts and gastronomy.

Culture when is discussed as tourist attraction it can be described as the manifestation in the form of music, literature, architecture, painting and sculpture, cuisine, theater and film, museums, handicraft and handicraft manufacturing sites, technology, art, science, as well as moral systems.

Culture however is confined as way of life of people belonging to same region, localities or country. These are the belief, traditions and other manifestations that the people inherit from their ancestors. Culture as part of tourist attraction; include the built constructions and human activities, which are resources from tourism point of view.

• **Natural Attraction:** Nature acts like a pull factor for tourists. Different natural features like landscape, national parks, wild life sanctuaries, biosphere reserves, climate, flora fauna and coast and islands are motivators for tourists to visit to the destination having these unique features. The natural attraction can be divided in terms of physical aspects (climate and landscape) and biological aspects (flora, fauna). These are the basic or core attraction on which service-providers supplement with additional benefits.

• **Dynamic Nature of Attraction:** In delivering the same core attraction to the tourists, managers take different course of action in terms of value added services, off-season festival of arts or discounted package. Destinations can be either nodal or linear in character. A nodal destination is one in which the attractions of the area are closely grouped geographically making them ideal for packaging by tour operators. Linear tourism on the other hand, is that in which the attraction is spread over a wide geographical area without any specific focus. Thus nodal attractions are static as they are the core attraction at a given place where as linear attractions depend heavily on the tour operator on its decision of choosing places for itinerary. While some nodal tourist attractions provide visitors a memorable experience for a reasonable admission charge or even for free, others can have a tendency to overprice their goods and services (such as admission, food, and souvenirs) in order to profit from tourists by offering a package.

Thus nodal attractions often is augmented with additional value added services like accommodation, food and entertainment etc. thus become dynamic characteristics of tourist attraction.

Further attractions which are event based unlike site attractions are not permanent by nature rather are temporary by nature. However absence of either site or event based attraction is practically not possible. Every site based attraction has some augmentation as discussed earlier. Similarly event, recreation and entertainment activities have some features, which are site specific. In case of recreation activities like site seeing, golf, swimming, tennis, hiking facilities are normally available in the fixed location, which may not always be created manually. Entertainment attractions like theme parks, amusement parks, casinos, cinemas, shopping facilities, performing arts centers, sport complexes though manmade by nature cannot be moved from one to the other place or sometimes insensible to individual demand. Events like mega events, community events, sports events, festivals, trade events too depend on the provision of minimum infrastructure, thus are not dynamic.

Other Dynamic Commercial Sectors

The main direct commercial sectors under the tourism umbrella: accommodation, transport carriers, attractions, tour operators & wholesalers, promotions & distributions, and retail services.

• **Travel Agency/ Tour Operators/ Wholesalers:** The definitions of these individual intermediaries don't come under the purview of this chapter. However these intermediaries sell travel related products and services, particularly package tours, to end-user customers on behalf of third party travel suppliers, such as airlines, hotels and cruise lines.

Unlike other retail businesses, they do not keep a stock in hand. A package holiday or a ticket is not purchased from a supplier unless a customer requests that purchase. The holiday or ticket is supplied to them at a discount. The profit is therefore the difference between the advertised price, which the customer pays, and the discounted price at which it is supplied to the agent. Thus the services of these intermediaries are dynamic and very sensible to the individual demands.

• **Accommodation:** Accommodation sector comprises widely different forms of sleeping and hospitality facilities, which can be conveniently categorized as commercial, and Non/quasi commercial sectors. Both commercial sectors and non-commercial accommodation units can be classified on the basis of serviced and self-catering establishments.

Generally hotels are the most significant and widely recognized form of overnight accommodation. However it may be difficult to distinguish hotels from other forms of accommodation units. In India, hotel as per tourism policy of government of India are the establishments other than holiday homes and paying guesthouses that provide accommodation and hospitality facilities for a quoted tariff to the visitors. At present there are about 100,000 hotel rooms in 1,800 hotels across the country as registered till 2004. Though the building of a hotel is static the services being provided them are flexible. The price decides the types of room and room services. Further the service and price vary from season to season based on demands. Seasonal discounts are common marketing tool for hoteliers to increase sale in the off-season. Thus as part of overall tourist experiences the role of hotels in the industry becomes dynamic.

Hotels attempt to standardize their room and service delivery as efficiently as possible through staff training and quality control procedures, but the human ingredient complicates the equation. As most services require interaction between the producer and consumer, each with their own set of expectations, it is highly unlikely that any product can ever be perceived equally by all customers.

• **Tourist Destination:** A tourist destination can be defined as particular resort or town, a region within a country, the whole of a country or even a region in the globe consisting of many countries or any other area, which is dependent to a significant extent on the revenues accruing from tourism. This significance level may vary from country to country as policy decision. The destination may contain one or more attractions and possibly some tourist traps otherwise known as family-oriented tourist attractions, which is an establishment or set of establishments that have been created to attract travelers or tourists and provide products for the tourist to purchase. Sometimes destinations are highly precise as in the case of a resort hotel, which provides a range of leisure facilities on site. In these cases tourists simply visit the hotel to avail the facilities these hotels provide. Hence the entire stay is spent in enjoying these facilities alone. Thus these tourist traps have tailor made services suiting the requirement of individual tourist.

Destinations are of two kinds: they may either be natural or constructed. Natural attractions are the mainsprings that drive many people to travel. The great national parks of USA, India, Canada, Africa, Japan and Australia are examples of it. Most of the destinations are maintained to some extent, whether they are natural or constructed. So the distinction between the two lies in the degree of human involvement in augmentation of the core attraction. A constructed destination can be cultural attractions like historical sites, architectural sites, monuments industrial sites and entertainment attractions like theme parks, amusement parks, casinos, cinemas, shopping facilities, performing arts centers and sport complexes etc. where the core attraction is human, its culture or its built constructions. Thus, in natural destinations there is a greater degree of static features involved where as in case of manmade destinations dynamic features are predominant.

• **Tourist Transport:** Tourist Transport system can include a variety of specific transport options for tourist activities to drive and promote alternative modes. These can include:

- Shuttle Services
- Taxi Service
- Cycling and Walking
- Parking Management
- Traffic Calming, Speed Reductions
- Access Management
- Vehicle Restrictions.
- Marketing to encourage visitors to arrive without a car
- Commute Trip Reduction programs for staff
- Freight Management to minimize truck traffic
- Aviation Transport Management
- Transportation Access Guides, which provide concise
- Directions to reach destinations by alternative modes
- Equipment Rentals (Bikes, Scooters, Skies, etc.)

Tourist Transport Management involves improving transportation options for recreational travel and reducing automobile traffic in the destinations. Tourist travel has predictable patterns and needs, and often occurs in areas that have unique environmental and social features that are particularly sensitive to degradation by excessive automobile traffic. Tourist Transport Management can preserve the amenities that attract visitors to an area, whether it is an historic city center or a pristine natural environment.

Traffic to resort areas often peaks at particular seasons and times of the week. Visitors have particular mobility needs (e.g., travel between transport terminals, accommodations, restaurants and shops, tourists attractions, etc.) and baggage requirements (skis, surf boards, gifts to carry home). Tourist Transport Management must take these travel patterns and needs into account. Unlike conventional modes of transportation tourist transport needs to look after various dynamic features like visitors mobility needs, baggage requirements and environmental demands.

• **Food Services:**

Food service industry consists of restaurants, travel food service and vending and contact institutional food service. Local restaurants are made up of establishments that include fast-food units, coffee shops, specialty restaurants, family restaurants, cafeterias and full service restaurants with carefully orchestrated atmosphere. Travel food service consists of food operations in hotels and motels, road side service to automobile travelers, and all food service on airplanes, trains and ships. Institutional food service in companies, hospitals, nursing homes and so on is not considered part of tourism industry.

The same food outlet doesn't provide same quality of food to all visitors who dine there. The service depends on the price, time and more over the taste of the customer. The menu too ranges from continental, Indian or any regional basis.

Check your answer with the one given at the end of the unit.

Economic and Operating Characteristics of Tourism Industry:

Of late tourism has matured into becoming a major industry. As an economic activity, it brings many positive and negative effects on the economy and society because of its pervasiveness. Further as a separate industry, it is spread across the country. Its economic and operating characteristics are described as follows.

- Operating sectors of Tourism Industry
- Events sector
- Attractions Sector
- Entertainment sector
- Adventure and Outdoor Recreation
- Transportation sector
- Tourism Services
- Food services
- Travel trade sector
- Accommodation sector

Economic Characteristics:

Tourism is basically an economic activity with having socio-cultural implications. All the countries formulate policy as a tool for economic development of the country.

• General Economic Conditions and Tourism Industry:

This can be understood by the recent performance of tourism industry in our country. There could be several reasons for the buoyancy in the Indian tourism industry. First, the upward trend observed in the growth rate of Indian economy has raised middle class incomes, prompting more people to spend money on vacations abroad or at home. Also, India is booming in the information technology industry and has become the IT center. Aggressive advertising campaign 'Incredible India' by the government has also had contribution in changing India's image from that of a land of snake charmers, and sparking new interest among overseas travelers.

• Tourism Contribution to the Economy:

It is not hidden that tourism is among important export industries in India as well as in the world. Even with comparatively low levels of international tourist traffic in India, tourism has already emerged as an important segment of the Indian economy. Tourism also contributed to the economy indirectly through its linkages with other sectors like horticulture, agriculture, poultry, handicrafts and construction. Foreign exchange earnings from tourism during 2003-04 were US $ 3,533 million (Rs 16,429 crore). Besides being an important foreign exchange earner, tourism industry also provides employment to millions of people in India both directly and indirectly (through its linkage with other sectors of the economy.) It is estimated that total direct employment in the tourism sector is around 20 million. Tourism contributes directly to the state exchequer in terms of different taxation like excise tax, entertainment tax, sales tax, income tax, Airport tax, corporate tax and VAT. In addition tourism helps in development of infrastructure through private and public participation which otherwise would have been solely a government purview.

• Regional Development:

Natural tourist destinations are normally located in economically backward regions in the initial phase of its development. Subsequently economic activities infused through tourism industry offers an ideal platform for less developed and economically backward areas. Thus tourism can help in balanced development of the country.

•Employment Benefits:

Employment in tourism industry can be expressed in three different angles. Direct employment arises from the need of direct service of the tourists. Indirect employment arises from the sectoral demand of tourism industry on the other sectors. Induced employment is the additional demand for manpower to cater to the needs of overall economy.

• Problem of over-consumption:

Tourism must be one of the few industries in which too many customers can be detrimental. This can apply to the social and environmental impact on local communities. There is some consensus that crude numbers are not a good indication of the contribution of tourism to a local economy. The more the tourists visit to a particular place the more expensive infrastructure has to be provided for them. That in effect may dampen the serenity and sublimity of environment after a certain point of the destination life cycle. The argument can be replicated in other areas of hotels and resorts.

• Tourism and profitability:

An irony of the hype of the surrounding of tourism is such that many sectors under the tourism umbrella do complain of getting poor profits. Travel agencies, hotels, tour operators and taxi operators have long been complaining about the low returns. Further after internet revolution and then reduction and reluctance of airlines giving commissions to the agencies many agencies have been out of business. Tourism industry still has not tackled the three issues that most affect profitability. These are: firstly, higher building costs, such that the capital outlay per room or bed is much higher; secondly, hotel and resorts operating costs are too high; thirdly, hotels and resorts have very seasonal and highly unpredictable occupancies and cash flows.

• Shift in Seller's market to buyer's market:

Tourism is one of the industries, which are experiencing the change from a seller's to a buyer's market. Customers are more aware with revolution in information, which results in increased customer demands for quality products in right price at their doorsteps. The stiff competition in the market threatens the very existence of service providers. As a result, marketing techniques have advanced than earlier, where managers have been accustomed to a fastidious and discriminating customer for years. Plainly, in the outbound market, the shift from a seller's to a buyer's market is taking place right now. Travelers' interests and needs are changing rapidly and the major wholesalers are struggling to respond effectively. Increasingly, today's traveler wants to make his or her decision about tourist activities, wants more free time and less expensive accommodation. As a result, the wholesalers are finding their market shares under threat from emerging discount travel companies.

Operating Characteristics

• Tourism as a service industry:

The tourism industry does not deal in goods. The tourism product can be categorised as intangible, invisible, perishable, inseparable and heterogeneous by nature. Its services include accommodation, transportation, facilitation and guiding and escort services.

• Tourism as an export industry:

Tourism is regarded as an export industry. As foreign tourists while visiting the country, bring foreign currencies with them exchange these for goods and services they consume in the country. While inbound tourism brings foreign currency along with it out bound tourism takes national currency out of the country.

• Heterogeneous Industry:

Tourism industry doesn't include any single service rather it is an amalgamation of many services like accommodation, transportation, destination management companies, VISA and passport services, entertainment facilities etc. Formulation of tourism policy in the country encompasses different ministries in the country like Civil aviation, Environment and forest, Labour, External affairs, Defense, Surface and Rail transportation, Rural development and so on in addition to the core tourism ministry.

• Highly Capital Intensive Industry:

Tourism is highly capital-intensive industry, which requires high initial capital allotment. A travel agency needs to have fleet of taxis and coaches in addition to certification and approval cost. A hotel needs huge initial capital for building.

• Value Addition and Customer Satisfaction:

As an export industry, the tourism sector adds value to the core product at every steps of its production process. Improving product and service standards is a continuous affair in the tourism business. In the tourism market products, which have customer requirements, are developed and augmented at every step of its production. The ability to meet the customer standards increases with increasing customer expectation.

• Dominant Role of Small-Scale Enterprises:

Tourism has been described as the classic small-business industry. Majority of tourism businesses in the hospitality sector employ less than ten persons. One of the reasons for the small business concentration is the ease of entry into the industry. Anyone with a four-wheel drive, a farm, or a yacht or a site in prime location of the destination can set up business targeting tourists.

• Decentralized Industry Structure:

Tourism is a diversified and decentralized industry. Different tourism products have a combination of different service providers like, hotels, airlines, destination management companies, marine parks or inbound operators and trade associations etc. The success of a tour package depends on the successful delivery of all allied services. Further in one sectors like trade associations also there are regional, national as well as urban associations like Hotel and Restaurant Association of India (HRAI), Travel Agency Association of India (TAAI) etc. Professional associations involved in tourism, such as the Tour Operators' Association in India (IATO), represent another interest group and the list goes on.

• Private Sector Driven and Public Sector Controlled:

It is the government that shapes the environment in which the tourism industry operates. They provide much of the infrastructure and services used by tourists and the industry generally - these include promotion and information services, the provision of roads, airports, railways and harbors, the management of national parks, visas and customs services, research and statistical data, education and training programs and various public amenities. Thus the government acts, as a catalyst in the functioning of the industry where the actual management lies with private players be it is a travel agency, hotel or transport operator. Generally the government provides relatively little assistance in the functioning of the tourism industry. For example the hotel industry in India has staged a long, hard battle to gain recognition as a service exporter such that it can be deserving of export grants.

• Demand Driven Industry:

This industry is marked by seer demand in the market. The demand decides the price in the industry. For example the introduction of low cost carriers, off-season discounts etc. The industry enhances the competitiveness since there is a perfect competition in the market. Beyond meeting the consumer's product or service requirements, the producer may have to implement international quality standards, such as HACCP. (Hazard analysis and critical control points) In addition, buyers may have firm-specific requirements related to consistency in quality and quantity of supply, which force companies to adopt management and production standards to improve efficiencies and profitability. These often result in improved competitiveness of firms.

• Labour Intensive:

Tourism as a service industry depends heavily on human factor. It provides job opportunities to skilled, semiskilled and unskilled employees. When compared to capital investment as compared to other manufacturing or service industry the rate of employment is higher in tourism industry. This industry is also one, which provides more employment opportunities for women.

• Technology Driven:

Tourism industry is sophisticated industry and technologically advanced industry. Even much before the introduction of Internet, Global Distribution System (GDS) was popularly used in the travel industry. With the advancement in the technology and particularly with the evolution of internet, there has been a drastic change in the functioning of tourism industry. Travel portal, online booking, eticketing, online billing and settlement plan etc. are examples of the advancement in use of technology in the industry.

• Dominant Role of Intermediaries:

Distribution channel in the industry can't be avoided at all. It is a travel agent, which facilitates travel of a customer who may not be aware about the alternative modes of transportation. A tour operator after assembling different services makes a package tour which includes all related services required by a tourist. Suppliers in the industry necessarily need intermediaries to reach the customers and vice versa. Thus the role of intermediaries is important.

• High Interdependency among sectors:

A feature of tourism is its high degree of inter-relatedness. For example, resort or hotel development cannot begin without adequate airports and roads to bring tourists to those properties. In India, tourism depend heavily on the success of other industries like software industry, Pharmaceuticals industry etc. Further tourists from different countries may like different form and level of infrastructure.

• Marketing Tourism:

The above discussion about the shift in consumer preferences leads to the issue of strategies of marketing for tourism products. Tourism is a relatively young industry and the learning curve for many parishioners is understandably steep. There are only a handful of tourism parishioners in India with more than a few years' experience in the market. These men and women have extensive contacts, where they visit regularly; they are sensitive to the needs of their customers, both the consumer and the wholesaler, and they are open-minded to change and to new ideas. For the relative newcomer, however, things are tougher. The challenge faced by the industry is the lack of marketing orientation by tourism promoters and suppliers. First, there is an emphasis on sales and promotion at the exclusion of a thorough understanding of the distribution systems in outbound tourism. Second, fierce price competition among individual suppliers, particularly in the hotel sector, is widespread. Third, there is an underutilization of market research into the changing trends in tourism. Fourth, there is a reliance on simplistic forms of demographic segmentation, such as honeymooners, retirees and baby boomers' market. Tourism managers need to adopt more sophisticated approaches to market segmentation that bundle together travelers' interests and motivations.

Further it remains the task of the individual suppliers to satisfy the needs of travelers once that decision to travel has been made. Since tourism is a small business industry, most tourism operators do not have the financial or managerial capability to take full advantage of the opportunities in the rapidly diversifying travel market. Thus there is a need of an intermediary promoting body in each country that will be charged with the responsibility of ensuring the offer and delivery of quality tourism product to all international travelers.

• **Relationship between locals and tourists**:

There are some general features of tourism that affect all destination communities in one-way or another. These include the transient nature of tourism and the relations between tourists and locals. A major factor affecting relations between locals and tourists, however, is the desire of the latter for a temporary change in their life situation. They seek escape from established routines, from the constraints of time and place, and the behavioural codes that rule their daily lives. They believe this change will recharge their mental and physical batteries so that they will be better able to cope with the pressures of their daily commitments. Thus becoming a tourist, however briefly, means shedding part of one's old identity and normal behavior. This involves adopting a new, temporary identity that necessarily incorporates some elements that are the opposite of the habitual personality and behavior. Many tourists, for various reasons, are occasionally most unpleasant guests. Yet those whose livelihoods depend upon their presence must somehow come to terms with their difficult behavior and cater to their strange needs.

• Creation of demand for exports products:

Tourists are introduced to new products in the host country, which may trigger a desire for the products once the traveler leaves the destination country. This often creates a demand for the product overseas – resulting in new export opportunities. There is also stronger brand recognition of tourism as a destination, which may drive exports through joint branding/marketing.

Summary:

The tourism industry comprises several main sectors, e.g. transport, accommodation, travel distribution, tourist attractions, tourism organizations etc. This module focuses on each sector's operational characteristics and the ways in which they interact in the production of tourism products and services. The economic linkage between the core travel and tourism sector and travel related services, is also discussed.

This module examines the structure and also the components, which are characterized by the static aspects of tourism industry and its operational aspects, organization and trends with functions of individual sectors in the tourism industry as well as the dynamic aspects of it. Each of the sectors under study is analyzed in terms of its business characteristics, yet the overall aim of the module is to offer a comprehensive introduction to the static and dynamic aspects of the business of tourism by examining as to how different sectors 'work' and interact within the tourism system. In addition the second part is devoted to the economic and operating characteristics, where the economic and operational dynamics of the industry have been discussed.

CHAPTER XI

BASIC TYPOLOGY AND THEIR USES

Introduction:

Tourism is a dynamic and complex product that is processed and delivered by the intervention of related and interrelated providers of services. This has become a massive business phenomenon that is regarded as the emerging economic engine for the host countries. Tourism has been recognized as an industry in many countries. There are a large variety of heterogeneous products and services, which are interlinked and complementary to each other. Tourism is an amalgam of products and services. Tourism products are intangible, perishable and heterogeneous in nature. A single agency cannot at all meet the needs and wants of tourists. It is a vibrant sector with the capacity of ample revenue generation for the benefits of the whole host community. In nutshell, business activities of tourism are unlimited. The systematic functioning of tourism system influences both the macro and micro business environment of tourism. This unit will highlight on the various typologies of tourism systems and their general and specific uses with the specific objectives of offering quality services to the tourists.

The Composition of Tourism Industry:

Tourism is often interpreted in terms of being an invisible and service oriented industry. Tourism however, is not a single industry in the conventional viewpoint. Tourism comprises a wide range of products and services whose limits for inclusion are very vast and extensive. From an economic and business perspective, an industry is defined as being a group of independent firms, all turning out the same product. It is clear that the focus of industry includes individual business establishments, which are grouped together in a network for generation of revenue received by all the economic units through the production and sale of a common product.

The Meaning of Tourism:

The World Tourism Organization's definition of tourism in 1995 state that the activities of persons traveling to and staying in places outside their usual environment for not more than one consecutive year for leisure, business and other purposes. The Tourism Society has also defined tourism in 1976, as tourism is the temporary short-term movement of people to destinations outside the places where they normally live and work, and activities during their stay at these destinations; it includes movement for all purposes, as well as day visits or excursions. The most intuitively logical definition is the one cited by Mathieson and Wall (1982) that tourism activity relates to: the temporary movement to destinations outside the normal home and workplace, the activities undertaken during the stay and the facilities created to cater for the needs of the tourist. Tourism has become an extremely dynamic system due to the globalization of trade and commerce, fast changing customer behavior, development of transportation and accommodation, basic sanitation and hygienic at the destinations and information technologies that all strongly influence the industry in a big way.

The Meaning of System:

Systems perspective focuses on as to how coordination can be established among primary, secondary and tertiary actors in complex innovation situations without one group or individual imposing their views. The system's approach aims for a way of assessing and dealing with complex real world situations. It aims at achieving the performance of tasks of each actor or stakeholder as part of a whole and to help in achieving a common goal. This approach is a practical means of studying the interconnectivity and existing linkages of providers of services and looking at composite inter-related issues and events from a holistic perspective. This holistic approach provides opportunity for a synergetic interaction of individual competence of inter-related actors in an area of common interest.

What is really essential to study tourism a system's approach? A system is a set of interconnected groups harmonized to form a combined objective and strive towards the accomplishment. It integrates another approach into comprehensive method dealing with both micro and macro issues in the tourism industry system. It can examine the tourist firm's competitive environment, its market and pricing structure, its outcome and its linkages with other institutions. It also emphasizes on the tourists and the interaction of the tourism intermediaries with the tourists. Furthermore, tourism system takes a macro point of view and closely examines the entire tourism system of a country, state, or area. This makes an attempt to find out the feasibility as to how it operates within and related to other systems such as legal, political, economic and social systems.

From a structural approach, a destination can be seen as a system composed by a number of elements, which share some kind of relationship in order to achieve common objectives. The system develops by taking external and internal inputs in to the process. It may be considered a complex adaptive system. A tourism destination comprises a number of elements like the tourism operators, the support structures, public and private organizations and associations etc. McKercher's (1999) model describes the following groups of components:

- Tourists and communication sectors linking tourists to the destination (both real and virtual)
- Local destination stakeholders; and tourism-related and non-tourism-related externalities.
- External tourism agencies and outputs from the system.

Essential Elements of Tourism Activity:

Tourism arises out of a movement of people to and their stay in various destinations. There are two elements in tourism one is the journey to the destination and other is the stay at the destination that includes diverse activities undertaken there by the tourists. The journey and the stay take place outside the normal place of residence and work, thus it gives rise to activities, which are different from the resident and working populations of the places through and in which travel and stay. The movement to destinations is temporary and short term in nature. The basic intention is to return home within a few days, weeks or months. The period of stays is limited and return is definite. Destinations are visited for the purposes other than indulging in permanent residence or employment activities.

Tourism definitions intend to dwell on the demand side of tourism activity rather than the supply side. It may be inferred that it is certainly difficult to distinguish which type of tourism related industries are catering tourists only and which are serving local residents and other markets along with the tourists. This makes defining the supply side of the system relatively hard. It is much easier to ponder over the demand side where those participating service providers in tourism can be identified more easily. These models incorporate elements of demand and supply which and when brought together by intermediaries, result in tourism activity. Many researchers have attempted to construct models of the tourism system. Let us have a glance on a handful of these systems.

1. Write five lines on the meaning of tourism and various elements of tourism Industry?

2. Write briefly the need for having a system to run tourism business?

Tourism as a Dynamic System:

Tourism can not only be called as an industry or even a conglomerate of different business sectors in the narrow sense but also in the broader sense as a full-fledged system that is managed by both the public and private sector enterprises. It is a service industry connected with most other sectors of the economy like the host community at both the broad and local levels, government through policy, planning, infrastructure development and the biophysical environment. The tourism industry is running with the support of the host community as workforce, the government as regulatory body and tourism intermediaries as service providers. It is necessary to find out tourism's multiplicity of backward and forward linkages that extend from the highly localized to the wider background taking on local, regional, national and international levels in areas such as the economic, the social, the cultural, the political or governmental and the environmental. As Gunn and Var (2002) point out in their research works that every part of tourism is directly and indirectly related to every other part and some of the parts are often invisible to others within the periphery of the system.

Leiper's Tourism System:

Let us begin with the Leiper's (1981) model of tourism system given in Figure-1. The model suggests a simple three-fold approach that comprises generating region, transit region and destination region. This is an attractive and discerning model, which can be adopted as a practical model for identifying the demand at respective regions. To study a tourist destination, it is important to view it as part of a tourism system as the one proposed by Leiper. While describing the components of the system such as the Traveler Generating Regions (TGR), the Transit Routes (TR) and the Tourist Destination Regions (TDR) one must analyze them under the influence of diverse environments. Tourism growth in a specific destination cannot be comprehensively measured unless the other regions, TGRs and TRs, as well as the environments influencing in each region are taken into analysis.

Tourism system is divided into three geographical components, the general focus remains on the environments of the system and how these affect tourism and at the same time how tourism affects the environments at each geographical component. The model has certain specific functions that all these regions are included in the analysis of the impacts. The environmental impacts should not only be considered to measure the growth of a destination, but also the environments should be analyzed comprehensively for each of the regions to fully assess the growth of destination.

Murphy's Psychological Factors:

One of the most practical tourism system models advocated by Murphy in 1985 has been presented in figure-2, you will see that the focus is given the psychological factors that influence demand (motivations, perceptions and expectations) and how these determinants of demand are linked by the travel intermediaries (i.e. travel agencies and tour operators) in the market place to the supply of tourist facilities. The Murphy's tourism system model can generally be used for the purpose of analyzing the demand and supply for the travel product and the involvement of travel agencies and tour operators in catering to the demand as key suppliers. The Murphy's model can be used for analyzing the demand and supply of the tourism products and more particularly the role of the suppliers is very significant as they create capital and resources to meet the demands. They also conduct the organized tour packages for the purpose of offering unique experience to the tourists. This model will be much useful for the tourism intermediaries to measure the magnitude of demand and accordingly they will work out strategies to meet the demands.

The model can be used for specific purposes for example Destination Marketing Organizations (DMO), Governments and tourism intermediaries assess demands in terms of motivations, perceptions and expectations and can take combined efforts to create facilities, accessibility and infrastructure to enhance the competitive advantage of the tourism products in the destinations can take the advantage of the model. The model is of much explicit use for travel intermediaries because they can better analyze the size of the market demand and supply.

Gun's Influence of External Environment:

Gun (1979) has developed a model which reflects the influence of the external environment and the two- way relationships between the various elements of the system. The tourism system model of Gunn is presented in figure-3. By acknowledging the mutual influence that certain elements have on each other, Gunn is emphasizing the interdependency and importance of various facets of the tourism system. The Gunn's tourism system model that states about the much influence of external environment on the functioning of the tourism system. The model includes attractions, transportation, information and services which influence the tourist motivations. Whilst the external environment that embraces political, economic, physical, natural and cultural factors has much influence on the total functioning of the tourism system directly. The external environmental factors have much control on the tourism system and they are the significant players in making the tourism system dynamic. In turn, tourists can be negatively affected at the destinations.

In essence, the system has certain general uses like the model will give proper guidance to the tourism intermediaries and Governments about various external environmental factors and how they determine the running of the tourism system. The model, on the other hand, can be used for specific purposes such as each service providers can be guided by the external environments and evolve suitable plan and programmes to deal with the influence of external environments. Tourists in general can get plenty of knowledge from this model that can better guide them to plan the holidays.

Mill and Morrison's Consumer Behavior:

The model suggested by Mill and Morrison in 1992 is given in figure-4. This model is cyclical in nature. The model suggests that each element of the tourism system reinforces and influences the next. According to Mill and Morrison, the key components of the system are the market, travel, the destination and marketing. To look at this in more detail, market demand is determined by a number of internal and external influences which affect the purchase of travel. This, in turn, influences the travel element of the tourism system since the demand for a product encourages the development of transportation networks to meet this demand. This in turn influences the type, nature and level of supply of tourist infrastructure and facilities at a destination. This sequentially influences the marketing strategy for a destination and the market segments. The way in which a destination markets itself and communicates its product-offering to its market can stimulate the level and type of consumer demand, which is influenced by a number of internal and external factors. The model can have certain general uses like total demand of the market can be studied by taking into account the external and internal factors. The model can specifically be used by the tourism promotional agencies and travel intermediaries (tour operators & travel agents) for evaluating the various levels of buying behaviours of tourists. More specifically, the model can guide the destination development and promotion agencies to undertake research and development for the tourism industry.

This model can better be adopted by the tour operators, travel agents, hotels, resort companies, transport operators, entertainment agencies, etc as a framework to evaluate the travel purchases of tourists. Accordingly, they can implement marketing strategies to position the product in the market. This model, in brief, explains about the stages through which tourism intermediaries can reach in the market place comfortably. In essence, this approach reflects a market –oriented view of the tourism system where the determining factor is consumer behaviour.

Westlake's Transport, Communication and Planning:

The model proposed by Westlake in 1985 explains about the dominant roles of transport in establishing linkage between demand and supply of tourism services. Westlake also focuses on the importance of the communication process between market and destination. In addition, the model highlights that the importance of planning and development strategies at the destination is to minimize the impact of tourism and maximize the positive significance of tourism activity. Westlake also links the effectiveness of planning and development policies to market. The destinations which effectively plan for tourism will be more likely to sustain demand and retain market share than those which neglect the sustainable planning and development of destinations.

The model has reflected on the significant roles of the transport and communication as a mediator between origin countries and destination countries. This model can be used for the common purpose of marketing the tourism product by identifying the demand and supply for transport and communication facilities at the destination area. The impact can also use for exclusive purpose of evaluating the positive and negative impact of tourism development. The model can be used particularly for the tourism planning and development as it suggests that transport is the most important factor that establishes links between origin countries of the tourists and destination countries.

Finally, Mathieson and Wall (1982) have suggested a complex tourism system that remains a simplistic overview of the structure of the industry. They have identified dynamic, static and consequential elements of the tourist system. The dynamic element is the demand for all types of tourism. The static elements are the characteristics of the destination (including political, environmental an economic influences) and the tourist and including socio-economic characteristics, type of activity and length of stay characteristics) which combine to constitute the destination, the pressure on the destination (in terms of length of stay, types of activity and levels of activity) and carrying capacity. The impacts of tourism are seen as the consequential element of the tourism system and this refers to the physical, social and economic impacts of tourism which need to be controlled by comprehensive management and planning policies.

All of the models offer a slightly different perspective on what the tourism system involves and how the elements interrelate and interdependent. However, as is usually the case, no one model can be classified as definite or absolute and it is essential, therefore, to consider them together. It is up to you to develop your own overview and your own conclusions as to what the tourism system looks like and how the various polices fit together.

A Synthesis of Models of Tourism System:

An attempt has been made in this unit to establish synthesis among the tourism system models and find out their basic differences in their approaches to run the functioning of tourism business. The intricacies of the tourism system have been explained with the help of various diagrams. A number of analogies have been used to explain about the tourism systems. Tourism is in effect thousands of independent components with a huge range of relationships that differ both quantitatively and qualitatively and each individual component affects others in direct and indirect ways. The geo-physical definition of tourism system propounded by Lieper (1989) can be synthesized with the Gunn's demand and supply system (1972), the Westlake's transport & communication model (1985) and socio-cultural element of Mill and Morrison's marketing-oriented system (1992). All these can be added to create the main ingredients for the complete tourism system which divided into the following seven structural components:

- The visitor generating region
- The transit region
- The destination region
- The support services sector
- The government sector
- The environment (bio-geo-physical region)
- The community

The Visitor Generating Region (Demand):

The population of a visitor generating region possesses two fundamental characteristics first is income levels high enough to allow for discretionary expenditure on non-essential items such as travel and the second is a propensity for recreational travel as an acceptable and desired form of behavior. Generally speaking, visitors from such regions can be categorized as domestic tourists or international visitors. They are disintegrated into different potential market sectors. Receiving countries classify visitors according to different criteria from those used by the marketing sector. Arrival registrations are completed at the point of entry and that have similar categories covering holiday, business, education, religion (pilgrimage), sport, conference, visiting friends & relatives.

Transit Region (Supply):

Major modes of transport transfer visitors through the transit region to their destination. The transit region supports these modes of travel by a host of transport-specific facilities such as airports, railway stations, road networks, ports, passenger terminals, fuel depots, engineering and repair facilities, and with a range of ancillary services and facilities such as restaurants, banks, accommodation, communications, retail shops, duty free outlets, bookshops, and bars. Heathrow Airport is an example of the transit region with its complex system of facilities and services that extend much beyond simply refueling aircraft.

The Destination (Supply):

The frontline industries or primary service providing sector consists of those businesses that operate directly with visitors. A common way of organizing our understanding of this part of the tourism structure is to divide them into the five 'A's as follows:

Accommodation - hotels, motels, resorts, backpacker hostels, B&B, caravan parks, etc.

Amenities - restaurants, sports facilites, theatres, casinos, etc.

Attractions - natural and cultural sites, historic, cosmopolitan and heritage cities, landscapes, theme parks, museums, events and festivals, etc.

Accessibility - travel agencies, tour operators, coaches, taxis, hire cars, cable cars, etc.

Activities - tour operators, ski fields business companies, yacht charters, bicycle hire, kayaking adventure companies, abseiling, Himalayan trekking companies, etc.

The Support Services Sector:

This sector brings the thousands of invisible operations into the system that provides goods and services to those operations that deal directly with tourists. But they do not deal directly with visitors. The frontline operators depend on inputs from a very wide range of suppliers of goods and services.

Whilst many of these secondary or support services businesses are heavily dependent upon tourism. They however have little or no realization that they are directly engaged in the business of tourism. For instance, a handicraft manufacturing unit may sell the products to the tourists. All handicraft items may be consumed by the tourism industry front line sector (tour operators, travel agents, hotels, resort companies, cruise liners, car rental companies, and railway companies. A typical front line operator of a small resort will have more than 200 suppliers of a wide range of goods and services. Both front line operators and support service businesses may be located in all three major geographic regions of the tourism system.

The followings are the specialist operators in the tourism system.

- In the visitor generating region (frontline operators such as travel agencies, tour operators, airline offices, and support services sector such as banks, insurance companies, suitcases manufacturers, etc.).
- In the transit region (frontline businesses associated with the transport modes, with facilities such as airports, and support services such as fuel depots and engineering repair businesses.
- At the destination (attractions, accommodation, activities, etc,) supported by a huge range of goods and services from the Support Services Sector.

Roles of the Government:

Since tourism is regarded as a private sector activity and the role of Government is time and again unnoticed or undervalued. In reality, governments take part in the tourism system more significantly through a wide array of functions that incorporate.

- Regulatory controls such as incensing laws for businesses, vehicles, companies and boats; business registration, taxation, foreign investment and building codes.
- Provision of national services for visitation such as customs, immigration and quarantine controls, law and order - including anti-terrorism measures.
- Policy formulation for economic, tourism, transport, foreign affairs, sport & recreation, telecommunications, etc.
- Planning for regional development and creation of zoning system for land use).

- National issues and interests for example environmental issues: legislation for conservation, protection and preservation of endangered species, threatened habitats, fragile ecosystems, coastal erosion, salinity; establishment of national parks and biosphere reserves, world heritage sites, etc. and health issues like the SARS, plague dengue, anthrax, bird flu epidemic.
- Infrastructure like roads, railways, airports, ports, communications systems, power, water, public transport, etc.
- Ownership of major resources like national parks, World Heritage Sites, city squares, national monuments, museums, a host of public spaces that have dual functions, e.g. as a parliament and as a tourist attraction, etc. Festivals and events such as republic day and Independence Day celebrations, New Year's Day fireworks, and so on.
- International agreements for visa, bilateral air services, anti-terrorism treaties, etc.
- International tourism marketing as the primary function and strong involvement in tourism planning and development.
- Disseminations of information services

Governments provide the policy framework within which tourism functions. Policies incorporate economic, social, and environmental objectives. Governments therefore undertake national and regional tourism planning. A major function in this regard is the development and maintenance of a national statistical database designed to measure many aspects of the contribution of tourism to the national economy.

The Environment:

The environment includes air, land and water. Landscape features constitute major tourist attractions in their own right, and also provide the habitats and ecosystems for the living marine and terrestrial organisms which support other attractions. Degradation of the natural environment constitutes one of the gravest risks to sustainability in tourism; a fact acknowledged by the tourism industry which has, in the last decade in particular, begun to take increasing responsibility for ensuring that its activities have minimal environmental impacts.

Role of Local Community:

Communities are considered as the hosts in tourism's binary division of residents and visitors. Communities consist of residents, rate-payers, families, individuals, community organizations, ethnically distinct groupings, and indigenous minorities as well as other kinds of social groupings based on common sets of identity (e.g. religious affiliations, sports associations, gender alignments, etc.). In the study of tourism, we are most concerned with social effects and impacts, cultural effects and impacts, community infrastructure, cultural landscapes, and identity of community place and space. Community-based culture is often a product or commodity for consumption by visitors, and socio-cultural impacts of tourism may create major problems for communities. Communities are embedded with a wide number of local organizations and non-profit organizations which have varying degrees of ownership over resources such as historic sites, festivals, gardens, museums, nature reserves, and which may provide a range of services to visitors, especially in the fields of interpretation and guiding.

Tourism covers a number of industries such as transportation, accommodation, food and beverage services, recreation and entertainment and travel agencies, and banks upon suppliers of a very wide range of goods and services from other sectors to function. Tourism measurements, in order to be credible and comparable with other industries in a country's economy must go after concepts and definitions consistent with internationally accepted macroeconomic guidelines such as the System of National Accounts. According to WTO (2002) the fundamental structure of the Tourism Satellite Accounting (TSA) depends on the balance existing within an economy between on one hand, the demand for goods and services generated by visitors and by other consumers and on the other hand, the overall supply of these goods and services. The initiative is to examine in detail all aspects of demand for goods and services which are linked with tourism within the economy and to assess the association with the supply of such goods and services within the same economy.

Summary:

Increasingly, tourism is recognizing that it has a responsibility to share the benefits of its activities with the poorest segments of populations. The key lesson to take from an understanding of tourism as a system is that it illuminates the way in which backward and forward linkages could provide opportunities for poorer sections of tourism communities and for intervention in enterprises not always recognized as part of tourism but which are nevertheless tourism-dependent in whole or in part for their sustainability and economic viability. When utilizing tourism as the access point for development intervention, it is thus necessary to look outside the square and identify opportunities associated with tourism which are not necessarily tourism businesses. When we begin to understand tourism as a system, we can also challenge the widely held criticism of tourism as a service sector which does not produce anything. Thus, when we look at tourism as a tool for poverty alleviation, we need to find out that we can look well beyond the front line sector to a multiplicity of opportunities for undertaking appropriate initiatives. As a new field of endeavor for development assistance, there is no systematic analysis on which aid donors can draw in developing their own policy. However, support for sustainable, pro-poor tourism fits comfortably with the guiding philosophy of many aid donors, and can make contributions to reduction of poverty, good governance, environmental sustainability, gender equity, rural development, health and education, infrastructure and private sector development.

CHAPTER XII

STRUCTURE OF TOURISM INDUSTRY

Introduction:

Tourism is one of the largest industries in the world. The industry is unique in many ways and has a complex structure and interrelationship among various components. Tourists visit the destination, which is a crucial component of tourism industry and the visit generates different types of impacts. The usage of the destination by the tourist is, hence, has lot of importance and relevance in the socio-economic context of a region. Hence, getting an idea about the structure of tourism industry, components of it, the nature of interrelationship among the industries, use of the destination by the tourists and the consequent effect on the economy in and around the destination, etc. is crucial for a beginner in tourism studies. This unit has been designed with that aim.

Tourism Industry:

Tourism industry is an amalgam of many industries. Tourism industry is defined as "the range of businesses and organizations involved in delivering the tourism product" and the businesses and organizations represent a key element in the tourism system. Complex linkages and interrelationships are existing among the various individual sectors of the tourism industry. For the generation of the phenomenon tourism, all the components of the industry have to act together and each has its own role and relevance. The industry has many characteristics and some of them are the following.

Seasonality

- High ratio of fixed costs to variable costs
- Pricing flexibility
- Fluctuating demand
- Perishable nature of the products
- Fragmentation of the industry, which, allied to its geographical dispersal acts to discourage the formation of industry associations.
- Intermediaries play decisive role

In order to understand the nature of tourism industry, a glance over the concept of tourism system will be useful. Tourism can consider as an activity as well as a process. Of the different approaches with regard to tourism system, the approach suggested by Leiper is simple and suitable for understanding tourism. He considered the phenomenon tourism as a system, which is functioning in various environments (such as Human, socio-cultural, economical, technological, physical, political legal etc). As explained above, this system is also having various parts/ elements, which are interacting with one another in generating the phenomenon tourism. As per this model, there are three major elements, and are illustrated below.

a. Tourists: - Tourist is considered as the main and most important element of the system. Without the presence of tourists, the system may not function at all.

b. Geographical Elements: - The various elements acting in the system related to geography are classified under this category. The front line geographical elements are further divided into three groups, which are as follows:

• **Traveler generating region:**

It is the area where the tourists are emerging from and is represented as tourism emerging markets. For example, if a foreigner is coming to India for visiting various places from U K, then U K is the generating region of that particular trip in relation to India various intangible factors present in this area 'push' to stimulate and motivate travel.

• **Tourist destination region:** This represents the 'end' of tourism, which the tourist is ultimately intended to visit. This region really attracts the tourists to engage in tourism. Leiper says that the 'pull' of the destinations energize the whole tourism system and demand for travel in the generating region.

• **Transit route region:** The area between tourist generating region and destination region is referred as the transit route region. This not only includes the short period of travel to reach the destination but also includes the stopovers, the intermediate places, which the tourist may visit enroute.

c. Tourism Industry:

This is the last element in the Leiper's model. As mentioned previously, tourism is a multi-sector industry that comprises of diverse range of sub-industries, which means that tourism industry is an amalgam of different industries. These provide different kinds of products, which are essential for the tourism process. Hotels, Restaurants, Airlines, Travel agencies, etc are some vital components. Such components can be located in different parts of the system. Hospitality industry is found in the destination region.

Transport sector is largely represented in the transit route region.

Al the elements of the system interact one another in various contexts like delivering the tourism products, transacting the products, etc.

'Push' and 'Pull' factors in tourism:

A large number of factors can cause a person to engage in tourism and such factors can be classified on different basis. When we classify them on the basis of location, some of them can be located in the tourism-generating region and some can be found out in the tourist destination region. The factors present in the tourist-generating region have the capacity to force a person to engage in tourism i.e., income level of person. If a person has more amount of discretionary income, it may encourage him to participate in tourism activities. Such factors, which can be located in the tourist generating area, which may force a person to engage in tourism, are referred to as 'push' factors. Apart from the factor mentioned above, mobility, educational attainment, paid holiday entitlement, family size, work related stress, etc could also be categorized under this heading.

On the contrary, some of the factors are seen in the destination region. For example, the cultural attractions of a destination can allure a person to visit there. Such factors are called as 'pull' factors. Some examples for this category are, climate, infrastructure facilities and scenic beauty.

Components of Tourism Industry:

The major sub sectors of tourism industry are the following.

Destination and attractions

Government organization

Intermediaries

Transportation

a. Road transportation

b. Railways

c. Air based transportation

d. Water based transportation

Accommodation

Entertainment and Recreation

Shopping

Hospitality

Infrastructure

Destination:

Destinations, as defined in the travel industry are specific areas that travellers choose to visit and where they may spend a significant amount of time. In the tourism system concept, destination is the end of tourism. Destinations are not simply transit or stopover points. The selection of a destination by a tourist depends upon the purpose and motivation for travel. Destination as distinct from origin or market refers to the place where tourists intend to spend their time away from home. This geographical unit visited by tourists may be a self-contained centre, a village or a town or a city, a region or an island or a country. Furthermore, a destination may be a single location, a set of multi-destinations as part of a tour, or even a moving destination such as a cruise.

Geographically, destinations can be small areas to large continents. For example Khajuraho in Madhya Pradesh is a destination with a limited area, at the same time, India as a whole is also considered as a destination. It is the area where a good majority of the components of the tourism system can be located. For example, accommodation and food industry can be seen here. The attractions are part of this component of the system.

A destination and the attractions there must have 'pull' capacity to induce visitors to come. This area is highly prone to impacts of tourism- both positive as well as negative. Hence, care has to be taken at the time of development for maximizing the benefits and minimizing the negative impacts. The people residing in and around a destination also have a role in making the tourism successful. Destination as a product has been defined as 'an amalgam of three main components: the attractions of the destination, the facilities over there and the accessibility to it. In recent years, environmental, cultural and social aspects have emerged as important dimensions in developing a destination.

Destination: Concepts and Models:

Tourism is geographically complex, and its different products are sought and supplied at different stages from the origin to the destination. It is not easy to classify that since spatial and characteristics diversity among destinations has become so great. There are several models seek to describe the tourism system relevant to the destination. The tourism system model explained earlier may serve to explain the basic feature of the generating and receiving function of origins and destinations. The routes and linkages may carry tourists from one place to the other and back again or to some third place. And a destination may have multiple destinations in it.

Some other models like structural emphasize the relationships between origins and destinations particularly in Third world tourism in core-periphery terms. The market is concentrated upwards through the local, regional and national hierarchy with international transfer occurring between national urban centers either as origins or destinations in such models. Evolutionary models emphasize dynamic, change and evolving movements or the development of destinations. A range of such models are there, like from pleasure periphery, to psycho graphic positions of destinations, to the life cycle of a destination, with emphasis on structural evolution of destination through time and space.

Destination Selection:

How does a tourist choose a destination? Several factors are there behind it.

"There is general agreement on the structure of the overall destination choice process as including some or all of the following: perceptions (belief formation) of destination attributes in the awareness set through passive information catching; a decision to undertake a pleasure trip (problem recognition/formulation); evolution of an evoked set from the awareness of set of destinations (search for alternatives) perceptions (belief formation) of the destination attributes of each alternatives in the evoked set through active solicitation of information (evolution of alternatives); selection of a destination(s); and post-purchase evaluation".

Attractions, one important group of factors, are those elements that draw a tourist to a particular destination. Attractions are mainly seen as natural or man-made. Scenery, climate or beaches are examples of natural attractions. Resorts or theme parks, etc. are the examples of man-made attractions. Amenities at the destination can be viewed as the elements within the destination or linked to it which make it possible for tourists to stay there and to enjoy and participate in the attractions. They include basic infrastructure, accommodation, transportation catering services, entertainment shopping facilities and visitor information at the destination. Amenities do not usually in themselves attract tourists, but the lack of amenities might cause tourists to avoid a particular destination because there provide the basic facilities which are regarded as contributing to the quality of the destination.

Accessibility of a destination is also a factor that contributes in the destination choice. Image of a destination also has a role in this context. Images can be regarded as "the ideas and beliefs, which tourists hold about the destinations". These images become the main determinant for maintaining or eliminating a particular destination as a possible choice, once the list of all known alternatives is subjected to a winnowing process using more tangible considerations (such as time and money). Price, the sum of what it costs for travel accommodation and participation a range of selected services when there, is another important factor in destination selection. The major factors are explained in detail later.

The Common Features of Tourist Destination:

The following common features of most destinations can be identified:

• Destinations are amalgams

• Destinations are cultural appraisals

• Destinations are inseparable that is tourism is produced where it is consumed

• Destinations are used not just by tourists, but also by many other groups.

Destination amalgam consists of attractions – whether they are having artificial features, natural features or events- that provide an invitation to visit. A tourist at a destination requires a range of amenities, support facilities and services. Accommodation, food and beverage sector of the destination not only provide physical shelter and sustenance, but also create the general feeling of welcome and a lasting impression of the local cuisine and produce. Apart from these, a range of retailing businesses will be there in a destination. Infrastructure and supper structure are the alternative ways of looking at the components of the destination. Infrastructure represents all forms of construction above or below ground needed by an inhabited area. It is mainly in the form of transportation, utilities and other services.

Tourists and visitors alike normally share it. Whereas superstructure is normally a private sector activity and it includes accommodation, built attractions, retailing and other structures. Destination can be naturally attractive like wild life sanctuary or they can be designed with manmade or artificial attraction like amusement parks, historical complexes or holiday villages. People and their custom and life style including fairs, festivals, music, dance and ornamentation can also be staged as attractions. Destinations and attractions sometimes cover a vast area. They encourage linear tourism, which is popular with motorists and coach tours. More than the site or event, the attraction of a destination lies in the image that the potential tourist has of a particular place. In fact, the image of a destination depends on a variety of factors like attitude of host population, civic amenities, natural surroundings, accessibility, food, etc. The image is neither constructed nor deconstructed overnight. It tends to build up over time. No destination can be popular unless it is accessible and offer services and amenities that the tourists demand. Essential services are accommodation and food, backed up by local transport, activities and entertainments.

The development of a tourist destination is not an independent product rather is an amalgam of several products acting as components. The element of intangibility is a crucial one to the destination. Perishability, seasonality, inseparability and heterogeneity, the characteristics of tourism products, have much relevance in the core of tourism destination also. As explained earlier, tourism destination, apart from just a place, comprises of different components or elements. All such elements can be summarized into four groups, usually represented as 4 As. These as represent Attraction, Accessibility, Amenities and Ancillary services, Let us go into the details of each element.

a. Attractions:

The explanation for attraction is given earlier. Attractions are the heart of the tourism industry. They are acting as motivators that make people want to take trips. Generally attractions are classified as either natural or man-made. Further classifications also be possible like, man-made attractions not designed to attract tourists (e.g.: Cathedrals, Archeological sites), man-made attractions designed to attract tourists (Eg. Theme park, Zoos), special events and festivals, complete natural environment attractions (eg. Beaches, seas, rivers), etc. Attractions have the 'pull' capacity by which tourists will be stimulated to engage in tourism and visit the particular place.

b. Accessibility:

Accessibility refers to the easiness in reaching a destination. A destination must be accessible if it is to facilitate visits from tourists. Most of the tourists will not be attracted to a destination unless it is relatively easy to reach. This means that the destination can be reached easily. This connotes that various transportation facilities have to be there at the destination or near to the destination. An airport, railway station, Bus stand, etc. near to the destination will increase accessibility. From such transport centers, transportation facilities are also needed to reach the destination. The frequency of various transport services is also a factor having a role in accessibility of a destination. But in some cases like adventure tourism, lack of accessibility may be an attraction.

c. Amenities:

Amenities are those essential services catering to the requirements of the tourists. In some cases, amenities are represented as infrastructure required for tourism. The amenities required for tourism include the facilities such as accommodation and food, local transport, information centers and the necessary infrastructure to support tourism such as roads, public utility services, and parking facilities. The required amenities will vary according to the nature of the destination itself. In adventure tourism, the required number of amenities is very less. If it is more, the destination will lose its charm. In some cases amenities themselves will the attractions. For example, the destination like France, which is famed for its regional foods, encourage tourists whose motive in traveling may be largely to enjoy the food.

d. Ancillary services:

Ancillary services refer to the auxiliary or the supplementary services offered at the destination. Local organizations are the best example, which usually offer various services to the tourists. The main services normally provided by the local organizations are listed below.

- Promotion of the destination
- Co-ordination and control of development
- Provision of information and reservation services
- Giving advice to the local businesses
- Provision of certain facilities (e.g. Catering, sports, etc)
- Provision of destination leadership.

Destination Life Span:

It has been reported that every destination has a life span and passes through various stages. Different arguments are there in this area, and some are against it. Butler has suggested a model representing the life span of a destination and is named as Tourism Area Life Cycle Concept (TALC). He has pointed out that there are six to seven distinguishable stages in the life cycle of a destination and the details of the stages are given below.

a. Exploration:

Here a small volume of explorer type tourists who tend to shun institutionalized travel will visit the resort/destination. At this stage the destination may not have much accessibility and facilities.

b. Involvement:

At this stage, local initiatives will begin to provide facilities and services for the visitors. The destination will gradually begin to develop. Outsiders will start to arrive and the volume of tourist arrivals will get momentum.

c. Development:

By the development stage large number of visitors are attracted and the control of the tourism at the destination will pass out of the hands of the locals. Government will start large-scale promotion and private enterprises will rush to begin establishments. The rate of increase in tourist arrivals will be high.

d. Consolidation:

In the later stages of the cycle, the rate of increase of visitor declines though the total numbers are still increasing. The resort, by now will be a full-fledged one.

e. Stagnation:

By the stagnation stage, peak tourist arrivals have now being reached and the destination is no longer fashionable. Now it will be relying upon repeat visits from more conservative travellers. The destinations will usually begin to show environmental, social and cultural problems at this stage.

f. Decline:

By this stage visitors are being lost to newer resorts and the negative impacts will be on the increase.

g. Rejuvenation:

Authorities of the destination, at this stage have to decide to rejuvenate/ re-launch the destination by looking at new markets/product diversification. Satellite destinations can also be developed. It has been found that rejuvenation strategies are difficult to implement.

Destination Elements and Tourist Flows:

The above-discussed elements of destination have very high influence in tourist flows. As explained earlier, tourism destination is the most important sub-element of the tourism geographical element as per the Leiper's model of Tourism system. This area (Destination) consists of different 'pull' factors as far as tourism is concerned. Apart from it, some of the industrial components of tourism are distributed in the destination. Each component, in one way or other, is related to each of the element of the tourism destination.

Out of the elements of a destination, attractions are the most important category which have an appeal to the tourists. Much of the attractions of a destination is intangible in nature, and depends upon the image, which the potential tourist has of it. India will be seen by one group of travelers as exotic and appealing, while others will reject the destination because of the negative image due to many reasons or its alien culture. Different destinations will have different attractions and the appeal these make and the influence these exert will also be different.

Anyhow as stated earlier, attractions share the maximum contribution in the total 'pull' factors of a destination. The attractions are the major factors in making customers'/tourists' view about the destination. Kerala has emerged as important destination in India recently and the share played by attractions of Kerala in the scenario is very high. Kerala encompasses many destinations with diverse attractions. Natural beauty, cultural diversity, greenery, etc. are very important components of Kerala's attractions and natural attractions like Beaches, Backwaters, etc are really capable enough to influence anyone from the world. Such specialties really have a big role in making a good image and positive tourists view about Kerala.

Accessibility is another important element of a tourism destination as well as a factor that has a big role in influencing a customer. In general cases, accessibility is an important factor for attracting tourists. But in some exceptional cases, the lack of much accessibility can also be an attraction. For example, an adventurous tourist trekking trip to Agasthyarkoodam (a hilltop point in Kerala) doesn't require transport facilities. If the accessibility is very high, it has been reported that, in some cases, it may cause crowding and congestion which may lead to the loss of charm and ambience. It should be noted that the 'perception' of accessibility on the part of the travelers is often as important as a destination's actual accessibility. For example many people in Britain perceive Corfu as being more accessible than Cornwall, in terms of traveling time. Such perceptions will undoubtedly affect decision-making when tourists are planning their travel.

Amenities are the essential services catering to the requirements of the tourists at a destination. For experiencing tourism phenomenon, amenities are necessary. Stay, local transport, shopping, etc are vital components of tourism process. For enjoying the same, amenities are required. Amenities contribute to the image of a destination. Thus it has a part in attracting and influencing tourists. Sometimes amenities alone become attractions. The topless, double decker bus services in some cities of Europe, traditional food outlets in France, house boat transportation in the backwaters of Kerala, etc. can be cited as examples for the same. Ultimately, it can be said that, amenities are highly essential as far as tourism is concerned and these can also influence tourists in making decisions. Apart from amenities, the ancillary services provided at the destination also can exert influences in making decisions. Such services will create more positive image among tourists and have a big role in tourist flows and tourists' views on destinations.

Destination Use by Tourists and Impacts:

Tourism is a multi-faceted, multi-dimensional activity with a large number of consequences on society, culture, environment and economic conditions of a country or a region. The second half of the last century has seen tremendous developments in the tourism sector, and initially it was considered as a smokeless, non-polluting industry. But later on, as years went by, tourism sector started to produce different issues in different spheres of life. The contribution of tourism towards the economic and regional development was quite significant. Thus, tourism produced both positive as well as negative impacts. Traditionally tourism has been viewed as a great force in promoting understanding among nations and within the national boundaries, facilitating national integration. Tourism has been accepted as an important catalyst for economic development recently only. The economic contribution is measured in different terms such as employment generation, foreign exchange earnings, income generation and output growth.

It is natural for people belonging to different cultures, life styles or social settings to interact and leave an impact on each other. In tourism this happens at a massive level. Tourists generally may try to explore the social life at the destinations, whereas the local community may attempt to imitate the life-style of tourists. Friendship making, learning from each other, better understanding among people, etc. are considered as positive impacts of tourism. At the same time, there are some impacts, which have been termed as negative impacts. Many examples can be cited worldwide for the negative impacts of tourism in the social and cultural spheres of human life. Adopting pseudo behaviors, involving in drug and mafia activates, inspiring prostitution tendency, loss of local and traditional culture, etc are considered as menaces due to tourism. Commercialization of art and art forms is another one, which can be added to the negative impacts or tourism. But, on the contrary, the preservation and maintenance of culture and cultural features are highlighted as very strong positive impacts of tourism.

Apart from the impacts in economy, society and culture of the host population, environment and ecology is another important area where tourism generates impact. Different kinds of tourism activities affect the natural and built environment. There is a complex interaction between tourism and the environment. Environmental impacts are inherently and irreducibly multi-dimensional. The OECD report on the environmental impact of tourism states: "A high quality of environment is essential for tourism while the quality of environment is threatened by tourist development itself, which is promoted because of its economic importance". In other words, tourism tends to destroy tourism itself. But at the same time, the opposite dimension of tourism industry- recreation in national park and conservation reserves-has been highlighted in tourism and environmental discussions. Impact of tourism to some extent varies according to the type of visitors attracted to an area and their activities while they are at the destination. The impact of tourism on any destination will be determined by a wide variety of factors and the major of them are:-

- The volume of tourist arrivals
- The Structure of the Host Community
- The Types of Tourism Activity
- The fragility of the local environment

Difference in socio-cultural characteristics between the hosts and the guests (local community and the tourists)

Apart from this, the interests of various stakeholders in preserving and maintaining local environment and culture are an important determinant in generating impact. The political factors, including policies also have the capacity to influence impacts of tourism. Tourism is functioning in different environments and all such have roles in determining impacts. The greater the economic and social diversity of the destination, the more facilities it has for visitors, the more easily it will accommodate additional tourists. In practice, it has been reported that the destination area's landforms and ecology, it's economic and social structure and political organization, all determine the form and structure within which tourist activity produces specific local results.

The carrying capacity of a destination has an important role in determining the impact of tourism. There are a variety of factors, which determine carrying capacity like social structure, culture, environment, political structure, tourist activities, tourist characteristics, etc. Such factors are classified as cither local factors or alien factors. The local factors and alien factors, manipulated by planning and the management of tourism development, will result in impacts on the social structure, culture, environment and economic structure. The details of carrying capacity and alien and local factors are explained later in this book. A schematic framework for identifying the relation between determinant factors and tourism impacts can be illustrated as follows.

The destination area's landforms and ecology and political organization determine the form and structure within which tourist activity produces specific local results. Given the interaction of the local and alien factors within the host environment the planning and management process should aim to secure the maximum positive benefits while incurring the minimum costs. Law (1985) has come up with a systems model (destination system model), which suggests that introducing or expanding tourism in any region/ area results in multifarious changes. Care has to be taken to control the factors leading to negative impacts and to enhance positive benefits. The following descriptions will give an idea about the various identified/ reported positive and negative impacts of tourism.

In many economies, the travel and tourism sector has for some time been recognized as a major area of activity which both draws upon the resources of those economies and affects their nature and development. In addition to this, tourism has been fit to use as a subject or agent of macroeconomic policies by the governments. Tourism often has a high involvement in policies related to employment levels or the balance of payments whose significance in modern macro-economic management is high. The governments see tourism as an engine for economic development.

The norms used in monitoring tourism are normally weighed on the upper side primarily for its role in foreign exchange earnings or tourism receipts. The economic benefits generate due to the spending by the tourists while they are on the tourism process. In the economic sphere, tourists spending can enhance an area by bringing wealth and catalyzing income, employment, and enterprise and infrastructure development. In contrast to the benefits on employment foreign exchange earnings and others, tourism is generating some negative effects also. The positive and negative economic impacts are discussed in detail below.

Tourist Visit and Impacts:

Economic Impacts-Benefits:

A range of tourism economic benefits are identified and the very important of such are as follows.

Invisible Export:

In the national context, tourism may have a major influence on a country's 'balances of payments. A country's balance of payments reflects it's transactions with the rest of the world, on part of its system of national and macro accounting. A country's balance of payments is important for the maintenance of the value of its currency in foreign exchange. Continuous balance of payment deficits for a country normally leads to an imbalance between the international supply of the country's currency and the international demand for it, in the direction of an excess supply. It may lead to the country's 'currency weaknesses. Developing countries use the strategy of development of tourism as an invisible export.

International tourists are generally buying services from another country and are therefore paying for 'invisibles'. When a tourist from UK comes to India, there is an invisible payment of Germany's balance, while India's balance gets an invisible receipt. Tourist expenditure is as 'real' as any other form of consumption, and international tourist expenditure can be seen as an invisible export from the host country. Usually, countries try to maximize their travel receipts through promotional and marketing strategies. A tourist spends money on various heads.

Accommodation, shopping, travel, entertainment, etc. are the major areas where tourist spends money. International tourist has to exchange the currency into that regional currency before making various purchases. Tourist can purchase goods and services from the host country by paying accepted international currencies also. Thus, the consumption of tourism products will generate activity, which can be compared to export, and even though most of the tourism products are intangible in nature.

In the case of domestic tourism, tourism expenditure is considered as an 'export' between the local regions, and perhaps an import substitute for the national economy. Domestic tourism encourages redistribution of income of the country.

Government Revenue:

Tourism activity is used by certain economies as an important resource for generating government revenue. Tourism generates tax income, some of which is directly applied and some computed indirectly. Most of the taxes come in the form of sales tax on various items the tourist is purchasing, like cigarette, liquor, accommodation facilities, etc. Tourists are paying taxes indirectly also by the consumption of various imported items. When we consider the direct, indirect and induced effects of the expenditure by a tourist, it can be inferred that he is paying taxes to government in different ways.

Employment Generation:

Tourism, in common with most personal service industries, is labour intensive. For developing and developed countries with high unemployment rate, tourism is considered as an attractive alternative. Tourism involves a wide variety of industrial sectors, and this makes it particularly difficult to derive estimates concerning the number of employees associated with tourism. In addition to this, tourism has a diverse range of linkages between tourism sectors and other sectors of the economy. Thus the employment generation happens not only in tourism industry alone, but even in all the allied and other sectors with direct or indirect linkages with tourism activities.

Tourism products mainly consist of service products and they usually tend to generate more employment opportunities. The concept of multipliers has the same impact in the employment sector as in income. Tourists staying at a destination create jobs directly in the industry. Apart from this due to the effect of tourist's stay; many other sectors indirectly related to tourism will be influenced to create more job opportunities. The direct employment generation includes employment in travel agencies, tour operators, transport undertakings, accommodation establishments and enterprises engaged in marketing destinations.

Indirectly tourism will cause employment generation in other sectors like financial institutions, organizations that supply raw materials to the tourism organization, etc. But still there are a variety of criticisms in this area in comparison with other industries such as; the tourism employment potential is seasonal, most of the jobs generated are only inferior employment, local population is often too small to fill the vacancies, etc. Counter arguments are these, but these are not discussed here in detail since such issues are beyond the scope of this.

Investment and Development:

The development and growth of tourism in particular areas will attract more private and public investments. The private and public sectors may be induced to invest even more in that area and this is what economists call as "accelerator effect". Thus if tourism to an area booms and the value of TIM (Tourism Income Multiplier) is high, more investments in both tourism and allied industries can be expected. Superstructure development is an important aspect in relation to a destination at this juncture.

Income:

Income is generated to the local community directly, indirectly and in induced forms. Income is created in different forms and in general it accrues from wages and salaries, interest, rent and profits. Since tourism industry consists mainly of service products, the greatest proportion is likely to be in wages and salaries as far as income generation is considered. And hence, the level of generation of income from tourism is closely bound up with the level of employment. Here the wage levels also have much importance. If it is high, income level will also be high. Income is also generated from interest, rent and projects on tourism business ranging from the interest paid on loans to an investor in infrastructure and superstructure to rent paid to a land owner for a car park or campsite. The sum of all incomes in an economy is called as 'national income' while the significance of tourism in a country's economy can be identified by its contribution on the proportion of national income.

Negative Economic Impacts:

Tourist expenditure has a 'cascading' effect throughout the economy. The benefit it is giving to the economy is described above. But, there are some negative impacts, which have been under wide discussion for a long term. Some of them are discussed here.

Migration of Labor:

When tourism development comes in rural areas, the possibilities will arise for migration of labor towards tourism sector. In such areas, primary sectors of production like Agriculture, Fishing, etc would have been the major source of employment before the arrival of tourism. But the introduction of tourism will generate employment opportunities there, and usually a share of the population employed in primary sector may move to tourism sector for employment since it may give jobs with better salary, etc. In tourism sector, they will be employed in non-skilled categories, but they might have been skilled employees in the former sector. This will affect labor in primary sector, which may suffer from lack of enough skilled labor. This will raise the cost of labor and ultimately the production cost. This scenario may happen in urban tourism also where labor units may be migrated from rural areas. The migrated labor units are likely to experience additional infrastructure pressure for health, education and other public services.

Opportunity Cost:

The concept of 'opportunity cost' was introduced by D.I. Green and popularized by Professor Knight. The opportunity cost of given economic resources are the foregone benefits from the next best alternative use of those resources. i.e., the sacrifice or loss of alternative use of a given resource is termed as 'opportunity cost'. The use of capital resource (in developing and developed countries, it is often scarce) in the development of tourism related establishments preclude their use for other forms of economic development. Hence, opportunity cost has to be considered in measuring tourism economic impact.

Displacement Effect:

While estimating the economic impact of tourism an allowance should be made for the 'displacement effect' when tourism development substitutes one form of expenditure and economic activity for another, it is referred as 'displacement effect'. In the context of tourism, it is usually referred to when a new project takes away business patronage from an existing one.

Tourist Expenditure and Generation of Economic Benefits:

Tourists spend money on a wide variety of goods and services. They spend money to purchase accommodation, food and beverage, transport, communications, entertainment services, goods from 'retail outlets' and others. A part of the money spent by the tourists will go out of the local economy for providing various services and goods. For example, a tourist is visiting India, and staying in a deluxe hotel, ask for Russian made Vodka, then the hotel will have to supply the same. Here, the money spent for the same goes out of the local/national economy. At the time of economic impact measurement this leakage of money is referred to as 'import'.

In tourism, the amount of leakage has to be taken into account so seriously and since, especially in developing and developed countries the leakage is high.

Tourist Expenditure is defined as the "total consumption expenditure made by a visitor or on behalf of a visitor for and during his trip and stay at destination". The consumption of the goods and services may not necessarily be by the visitor himself and the expenditure may not necessarily be undertaken by the visitor himself. For example a groups tour, where expenditure can be done one or two individuals, not by all. International tourist expenditure is usually considered from the perspective of destination country for inbound visitors, and from the perspective of the origin country for outbound tourists. International tourism receipts are defined as "the expenditure of international inbound tourists, including their payments to national carriers for international transport". Expenditure pattern can be classified into three as pre-trip, on-trip, and post trip expenditures.

Tourist Expenditure Pattern:

The money spent by a tourist will generate additional demand in the economy. A country is mainly benefited from tourism by the tourist expenditure. The economic contribution of tourism is an important area to be measured. This statistics concentrates in that area. All the expenditures by the tourists will be considered in this statistics except payments made to international airlines.

The full assessment of economic impact must take into account all the aspects including the following.

- Indirect and induced effects
- Leakage of expenditure out of the local economy
- Displacement and opportunity costs.

Economic Benefits are generated not only in the tourism sector itself, but it passes to other sectors also. Thus economic benefits are generated in three levels. Direct, Indirect and Induced. The direct level measures the economic benefits coming to the tourism industry directly (in the frontline establishments). It is the value of tourist expenditure less the value of imports necessary to supply those 'front-line' goods and services. The direct impact is likely to be less than the value of tourist expenditure. The direct impact depends on the capability of the local economy to provide for tourist's demands from its own production sectors.

The establishments which directly receive the tourist expenditure also need to purchase goods and services from other sectors within the local economy. For example, Restaurants will have to purchase food raw materials from retail shops there. The suppliers to those frontline establishments will need to purchase goods and services from other establishments and the process continue.

The generation of economic activity brought about by these subsequent rounds of expenditure is known as the indirect effect. During the course of direct and indirect rounds of expenditure, income will accrue to local residents in the form of wages, salaries, rent, and interest and distributed profits. This addition of income to the local income will, in part, be reinvested in the local economy on goods and services, and this will generate yet further rounds of economic activity. This phenomenon is referred to as 'induced effect'. Thus, while we consider the economic impact of tourism, all the three kinds of economic effects have to be taken into account.

The calculation of level of tourist expenditure is easy, but at the same time, measuring of economic impact of tourism is far more complicated. Usually the estimation of economic impact based on tourist expenditure is inaccurate and misleading. At the national level, the world Tourism Organization (WTO) publishes annual tourist statistics for countries throughout the world. These statistics are only showing the tourism receipts/ foreign exchange earnings. This cannot be taken as a parameter for understanding economic impact. In order to translate tourist expenditure data into economic impact information, the multiplier concept has to be taken into account. Tourism benefits and impacts are not only occurring directly, but indirect and induced effects are there. Appropriate multiplier values have to be calculated for the full assessment of economic impact. Multiplier is one of the most widely considered economic concepts in tourism. Hence it is essential to learn the multiplier concept in tourism.

Multiplier Effect and Tourism:

Multipliers are known as a means for estimating how much extra income is produced in an economy as a result of the initial spending or injection of cash. Concept of multiplier is based upon the recognition that sales for one firm require purchases from other firms within the local economy. This tells that the industrial sectors of an economy are inter dependant. Changes in the level of activity in one industry/ sector lead to changes in the level of activity in other industries / sectors. That means, it could create a ripple effect, also called multiplier effect throughout the economy. The firms in the sector /industry, purchases not only the primary inputs such as labour, imports, etc, but also intermediate goods and services produced by other establishments within the local economy. In simple terms, the term multiplier refers to the ratio of two changes. Change in one of the key economic variables (such as income) to the change by the development. The multiplier can also be expressed in terms of the ratio of direct, indirect and induced changes in the economy to the initial (direct) casual change.

In the case of tourism the concept has much relevance. Tourist expenditure has a cascading effect throughout the economy. Because firms in the local economy are dependent upon other firms for their supplies, any change in tourist expenditure will bring about a change in the economy's level of production, household income, employment, government revenue and foreign exchange flows. Tourist multiplier measures such changes. The following diagram will represent the multiplier effect in tourism.

Tourist is spending money in the front-line establishments (Eg: Hotels, Airlines, etc), which provide the tourist with their goods and services. The money received by the organizations will be re-spent. A portion of the money will leak out directly from the economy in the form of 'imports'. For example, a hotel is purchasing a foreign-made liquor to supply to the tourist, then the money paid for the same will leak out of the economy. This phenomenon is usually represented as 'leakage'. These imports may be in the form of food and beverage also when the tourist eats, but that are not provided locally. Here the value of tourist expenditure that actually circulates in the local economy is immediately reduced. The remaining sum of money will be used to purchase locally produced goods and services, labor and entrepreneurial skills and to meet the government taxes, licenses and fees. From the local businesses also, the money is re-spent.

Again some part of it leaks out of the local economy in the form of imports. Some part of it will go to the government. A good share of the money is again passed to the local business. Thus, the indirect impact arises. This process will continue. During each round of expenditure, some portion of money accrues to local residents in the form of income (wages, salaries and profits). Either households or businesses will save some of the money. This is also a form of leakage. If the money is re-spent again leakage happens and some part goes to government. This spending of income accrued as a result of the initial tourist expenditure will generate further rounds of economic activity and is referred as induced effect. Measurement of economic impact of tourism has to take into account the flow of money through various sectors of the economy and the corresponding generation of different rounds of expenditures, which include direct, indirect, induced effects.

Different Types of Multipliers:

In order to translate tourist expenditure data into economic impact information the appropriate multiplier values have to be calculated. The term tourist multiplier refers to the ratio of two changes - the changes in one of the key economic variables such as output (income, employment or government revenue) to the change in tourist expenditure. There will be some value by which the initial change in tourist expenditure must be multiplied to estimate the total change in output. This change is referred to as output multiplier. Similarly, there will be a value that, when multiplied by the change in tourist expenditure, will estimate the total change in household income. This is referred to as income multiplier. The major types of multipliers are listed below.

Output multiplier:

This measure the amount of additional output generated in the economy as a result of an increase in tourist expenditure. That means it measures the size of added output produced in primary and all the secondary rounds in an economy due to an increase in tourist spending. This is different from transactions multiplier which is concerned with the changes in total volume and value of sales.

Income Multiplier:

This measures the additional income (wages, salaries, rent, interest, distributed profit, etc) created in an economy as a result of an increase in tourist expenditure. Such an income is to be considered only in the form of disposable income, i.e., the income which is available to the households either to spend or save. It can also be measured as national income. Here, the income accrued to non-nationals is not included since major part of it is repatriated. On the other hand, the secondary economic effects created by the re-spending of non-nationals income within the area must be including within the calculations.

Employment Multiplier:

This measures either the total amount of employment generated by the increased tourist expenditure or the ratio of total employment generated by this same expenditure to the direct employment alone (i.e., employment generated during the first round in the directly tourism- related sectors). Employment multiplier provides useful sources of information about the secondary effects of tourism, but their measurement involves more heroic assumptions that in the case of other multipliers, care is needed in their interpretation.

Government Revenue Multiplier:

It is a measure of the impact of an increase in tourist expenditure on government, public revenue in all forms and from all sources. This multiplier may be expressed in gross terms – that is, the gross increase in government revenue as a result of an increase in tourist spending –or in net terms, when the increase in government revenue is reduced by the increase in government expenditures associated with the increase in tourist activity.

Summary:

Tourism is has become the largest industry in the world, particularly in terms of employment generation. As the sector grows, the structure of it gets more complex. The tourism industry is considered as an amalgam of a range of industries with strong interrelationships. Destination is an important element of tourism industry and the reison de etre of tourism phenomenon. The flow of tourists and the corresponding usage of it results in a range of impacts. The benefits of the usage of destination, particular economic are the main reason why tourism has been considered as an important industry in this modern world. This chapter discusses the nature, structure, and elements of tourism industry. The discussion also focuses on destination, tourist flow into a destination, benefits and impacts of such flows as well as the generation of economic benefits.

CHAPTER XIII

FACTORS STIMULATING GROWTH OF TOURISM

Introduction:

Travel has been a nomadic urge in man but due to 'antediluvian means of transport', 'lack of amenities, safety and security' and, 'non-availability of adequate means' during earlier phases of history, it largely remained the privilege of influential and well-to-do class of society who could afford to buy the conveniences. Middle ages, for the first time observed the emergence of a new class of travelers, i.e., adventures and explorers. Strongly motivated by 'curiosity' and 'quest for knowledge', these inquisitive souls, despite their limited means, used to set-out on long and arduous voyages, bravely facing the enroute risks and discomforts. Thus, daring spirits like Marco Polo, Columbus and Vasco-de-Gama added new dimensions to travel, in terms of activity, concept and philosophy. Renaissance in Europe followed by Grand Tours and subsequently, the development of spas, beaches and resorts as health destinations gave further momentum to travel and tourism.

In fact with the varying socio-cultural, economic, environmental, political and technological dimensions the motivations and determinants have kept on, and will continue to be highly dynamic.

Push and Pull Factors in Tourism:

Let us try to understand as to under what circumstances do we take a decision to travel? At any given time in our family life cycle, we experience different sets of liabilities and, of course, liberties. These differ in diverse stages; like when we are settled in an occupation, drawing handsome salary, though married, but yet to extend our family; we enjoy more financial and social freedom and at this stage there are more possibilities of using our leisure time for touristic pursuits compared to the stage when we have kids, and that to at crucial juncture of their studies. Further, at times we are compelled by social obligations to undertake a journey; like some important function in our family or compulsory visit to some religious place. Many a times our profession makes it necessary to frequently go out of the place of work. Then there can be monotony due to the same routine. In present era stress and strain are also regarded as prominent factors. Whatever is the case, the fact is that at any given time many pressures keep on working on us to make us to realize that we have to take a break. All these pressures or reasons are generally called Push Factors.

Once we realize the need to get involved in some touristic pursuit and identify the exact need niche, we start collecting information about possible alternatives that can fit into our requirement spectrum and in the process we come across a number of options. For example, a person residing in Delhi might like to beat the heat in summers. Obviously the best way is to go to some hill station. Well, he might go to Nainital, Mussoorie, Shimla or, say, Jammu & Kashmir. Each of these places offer different attractions, have different tourism appeal, the expenditure might also vary from place to place and the distance factor also comes into the frame. Depending upon our motives, budget and time available, we chose one or more than one out of these. In fact all these options have different tourismagnetism, or in simpler words possess diverse levels of attraction. These alternatives are kept in the category of Pull Factors. So, we have understood that any tourism related decision is the outcome of interplay between Push and Pull factors.

The amazing fact associated with tourism is that; in the first place, people travel to various destinations due to uncountable and unimaginable number of reasons; secondly, in most of the cases a touristic pursuit is an outcome of combination of more than one motive, meaning thereby is that when we select a destination we look for multiple purposes – for example, while planning to go for a vacation we, the Indians, probably would prefer to go to a place which can provide us (if we are going due to religious reasons) with opportunities to visit a (or number of) religious place (s) along with some other leisure, cultural or natural attractions, in addition to friend or relative living nearby; and, most interestingly, the wants and needs might vary with additional trips to the same place. However, a person going to a destination due to only and only a single reason is called a Special Interest Tourist and the phenomenon Special Interest Tourism, commonly expressed by the abbreviation "SIT".

Motivations to Travel:

As discussed above there can be thousands of reasons behind the travel especially meant for touristic purposes. And, honestly, it is extremely difficult to enlist all of these. Therefore, the various scholars from the field of tourism have suggested diverse categories to enlist the same. Following the categorization proposed by McIntosh, we will now learn about the various broad classes of motivations which are as follows:

- Socio-Cultural Motivators,
- Physical Motivators,
- Inter-Personal Motivators, and
- Status & Prestige oriented Motivators

To begin with, and keeping in mind the strongest appeal of Indian tourism, let us look into the first category, viz. Socio-Cultural motivators. Whenever one undertakes a journey due to something related to either religion (visit to shrines, or for example), or monumental attraction (e.g. Taj Mahal), or historical connections (Port Blair), or fairs and festivals (Suraj Kund Craft Mela or Goa Carnival), or social ceremonies (marriage), or to study the life style of a particular group etc., the movement is caused by this set of motivators. Meaning thereby is that the tourists seek either social or cultural experience in this case. Countries like India are depending upon their extra ordinarily rich cultural treasures to woo tourists from all around the globe.

The second category, i.e. Physical Motivators has three dimensions, viz. visit to a place to either challenge our physical strength, or participate in or simply watch some sport, or physical well-being. This can be taken as the oldest set of motivators (Do you remember the organization of Olympic Games, and that too in B. C. period?). To challenge physical strength relates to getting involved in such activities where you require lots of stamina and courage, like the hard adventure sports. Adventure, undoubtedly, has gained a prestigious place in last two decades amongst the favorite activities. One because one explores new dimensions of ones' unlimited strength, and also due to the fact that adventure provides an opportunity to enjoy nature in its virginity.

Being a part of any sporting event (active or passive) has been traditionally inherited by all of us – actively when we participate in this and passively in case of only watching the sport as audience. I would like to remind you the noisy groups supporting their countries or teams that can be easily seen in cricket or football matches all around the world. In fact these people have tremendous impact not only on the economy of the area visited, but also on the general standard of living of the residents of the place because we have to have supporting infra and super structure to accommodate them. Thirdly, physical wellbeing which has two dimensions, namely bodily health & spiritual vigor. You know, we have entered an era when a new term has been coined in tourism; this is Wellness Tourism. Getting rid of ailments in climatically favourable environs has always persuaded people to go to other places (like people used to go to SPAs in ancient periods) and the same trend is continuing even today. In fact India has taken great leaps in this field by offering quick and comparatively inexpensive treatments on one hand, and state of the art facilities on the other. Health tourism, thus, is another bright shining in the Indian skies. Let us not forget we are living in the country which is equally known for the Ayurvedic treatment, as well as for Yoga & Meditation.

Coming to the third category, i.e. Inter-Personal Motivators now. Its' a bit intricate to understand this particular one. When someone travels due to various very personal reasons, without being forced by external factors, these motivators are said to be working upon the person. Two most commonly observed phenomena in this category are:

- **Visit to Friends & Relatives (VFR)**
- **Root Syndrome**

VFR includes the persons who visit a given place to meet their near and dear ones. Very frequently occurring a phenomenon in our country too, VFRs' have their own importance in the growth of tourism, as well as economic contribution. Many a scholars hesitate in recognizing VFRs' as conventional tourists, but the fact remains that though such tourists depend upon their hosts for only one component of tourism industry, namely accommodation, they use majority of the remaining components as the other segments do. Think about the situation when you go to a friend of yours' residing in Shimla. Though you will stay with him, yet you will visit different attractions in and around Shimla, probably use taxis or coaches for your intra-destination travel, purchase some souvenirs as well, visit some restaurants etc. meaning thereby is that you will, as a tourist, contribute to the economy of Shimla........and economic gains by the destination region is one of the major objective of tourism development.

Root Syndrome is the situation where one migrates to some other place and wishes to visit his or her native place as a tourist at some later stage. Another dimension to this consists of the later generations of these migrants who keep on hearing stories about the place they had belonged to and develop keen interest in experiencing the same thing(s) themselves also. For example the children of NRIs' coming to India to experience various colours and celebrations. In fact this is a very important segment, because they have high spending power and might come in large numbers, if properly approached with effective marketing and promotional strategies. China has made exceptional growth in this segment and that too in last two decades. Majority of the international tourists visiting China consist of Non Resident Chinese. Department of Tourism, Government of Uttar Pradesh has also launched a scheme to attract Non Resident Indians, viz. "Trace Your Roots". Other Indian states can also plan something on these lines to enhance their market base.

The forth category, proposed by McIntosh, revolves round Status & Prestige Oriented Motivators. There is a very old saying "travel to learn and learn to travel". In the present era of LPG (i.e. Liberalization, Privatization and Globalization) the whole world has become a small village where people from different backgrounds, and nationalities, have commercial interests and accordingly the idiom has to be amended a bit. Now it should be re-stated as "travel to learn & earn and learn & earn to travel". Obviously, knowledge and economic status are two most essential factors to fetch status and prestige in the society and, therefore, the number of such people is ascending year by year. Country like India have been major gainers of this phenomenon, where global investment has increased manifolds in last couple of years and as a consequence business oriented travel has also ascended.

Apart from the above, a section of the tourism experts is of the view that we must add one more category to the above list, which is Fantasy. In fact a lot of people undertake journeys for reasons different from the above mentioned ones. Many a times we dream about activities that are off-beat or unusual or are different from the routine ones. For example, the couples who go for honeymoon don't fall in any of the above mentioned categories, because their reasons to travel are different. Similarly, the persons who go to amusement parks mainly look for thrill and excitement. Then there are adventurous souls like space tourists who might be looking for the privilege of being the fore-runners in this field. In all the above cases, the travels are due to extremely unusual reasons- the reasons that are a part of far imaginations, the fantasies. We all keep on dreaming about bizarre things and at a point of time the curiosity crosses the bearable threshold of inquisitiveness to such an extent that we have to take some action to satisfy the need niche.

When do people travel?

Thanks to the ever greater automation, particularly on the industrial front, that more and more people have now disposable income and leisure time on the one hand, and strong desire to escape such by-products of industrialization and urbanization like noise pollution, over-crowding, routine, monotony and boredom on the other thus making travel and tourism both a 'convenience', as well as, 'compulsion' to the modern society (Kandari, 1984).

Let us now try to enlist some of the major prerequisites which are vital possessions required by any person to qualify to get involved in the phenomenon of tourism. These include, as briefly mentioned above:

Disposable Income: Disposable Income refers to that fraction of the income that is left with a person after fulfilling all the social, i.e. necessary, obligations and can be spent by him or her as per ones' own wish. Disposable income essentially has correlation with the motivations of the tourists, because this amount is to be spent on leisure activities.

Discretionary Time: Discretionary Time means the period that remains with a person which he/ she can spend as per his/ her own discretion or desire without having any out-side influence. The more the discretionary time, the higher is the urge to get involved in touristic pursuits.

Need or Desire: Need or Desire are the factors that basically design and direct our motivations. When the persons travel due to need or compulsion; whether social, occupational, or well-being; the phenomenon falls in the category of "Compulsive Tourism" and in case of travel undertaken due to some desire, or combination of desires, the practice is termed as "Impulsive Tourism".

Social Sanctions: is the recent addition (of 90's to be specific) to the list of prerequisites for travel and tourism. These relate to all the three regions that constitute a tourism system, viz. Tourist Generating Region (TGR), Tourist Transit Region (TTR) and Tourist Destination Region (TDR). Social sanctions refer to the open-ness / flexibility / hospitability of the society of these three regions to either allow the people living at TGR to freely move out to other destinations or to explicitly welcome the ongoing or incoming tourists (w.r.t. TTR and TDR, respectively). Values, ethics, social norms, education level etc. are the governing factors of social sanctions.

Determinants:

Determinants refer to the factors that shape or regulate demand or supply of tourism, i.e. are responsible for growth and development of demand and quantitative, as well as qualitative, supply provided by any destination. These are called determinants because these determine the typology and level of either demand or supply. Let us have an insight into some major ones related to demand and supply, respectively. Undoubtedly, the origin of modern tourism and its speedy growth can be attributed to the remarkable achievements in the field of science and technology. To quote Singh (1975) 'modern tourism is a direct product of economic and social progress promoted by technological and scientific advances, higher real income, longer leisure time, demographic expansion and increasingly cheaper and varied tourist-plant facilities that provide the essential conditions for the growth of tourism'.

Researchers have proved that, "the inhabitants of large urban and industrial cities are most eager escapers from their environment on weekends and annual holidays" (Wahab 1971). Consistent innovations in the field of transport and communication have particularly contributed to the dynamically increasing propensity to travel. Now people have a natural access to faster, cheaper and safer means of transport and an equally effective communication system. 'Time-distance gap' in real terms has considerably narrowed-down, thus converting the world into a close neighborhood.

Role of 'education' and 'awareness' too has been vital in promoting travel and tourism in a big way. To quote Hellen (1966), "The spread of education has created cultural awareness and has stimulated desire to travel". In fact, the frontiers of awareness have considerably enlarged over the years and as a result alongside, the usual cultural, political and business reasons, 'environmental', 'biotic', 'geographic', 'social', 'scientific', 'technological' and 'economic' perspectives, too, have begun to strongly motivate people to travel. Development of newer attractions and destinations, improvement in tourist-plant facilities and services, availability of competitive tourist supplies both in terms of quality and prices and effective marketing strategies being adopted by tourism developers and private sector enterprises are further tempting more and more globe trotters to set-out on recreation, pleasure and/or adventure trips or explore nature and culture.

Determinants of demand:

I. Income:

Income is the most vital factor affecting demand, as this is directly proportional to the spending power of the persons. If the income rises, the demand for goods and services rise too. However this has a relation with the quality also. The demand for superior goods and services will rise with the increase in income. A careful analysis of tourist generating regions reveals that the top slots have been shared by the countries with strong economy and currencies.

II. The number and price of related services and products:

The higher the price of alternative goods or services, the higher the demand will be for product or services in question. That means if the price of coffee rises then the demand for tea will increase.

Complements: as the price of complements rises, demand for the complements falls and so too will be the demand for the good in question. If the price of petrol rises then demand for cars will fall.

III. Tastes and Fashions:

Tourism demand is highly dynamic and is extremely sensitive to the variations in tastes and fashions. Mainly World Tourism Organization, World Travel & Tourism Council and Ministry of Tourism, Government of India keep the record of the apparent trends that might affect the growth and development of tourism in the country. Tastes and fashions are usually affected by advertising, trends, health considerations etc.

IV. Expectations of future price changes:

Prospects of fluctuations in prices of services and goods might influence the decision making to a large extent. If people expect prices to rise in the near future, they will try to beat the increase by buying early and vice versa. It has been observed that in many cases the tourism related decisions are deferred due to perceived (or actual) changes in prices. Generally any increase in prices has a short-term impact on demand. After a small span of time tourists accept the changes and once again retort to their planned schedules.

V. Population:

The size and makeup of the population has a reverberating effect on demand. In fact, the size of population is directly linked with propensity to travel (assuming that the economic health of the place good). Again, the age-wise distribution of tourists has a bearing with the type of demand. Like younger population might be interested in adventure based tourism products, whereas the senior citizens are more inclined towards leisure tourism.

Determinants of Supply:

Costs of production:

Cost of production is the most important criterion which regulates the supply of tourism product, services or facilities. Cost, in case of tourism also, is inversely proportional to the volume of production. In simpler words, if an accommodation is experiencing 80% occupancy, the costs will reduce compared to the option which has only 40% occupancy rate. Costs are affected by changes in input prices, wages, raw material, technology, organizational changes leading to increased/ decreased efficiency in addition to Government policies including taxes and subsidies.

• **Profitability of alternative goods in supply:**

If an entrepreneur makes a greater profit from accommodation units compared to that from tour packaging, supply of the later will decrease while that for former will certainly increase?

• **Environmental conditions, Nature, random shocks:**

The worst factors that affect supply in the field of tourism revolve around calamities, geo-political disorders, industry's working ambience etc. thus weather, earthquakes, wars and problems like industrial disputes are perceived as dark shadows in case of tourism industry.

• **Expectations from future prices:**

If the price of a good is expected to rise the supplier may hoard stock (reducing the supply now) in order to benefit later (increase in supply).

• **Profitability of goods in joint supply:**

Joint supply, in tourism sector, is a very common incident Meaning thereby is that suppliers of different components join hands to offer a complete and more satisfactory product. Tour packages are the best example to support this statement, where we find an effective involvement of hoteliers, transporters, guides & escorts, souvenir providers, entertainers and many more to ensure the supply of a package. Joint supply on one hand guarantees higher appeal in the product being hassle free & cost effective, and on the other assures sustainable business volumes to the suppliers.

• **Technology:**

A small stroll in the history reveals that with every technological advancement (may be in transport or communication or information technology) the supply in tourism industry has made steady strides. Simply because advanced technology ensures higher yields, quickness of service, better safety standards and, above all, lower production costs.

Summary:

Well, the nitty-gritty of the discussion made in the foregoing text emphasizes upon, first of all, the very mechanism of traveling. Whenever we take a traveling decision we have clear-cut or well defined reasons to leave our place (s) and, concurrently the options in the form of destinations. As discussed in the first part of this Unit, the reasons to leave our place are described as push factors, while the options form a gamut of what have been described as pull factors.

In the second part inspirations behind the touristic pursuits, along with the stimulating factors have been discussed in details. To have an insight into this, the classification of the motivational factors suggested by McIntosh, in addition to Fantasy, was taken as the major criteria. This included four categories of motivators, viz. Cultural, Physical, Inter-Personal and Status & Prestige.

In the succeeding fraction, the very pre-requisites, i.e. the basic requirements; which are necessarily needed to be fulfilled by any person to qualify as a tourist; have been discussed. In simpler words, the role and importance of money, time, need or desire and social approval has been highlighted, which are must for the phenomenon of tourism to occur. And in the last part, all the variables related to society, economy, technology etc. that might influence the demand and supply in the field of tourism have been discussed. These include population, income, State-of-the-art in the field of technology, cost of production – to name a few. These variables are commonly known as determinants and are indicative of the levels of qualitative and quantitative demand and supplies.

CHAPTER XIV

TOURISM DEMAND AND SUPPLY

Introduction:

The success of any business depend upon the equilibrium that has to be created between the products, attractions, facilities and services which can be, or are, offered by the destination and the level of interest and acceptability these generate amongst the groups of persons to take a positive purchase decision. Further, an economic system comprising of spectrum of different activities positioned in different locations generates movements that must be supported by the tourism system in order to fulfill the expectations and needs of the visitors. Without movements infrastructures would be useless and without infrastructures movements could not occur, or would not occur in a cost efficient manner. This interdependency can be considered according to two concepts, which are tourism demand and supply. In this module we are going to have an insight into these two most vital pillars of tourism industry.

Tourism Demand:

Let us begin with understanding the very concept of tourism demand. Interestingly, tourism demand is perceived differently by different persons. Some of the definitions are being noted down to have an insight into the assortment of expressions regarding this term:

Dictionary defines:

"Demand as the desire of people for particular goods or services"

Economists consider demand to be **Tourism** "The schedule of the amount of any product or service that people are willing and able to buy at each specific price in a set of possible prices during a specified period of time."

Geographers view tourism demand as:

"the total number of persons who travel, or wish to travel, to a specified geographical area; in a given duration of period; to use tourist facilities and services at places other than their places of work and residence."

According to Goeldner and McIntosh:

"Tourism demand for a particular destination is a function of the propensity to travel and the reciprocal of the resistance of link between origin and the destination areas."

Thus D= f (P/R)

Tourism demand, thus, can be understood as an expression of the tourism and travel related needs, even if those needs are satisfied, fully, partially or not at all. Further, most commonly, it is expressed in terms of number of people, volume, or tons per unit of time and space.

Conclusively, tourism demand can be defined as:

"Either the number of tourists who visit or may visit a particular attraction or region, with a definite set of expectations, OR the volume of services/products/facilities that is purchased or might be purchased from a specified geographical area, for a certain price-range and in a given period of time."

Types of Tourism Demand:

Scholars have categorized tourism demand in different manners. Following are two most commonly established categories of the same:

I. On the basis of actual or perceived purchase:

Many a times the actual volume of services, products or attractions purchased, or utilized, from an ear-marked geographical area, during a specific time period and at a given prize range is considered to be the demand for the said products, services or attractions. In such a case the generated, or measured, demand is categorized as effective or actual demand. There can be another situation where we anticipate the volumes that might be used or purchased by the traveling tribe in future. Obviously such estimations are based on application of tested and tried measures of forecasting. The probability factor is quite high in this case. This type of guesstimated demand is kept in the category of potential or latent demand.

II. On the basis of cause and effect:

At times the reasons behind taking a travel decisions might be controlled by our very own desires to go to a place to, may be, relax or break the monotony or get involved in activities we like, i.e. our decisions are not influenced by any external pressures. Such a touristic occurrence is usually put in the category of impulsive demand.

The contrast to it is the situation where one has to compulsorily undertake a travel as a tourist. Example of this type of phenomenon is travel due to business or unavoidable social reasons. This type of travel is a consequence of what is called compulsive demand.

Factors Influencing Demand:

Change is the name of the game and every entrepreneur plays the same. Every industry is influenced by variations and these have higher degree of effect in case of service industry, mainly because of higher degree of intangibility. By now you might have understood that tourism has emerged as one of the major service industry all around the world. So, any internal or external change, in TGR, TTR or TDR, affects tourism and travel industry too immensely. Holiday demand is driven by needs, motives, and expectations, its realization depends on the individual economic situation and the freedom to travel.

Thus:

External factors may have an impact on tourism demand by affecting the ability to travel (freedom, time, money, fitness) and the motivation to do so.

Consumer Behavior is not a reaction on a single factor but on the whole set of influencing external factors. In addition it is driven by internal factors (e.g. motives, abilities etc.). Thus, the impact of a change in a single external factor is limited. We have experienced in past that the tourism demand has either gone up or down with even slight alteration in socio-cultural, political, climatic or even economic set-up. Now the question arises as to how these developments have an impact on tourism demand. In the following discussion, we are going to discuss the same.

Economy: Economic health of the Tourist Generating Region (TGR) is the most important factor affecting tourism demand. Simply, the stronger the economy = the higher would be the income = more would be the disposable income and resultant spending power = elevated will be the travel propensity and, hence, tourism demand. The contrast in economic conditions will result in just the reverse equation.

Politics: This factor has two dimensions, viz. political stability (which results in creating a conducive environment for outward or inward movements) and political willpower to promote tourism (this will be helpful in laying down tourism and tourist friendly policies and, obviously, will result in increased touristic appeal).

Crisis and threats: Crisis and threats are the most unforeseen of these factors. Nobody can predict with surety as to when a calamity would take place. For example, there can be out-break of an infectious disease, or sudden tsunami, or landslides, or a parallel to 09/11 episode etc. the best and most effective measure is to be ready with effective and implementable crisis management strategies.

Demographic Change: Demographic factors include variables like age structure, education level, occupation etc. Tourism demand varies with changes in these. For example, statistics have revealed that the demand is ascending in the age brackets of 25 – 34 years and 55 – 64 years due to lesser liabilities and better financial and physical health of the persons in these age groups. Education, for that matter, enhances knowledge and working spectrums, as well as level of awareness; all these factors combined together enhance the chances of increased tourism demand. As discussed earlier, sometimes in order to enhance the business, occupational compulsions increase the propensity to travel.

Technology: This point has also been discussed; any advancement in any technological area had always had, and will have, a positive impact on tourism demand.

In addition to the above, we have to take into account the influences coming from general changes in consumer attitudes and, finally, the tourism industry itself, of course influencing the demand side of tourism (e.g. standardization of products, information channels, capacities and price strategies).

As we can't limit our attention to a single external factor and its impacts, we look at several of the emerging factors, new trends in tourism emerging from the whole set of influences and the endogenous dynamics of tourism. These emerging trends will not change tourism overnight. Trend research has shown that the future developments will most probably come as a step-by-step development, not as a revolution.

Giving the global and nearly unlimited offer in tourism with capacities still on the rise the power in the market is clearly with the consumer. He will only choose products which fit into his motivation and expectations. Taking the efforts to reduce seasonality in tourism as an example, we clearly see that the limitations to these efforts are only partly due to e.g. school holiday regulations but predominantly due to the motivation of spending a holiday under nice weather conditions.

Tourism Supply:

Tourism supply is the expression of the capacity of tourism related infrastructure and tourist plant facilities (this includes accommodation, F and B facilities, Guiding and Escorting services etc.), generally over a geographically defined tourism system, in different price ranges and for a specific period of time. Therefore, supply is expressed in terms of infrastructures (capacity), services and networks. The number of passengers/ volume that undertakes any movement for touristic purposes per unit of time is commonly used to quantify transport supply. Further, tourism supply can be simplified by a set of functions representing what are the main variables influencing the capacity of any given tourism system. These variables are different for each component.

So, tourism supply refers to the amount or volume of the goods, services and facilities; in addition to the level of comfort and conveniences (i.e. infra and super-structure) and the spectrum of attractions and activities that a destination system can offer to the groups of tourists during a given unit if time (period), at a specified price range, in order to satisfy sets of varied needs and requirements.

The Supply Chain:

The supply chain comprises the suppliers of all the goods and services that go into the delivery of tourism products to consumers. It includes all suppliers of goods and services whether or not they are directly contracted by tour operators or by their agents (including ground handlers) or suppliers (including accommodation providers). It should also be considered that some tourism goods and services are supplied direct to tourists and are purchased by consumers themselves and it should not be forgotten that tour operators can influence their customers in this area too. The initiatives reviewed in this report focus on improving benefits to the destination, consumers and the tourism industry. These initiatives are focused around four main points in the tourism supply chain:

- Accommodation
- Transport
- Ground handlers, excursions and activities
- Food and crafts

Supply chains operate through business-to-business relationships, and supply chain management delivers sustainability performance improvements alongside financial performance, by working to improve the business operations of each supplier in the supply chain. Tour operators have enormous influence over activities throughout the tourism supply chain, since they direct and influence the volume of tourism, the tourist destinations and facilities that are used. Tour operators can use this to help in promoting general improvements in sustainability performance as part of good commercial practice.

In planning actions for sustainable supply chains, tour operators and The Travel Foundation should note that there are examples of good practice throughout the direct supply chain of tour operators as well as in a variety of tourist destinations but these are only implemented by some companies and many others can learn from them. It will be easiest to implement sustainability requirements in accommodation and most difficult in transport, most visible in excursions and activities while most beneficial to the local economy when this supports food and craft production. Destination sustainability efforts will require wider stakeholder partnerships and if only for this reason will be more time consuming to implement.

A secure income stream, with stable contracts and foreseeable contracting conditions including prices is paramount, both to facilitate the necessary investments by the supplier, and to cement the trust in the relationship. Projects require time for companies to build knowledge and develop relationships, and tour operators tend to require a steady and significant volume of operations with a supplier or destination if they are to make a significant contribution and expect changes in local operations.

Three conditions in the tour operator-supplier relationship are particularly important for the success of supply chain initiatives: long-term partnership, fair pricing and a consistent volume of operations.

Successful supply chain relationships between companies and their suppliers are developed and implemented according to a defined series of steps:

1. To establish a sustainable supply chain policy and management system.

2. To support suppliers in reaching Sustainability Goals, including raising awareness on sustainability issues amongst suppliers and demonstrating why sustainability performance is important

3. To integrate sustainability criteria into suppliers' contracts and preferentially

contract suppliers that meet those criteria. Tourism supply chains involve many components - not just accommodation, transport and excursions, but also food and beverages, souvenirs and handicrafts, and the infrastructure that supports tourism in destinations.

Components of Tourism Supply:

Components of tourism supply basically refer to the organizations or individuals who are instrumental in materializing the ultimate product, say for example tour package. Keeping tour packages in the focal point, let us discuss the components of the supply. The components, in this case, consist of attractions, accommodation, transportation, refreshments, shopping and entertainment and recreation. Following is the description of these:

ATTRACTIONS: Being the basic pull factors, attractions are the core of touristic experience. The very nature of the attractions is responsible for the image creation of the destination.

Typology:
- Natural
- Built/ Man-made
- Entertainment
- Sports and Sports facilities
- Rides and Transport

ACCOMODATION: Accommodation is supposed to be the most vital component, as safe and comfortable accommodation tops the list of need hierarchy of the tourists. Usually this particular component acts as a catalyst to get a favorable response from the target segment and accounts for approximately 33% of the total trip expenditure (Cooper et al).

Typology
- Hotels and similar establishments
- Supplementary accommodation
- Alternative accommodation

TRANSPORTATION: Right from the ancient period accessibility and mobility have hold a very high importance in tourism development. Safety, comfort, speed and costs have been the crucial attributes for this particular component. Interestingly, transportation has the potential of being an attraction in itself, for example Palace on Wheels, Euro-rail etc.

Typology
- Land transport
- Air transport
- Water-based transport

REFRESHMENTS:

There is a popular saying that "Road to heart goes through the stomach" and the same stands true in case of tourism as well. Being the necessity of the traveling tribe, refreshments are the inevitable component of the packages and are instrumental for both the favor and abhorrence of the tourists and, thus, can make or break the tour.

Typology:
- Different plans: AP/ MAP/ EP
- General and theme restaurants
- Fast food establishments
- Pubs

SHOPPING: Shopping, in Indian context, has been the most used and abused component. Used, because everybody looks at it as a source of long cherished memories and, hence, shopping is an integral part of the vacations. Usually tourists look for unique and indigenous souvenirs and, therefore, can be an effective contributor to the destination economy. And since there is no specific mechanism regarding commissions and pricing, cases of fleecing and over-charging are quite frequently observed.

ENTERTAINMENT AND RECREATION: Tough generally not included in itineraries prepared in India, entertainment and recreation are the extremely essential components of the packages. After the tiring day trips, everybody looks forward to an unwinding evening. In fact carefully planned entertainment features can become an attraction themselves and, if the local artists are hired, can lead to more economic benefits for the regional economy of the destination.

Unique Characteristics of Tourism Demand and Supply:

To understand and appreciate the difficulties involved, it is necessary to consider the characteristics of demand and supply with specific emphasis on tourism and travel.

Demand:

Before going further, it is very important to have a clear idea about tourism demand. Following are some of the prominent characteristics of tourism demand:

• Spontaneity and uncertainty:

Tourism demand is characterized by great deal of uncertainty and spontaneity, i.e. it is very difficult to predict the requirements for any given period. Past trends are useful but not very reliable. When demand is greater than the supply, customers are usually unhappy. In a perfect match of supply and demand the load factor would be 100%, anything less gives an indication of over capacity.

• Variability:

Tourism demand is not same each hour of each day of each month. It remains fluctuating and is marked by crests and valleys. More capital needs to be invested if we want to cover demand in peak times. The Pricing strategies have to be planned strategically. Attempts of marketing like- peak pricing, mid-season pricing and off-peak pricing are commonly adopted in tourism and at times work as an attraction also due to lucrative tariffs.

• Segment-wise multiplicity of demand:

Any tourist destination, product or attraction has multiple usages at any given point of time. Meaning thereby is that a place or attraction or facility is frequented by groups of persons with different sets of motivations and requirements. Consequently, we experience a gamut of demand generated by the same destination or resource or attraction. For example, throughout the year Goa attracts millions of tourists. Now at any period of time some of the tourists are interested in sun bathing, few are keen in cultural panorama of the state, many might be present due to business or corporate meetings, while there might be groups enjoying the beverages and cuisine of the place. The motivations, frequencies and responses to price change are different in different segments.

• Elasticity:

The sensitiveness to the price change in generally termed as elasticity. The Elastic demand is sensitive to substitution and an inelastic demand is not. Pleasure travel is more elastic, than business travel that means the primary or impulsive demand is elastic and derived or compulsive demand is relatively inelastic.

• Ever increasing competition:

One of the note-worthy attribute of tourism industry is that it lacks patronage, i.e. tourists tend to use the services that provide them the best benefits irrespective of the company. Obviously, value for money and quality of services top the list of the factors affecting the decision making of the customers. Interestingly every year many new players, with innovative ideas, are joining the main stream. This causes a situation where competition touches new heights; means the business ambience is highly competitive and any intelligent move by a player might affect the whole equation. We need to apply strategic policies, which are bound to change with the emerging conditions. Like different trains operating between two points pose stiff competition to each other. Small change in departure time can capture significant number of passengers.

Supply:

Tourism supply, curiously, is much different from that for fast moving consumer goods (FMCG) or any other type of product. Let us discuss some of these.

• Pricing flexibility:

The price of the supplies in tourism varies due to certain factors. For example, price generally reduces with the size of the group. That is, with increasing number of group members the price decreases. Else, depending upon the type of season; i.e. peak, middle or lower; the price is, respectively, highest, moderate and minimum.

• **Perishability:**

Every component involved with tourism supply has specific capacity. The percentage of this capacity which is used (or sold) on a specific day gets converted into actual sale and remaining part is business lost forever because, unlikely to the consumer goods, the lost sale cannot be compensated in future. In other words supply cannot be stored for future use. So management has to sell, sell and sell. Say, if an aircraft having 100 seats has only 60 passengers on a particular flight cannot sell the unsold 40 seats in the next flight.

• **Independent, yet complementary components:**

The components, which when combined together ensure a wholesome tourism product; can effectively work independently as well. For example, a hotel can be promoted without it being packaged with transportation or any involvement of a tour operator, yet the association results in ensured and better business yields because these components are complimentary to each other and, together, increases the value, in addition to attractiveness, of each other. The independent nature of these components also makes the coordination quite challenging. Thus, ensuring a smooth coordination between these components calls for lots of effective managerial skills.

• **Fixed in space:**

The supplies in case of tourism cannot be carried physically to the customers. Rather the users have to come all the way to the product, facility or attraction to utilize the same. For example, we cannot take Taj or Hotel Maurya Shereton to the place where our clients are located. This is, obviously, different from the consumer goods (say tea leaves) which can conveniently be taken to the place of location of the clients.

• **Inflexibility in shorter period:**

Demand is instantaneous but Supply is not. There is long time between planning and placing order for a component, between placing order and getting it, between putting it into service and scrapping it. Thus demand can shift quickly, but it takes great deal of time to adjust supply.

• **High ratio of fixed costs to variable costs:**

Tourism is highly capital intensive- the accommodation units, infrastructure, manpower etc. cost great deal of money. Because of high level of costs, the incremental costs of operation are small.

• **Combination of tangibility and intangibility:**

Tourism supply is a curious combination of tangible (that can be physically touched and felt) and intangible (that can't be physically seen or touched, but experienced). Though the food in a restaurant can be put in the category of tangible things, yet the ambience is a good example of intangibility.

Measuring the Tourism Demand and Supply:

Measurement of tourism demand is a cumbersome process. One has to apply extremely effective methods to calculate the demand. This process being a futuristic one, there is always a high degree of probability. Meaning thereby is that it is very difficult to estimate the demand accurately. Refer to the characteristics of demand discussed earlier to assign reasons behind this fact.

What is measured?

• **Volume statistics:** refer to the calculation of the number of tourists coming to or going out of a place. So, this measurement gives us an idea about the movement of inbound (i/b) and outbound (o/b) tourists. This is enormously significant, keeping in mind that the number of tourists, inbound or outbound, provides us the lead to the level of infra and super structure, facilities and activities to be planned to accommodate the tourists.

• **Value (expenditure) statistics:** is an indication of the monetary gains a destination does make as a result of visit of tourists. This also includes gathering the information on the spending power and expenditure pattern of the tourists. Spending power indicates the amount of money that could be spent by the tourists on their touristic pursuits. Whereas expenditure pattern is the detail of component-wise expenses of the tourists (means how much a tourist spend on accommodation, transportation, food and beverages, shopping etc.)

•**Visitor profile:** Usually it is stated that "a tourists' brain is like a black hole". It is very difficult to predict as to what is going on inside the tourists head and heart? Simply putting, it's very hard to ascertain the perceptions, expectations, likings and dis-likings of a tourist or group of tourists. Therefore, it becomes mandatory to keep a record of the behavior and requirements related aspects of the tourists. Study of visitor profile provides us with the vital qualitative insight into the psyche of the tourists, which is important to establish equilibrium between demand and supply in order ensure higher levels of customer satisfaction, as well as being optimally benefited a link in the supply chain.

Why is Tourism Demand and Supply Measured?

The following are the major reasons behind measuring tourism demand and supply:

- To assess the contribution of tourism to indigenous community
- To assist in preparation of effective area and product development policies and planning
- For marketing and promotion
- To study the trends
- To predict the changes in future

Methods of Measurement:

Volume Statistics

- **By using counting procedures at entry and exit points:**

This is one of the most commonly used procedures and is highly effective in case of the destinations and attractions which have well defined and manned entry and exit points. The counting provides the month-wise number of the persons who have thronged a particular area and the same is translated into demand.

- **From records of international carriers:**

All the carriers (i.e. Airlines) have precise information on the number of passengers visiting a particular country, as the passengers are supposed to fill up embarkment and disembarkment cards while boarding and getting off a flight. The VISA reveals the reasons of the trip(s).

- **From records of Government offices:**

Almost in all the countries, the Government establishments keep a record of the tourist traffic, and that too is analyzed under different parameters; like country and region of origin, age-group, interests and motives etc. In India Department of Tourism, Govt. of India and some of the State Governments maintain such records that are very effective sources of information about the present demand, and when statistically analyzed for trends can give clues about the future demand, as well.

- **Collection of registration records at accommodation establishments:**

Another popular way of gathering information that can be interpreted in terms of tourism demand related to the volume of the visiting clients.

Value Statistics

- **Through sample surveys:**

Very commonly used a technique. In this the researcher picks up samples; i.e. respondents; randomly and seeks information from them. One has to be extremely conscious about the questions to be framed, because there are chances of misinterpretation of on the part of the respondent.

• By analyzing Forex statements:

The foreign exchange statements of the tourists provide information on the expenditure and expenditure patterns of the tourists. This is a very effective method, as this lead the way to the level and typology of infra and super structure to be created to cater to the tourists, in addition to the foreign exchange earnings of the destination and transit regions.

• By conducting surveys of suppliers:

The volume of the products or services sold is directly proportional to the demand generated. Hence, this method too has proved to be an important one to gather the required information.

Tourist Profiles

• By conducting tourists' surveys: Surveys of the tourists may reveal information on their personal profile, expectations and buying behavior. Though commonly used, yet is complex one as it is difficult to seek time and correct information from the tourists.

• Through study of the tourists' behavior at establishments and attractions: This basically is an observational technique. In this tourists are closely watched and their behavior is studied on the basis of certain pre-established yard-sticks. The observers need to be highly knowledgeable about human behavior and should possess analytical skills.

• From the information provided by the suppliers:

Suppliers are enormously vital source of collecting information on tourist behavior, as these are a link between demands and supply and do know about the present and future trends. In fact information provided by the suppliers is translated in terms of the qualitative demand and is highly useful to impart lead to plan the future supplies effectively.

Summary:

We have tried to understand the very concept of tourism demand, supply, their typology, the factors that have an impact – positive or negative – on these two important aspects and measurement of tourism demand, along with the techniques/ methods applied for the same. In nutshell, tourism demand can be described as the amount or volume of products, services or amenities that are, or will be, purchased or consumed from a well-defined geographical area, within a given price-range and during specified period of time, which usually is one year. In case of tourism supply, we focus on the amount or volume of products, services or amenities that are, or will be, offered from within a well-defined geographical area, in a given price-range and during specified period of time, which usually is one year; in order to satisfy tourists' needs and wants. Depending upon the criteria affixed, demand is classified as actual or potential/ latent and compulsive or impulsive. Coming to measurement of tourism demand, by now you might be aware that measurement in this case is either value based or volume based or behavioral. In assessment of value, we concentrate on economic gains, whereas in volume statistics the emphasis is on the number of tourists. In the third category basically the profile of tourists is studied as it has extremely close relationship with the expectations and post-tour satisfaction level. One thing that you must not forget is that the measurement of tourism demand is both Qualitative and Quantitative.

CHAPTER XV

TOURISM STATISTICS

Introduction:

Tourism has been identified, out of all the service industries as the most dynamic sector. That means tourism industry is highly vulnerable to the slight changes occurring at the place of operation (i.e. destination region) or right at the point of origin (i.e. tourists generating area) or, even, at the places those the tourists have to go through during their journey (i.e. transit cities). So, it becomes extremely crucial to have a tab on the changes that all such situations cause on touristic movements and the resultant economic gains to TDR (Tourist Destination Regions) and TTR (Tourist Transit Regions). In this unit we are going to have an amongst the groups of persons to take a positive purchase decision. Further, an economic system comprising of spectrum of different activities positioned in different locations generates movements that must be supported by the tourism system in order to fulfill the expectations and needs of the visitors. Without movements infrastructures would be useless and without infrastructures movements could not occur, or would not occur in a cost efficient manner. This interdependency can be considered according to two concepts, which are tourism demand and supply. In this module we are going to have an insight into these two most vital pillars of tourism industry. Idea of the number of tourists that is moving around the globe, to India and within India, along with the economic dimensions of these movements.

International Tourism at a Glance (Volume and Value Statistics):

The pace of growth in worldwide tourist traffic over last few decades, more so, after World War II has been virtually dramatic, which is well evident from the fact that as against 14.4 million and US $1.4 billion in 1948, the tourist traffic and tourism receipts respectively touched 831million and 754 billion US$ mark by the year 2006.

Three decades, spanning between 1960 and 1990, particularly witnessed an unprecedented surge in the growth of international tourism, both in terms tourist traffic and receipts. Early eighties (i.e., 1980-84) has been an exceptional period for observing very low to negative growth on account of global recession caused by sharp hike in oil prices. During the subsequent years also tourism growth has been substantive, and more so in the year

2000 which recorded annual increase of 7.25 % and 4.40 % in tourist traffic and tourism receipt, respectively – thanks to the Millennium Boom.

Although the evolution of tourism in the last few years has been irregular, UNWTO maintains its long-term forecast for the moment. The underlying structural trends of the forecast are believed not to have significantly changed. Experience shows that in the short term, periods of faster growth (1995, 1996, and 2000) alternate with periods of slow growth (2001 to 2003). While the pace of growth till 2000 actually exceeded the Tourism 2020 Vision forecast, it is generally expected that the current slowdown will be compensated in the medium to long term.

UNWTO's Tourism 2020 Vision forecasts that international arrivals are expected to reach nearly 1.6 billion by the year 2020. Of these worldwide arrivals in 2020, 1.2 billion will be intraregional and 378 million will be long-haul travelers.

The total tourist arrivals by region shows that by 2020 the top three receiving regions will be Europe (717 million tourists), East Asia and the Pacific (397 million) and the Americas (282 million), followed by Africa, the Middle East and South Asia.

East Asia and the Pacific, Asia, the Middle East and Africa are forecasted to record growth at rates of over 5% year, compared to the world average of 4.1%. The more mature regions Europe and Americas are anticipated to show lower than average growth rates. Europe will maintain the highest share of world arrivals, although there will be a decline from 60 per cent in 1995 to 46 per cent in 2020.

Long-haul travel worldwide will grow faster, at 5.4 per cent per year over the period 1995-2020, than intraregional travel, at 3.8 per cent. Consequently the ratio between intraregional and long-haul travel will shift from around 82:18 in 1995 to close to 76:24 in 2020.

Tourism demand depends above all strongly on the economic conditions in major generating markets. When economies grow, levels of disposable income will usually also rise. A relatively large part of discretionary income will typically be spent on tourism, in particular in the case of emerging economies. A tightening of the economic situation on the other hand, will often result in a decrease or trading down of tourism spending.

Going by region-wise performance in terms of tourist arrivals during 1999-2005 period reveals that Americas had been the worst sufferer, witnessing negative growth of -5.1 %, -4.7 % and -3.1 %, during three successive years, i.e., in 2001, 2002 and 2003 followed by Europe (-0.5 % in

2002), Asia-Pacific(-9.0 % in 2003), Middle East (-1.0 % in 2001) and, India (-4.2% and -6.0% in 2001 and 2003) while Africa remained least affected with no negative growth(Table-1.2;). In terms of Tourism receipts also, Americas had negative growth of -7.8 %, -6.7 % and -0.3 %, respectively in the year 2001, 2002 and 2003, while for Europe and Middle East only year 2001 proved to be the lean year with -1.7 % and -3.3 5 growth. Asia-Pacific marginally escaped negative growth but Africa as in case of tourist arrivals, again remained unaffected. On the whole, the above trends have been along the anticipated lines and Americas, for the obvious regions was expected be the most looser.

Interestingly, tourism effectively bounced back from its recession phase in the year 2004 & 2005, recording respectively 10.9 and 5.6% growth over the preceding year, in terms of tourist traffic and tourism receipt. Region-wise, Middle has been the leading achiever followed by Asia & Pacific, Americas, Africa and Europe respectively observing 26.0%, 21.9%, 11.4 %, 8.4 %, 8.2 % and 6.4 % growth in terms of tourist arrivals and, 30.9 %, 24%, 15.4 %, 19.6 % and 15.3 % in terms of tourism receipts in the year 2004 as compared to the previous year. Talking in net terms, arrivals Middle East and Asia & Pacific followed by Europe and Americas led the trends with increase of over 33 million, 19 million and 12 million tourists, respectively. However, in terms of the net receipts, Europe with increase of over 43 bn US $ has been the top achiever followed by Asia & Pacific and Americas respectively observing net gain of about 30 bn US $ and 16.5 bn US $.

Interestingly, the affluent countries of Europe and America have been traditionally acting both as effective tourist markets and destinations. However off-late, as also revealed by table 1.2 and figure 1.5, 1.6 and 1.7, that the trends have started changing in favor of developing countries, particularly those located in Asia Oceania and African region. This change is evident from the fact that while in the year 1960, Europe and Americans accounted for 72 % and 24 % of the international tourist arrivals and 60% and 36% of the tourism receipts their share has gone down to 55.37 % and 16.4% in terms of tourist arrivals and, and 36% and 26% respectively in 1990. In contrast, the share of Asia–Oceania regions in terms of world tourist arrivals and receipt, during this period, has increased from 1.2% and 3.3% in 1960 to about 12% and 15% respectively in 1990. The Indian tourism sector touched new heights in 2005, registering about 13.5% growth in tourist arrivals and about 20% increase in foreign exchange earnings, according to a release from the Union Ministry of Tourism. This gains significance since the average growth in global tourism was 5 percent, regional tourism trends for 1970-98 periods' further support the view that the traditionally popular destination regions are steadily losing their share to the emerging ones. Table 1.4 below clearly indicates that the share of developed regions of the world will diminish from the present 79.1% to 64.2% by 2020, whereas for the Less Developed regions of the World the share shall increase from the present 21.9% to 35.8% during the same period.

An interesting fact which comes to the fore is that the major tourism destination countries and regions have so far been traditionally leading global tourism markets in that order. Thus, obviously Europe and Americas are the top tourism generating regions of the world. Till late sixties, these two regions were together accounting for about 96% of the total international tourist arrivals and approximately 90% of the global tourist departures. However, over last five decades their share has been witnessing consistent decrease in both perspectives. Consequently, by the year 2004, their share came down to 71.77 % and 73.57 % in terms of tourist arrival and tourism receipts, respectively. In contrast, the performance of such emerging economies like Japan, China, South Africa, South Korea and Countries of Middle East and South East Asia has been steadily improving, to the extent that China now occupies top fourth position in terms of tourist arrivals, displacing such traditionally popular destination countries even like Italy and U.K.

Authentic tourism statistics for the year 2007 is yet not available. However, on- hand information for on the motivation is concerned, leisure tourism seems to be outperforming business tourism, perhaps receiving a strong boost from the increasing availability of low fares for short-haul travel and by pent-up demand still being released for long-haul destinations, though anecdotal evidence points to a recovery in demand for business tourism, including the meetings, incentives, conferences and exhibitions (MICE) sector. Cruise tourism also seems to witness above-average growth during the year.

Tourism experts, economists and futurologists unanimously speak in favour of sustained propensity of tourism during the years to come. Estimations made by the leading tourism institutions as well as eminent tourism scholars unanimously speak for per annum growth in international tourist arrivals between 4.5% to 5.5% after duly considering the past trends vis-à-vis potential influencing factors. There had been many factors influencing tourism trends in past which may continue to influence tourism trends in future, as well. The generic factors that may influence the future tourism trends have been nicely summed up by Robert Came (1969) in his article, the 'Future of Tourism', as under:

- The world's population is growing at an extremely fast pace and the average length of life will be nearly 80 years.
- Per-capita income will grow swiftly and will reach extremely high levels in the industrialized countries
- "The-Distance" in space will be all but eliminated, and this will result in comparatively lower transport costs.
- The widespread automation of productive processes will lead to a great increase in the leisure activities because of the growing amount of "free time".
- The rural population will shrink nearly everywhere in the economically developed countries, approaching the level of the United States where at present less than 10 percent of the total population i.e., about 5 percent of the active population is employed in agriculture.
- The population employed in the secondary and tertiary sectors will consist almost entirely of persons living in towns who, hand in hand, with increased spatial mobility, will have greater occupational and social mobility.
- Congestion of tourist traffic shall create problems in traffic in time and space. Greater educational opportunities and in-depth information will lead to increased curiosity and that in turn, to a greater desire for knowledge.

All the eminent futurologists including Fraustie, Came and Kahn promise for more leisure available to the society in coming times, which will obviously have a major impact on tourism growth. The quote Fraustie (cited in Singh 1982): "It is generally expected at present that fairly in near future the average citizen of economically developed country will be able to meet his needs by working thirty hours a week. Thus the time that an individual will devote to productive activities in future will take up about 6% of his existence".

Tourism is likely to grow with dramatic pace in the years ahead is aptly evident from the prognosis of WTO made in its report on Tourism 2020 Vision. According to it, international arrivals are expected to reach over 1.56

billion by the year 2020 of which approximately 1.18 billion will be intra-regional and 0.38 billion long-haul travels. The report further estimates that Long-haul travel worldwide will grow at a relatively faster rate (5.4 per cent per year) compared to intra-regional travel (at 3.8 per cent). Consequently the ratio between intra-regional and long-haul travel will shift from around 82:18 in 1995 to close to 76:24 in 2020. Consequent to the changes in favour of inter- regional traffic trends and the growing tourist desire to explore newer destinations vis-à-vis the on-going concentrated efforts being made by the developing economies, tourism is likely to grow in the developing regions of the world with faster rate as compared to the developed regions.

Thus according to WTO forecasts, with estimated growth rate of 8.10 % per annum during the first decade of the present century, the share of the former may rise to 30.21% by the year 2010 as against 21.55% in the year 2000. In contrast, developed economies may witness annual growth of 3.29 % during this period, thereby losing their share from 78.45 % in 2000 to 69.79 % in the year 2010. It has also been predicted that by 2010 the Americas may lose its number two position to the East Asia and the Pacific region which is expected to receive 25 per cent of world arrivals in 2010 and 46 per cent in 2020 with the Americas share decreasing from 19 per cent in 1995 to 18 per cent in 2020.

As cited in the foregoing also, the shift in tourist traffic trends towards developing regions especially those located in Asia Pacific Region can be attributed to such factors like, (a) consistent improvement in the support infrastructure, (b) organized efforts being made to promote tourism by using effective marketing tools, (c) increasing social awareness about tourism and its multifold benefits, (d) adoption of entrepreneur-friendly policy by the governments, including provision of a series of fiscal and non-fiscal incentives, particularly to the effective and potential tourism and hospitality sector enterprises, (e) stronger motivation among the tourists to explore newer destinations and enjoy exotic experiences, (f) emergence of a stronger market for adventure tourism, rural and ethnic tourism, wildlife and wilderness tourism and eco-tourism, for which there exists tremendous scope especially in southern hemisphere, incidentally where majority of the developing countries are located. Of course, technological advancements especially in the field of aviation and communication are also supporting the cause of developing countries by effectively narrowing down the time-distance gap. In nutshell, international tourism is expected to steadily flourish in regions, nations and destinations which need it most for their all-round development.

Indian Context (Volume and Value Statistics):

India is credited to pioneer the concept of tourism in the form of pilgrimages, as early as during Vedic Era. Accounts from the Epics and Puranas reveal that the tradition of religious travels flourished all through the ancient times, and that, sincere efforts were made by the contemporary rulers to develop wayside facilities and amenities, especially enroute the sacred centers. In fact, aware of the paramount contribution of 'travel' in broadening the horizons of knowledge vis a vis forging social integration, it was intelligently blended with religious dicta so as to make traveling a social movement. 'Indra (wise qualities!) is the friend of travelers, therefore travel' has therefore God)'jealously preached by the scriptures to inculcate healthy guest - host relationship, been propounded in the Aieterya Brahmina in order to instill social attitude for 'Charevati Charevati (keep on traveling and traveling). The principle of 'Atithi Devo Bhav(Guest is God) is still valued by the society though the rising materialism has considerably eroded it.

While the glorious tradition of pilgrimages has steadily prospered over the years, international tourism is yet to come of age in the country despite its vividly varied and rich touristic appeal. As evident from the Preamble of National Tourism Policy (1997), India is aware of its tremendous tourism resource treasure vis a vis the strength of tourism as tool to holistic development, and is therefore vying to achieve its rightful share in international tourism.

Evidently, the significance of tourism is comprehensively acknowledged and appreciated by the government of India. In fact, efforts to promote neo-tourism in the country date back to 1945 when a committee under Sir John sergeant was constituted to find ways and means to promote this industry. Though no budget could be allocated to it in the First Five Year Plan, tourism became an important constituent of national planning, onwards the second five year plan. The strong desire of country's policy makers to promote tourism is aptly illustrated by the various actions taken to this effect, ranging from 'creation of regional tourism offices in the country and abroad, setting–up NCT; inception of institutions like DOT, ITDC; State Tourism Departments, State Tourism Development Corporations, IITTM, TFCI, and National Council of Hotel Management, Catering and Nutrition; Launching special operations schemes viz; Operation US and Operation UK; and Organizing India festival abroad to penetrate potential markets;

awarding industry status to tourism; celebrating visit India year(s) and above all putting tourism under an exclusive Ministry at the Centre and in some states.

Today, India has virtually the most intensive organizational structure of tourism the world. As a result of these efforts international tourist arrivals have steadily increased over the years, registering an average annual growth rate of about 10% during 1950-1990 period. In net terms, the tourism arrivals touched 3.37 million mark in 2004 as against 16829 arrivals in 1951. Though, country's share in the international tourism is still too meager, 0.44% in terms of tourist arrivals and 0.77% in terms of tourism receipts, the recent trends strongly indicate towards consistently better performance. During 1991 – 2006 period, despite negative trends in the year 1993 (assassination of Sri Rajiv Gandhi), 1998 (General Elections), 2001 and 2002 (after effect of Iraq War, September 11 incident, and terrorist attack on Parliament), tourist arrivals marked net increase of about 1.68 million, during this period.

Putting in other words, with an average annual growth of about 6.11%, the tourist arrivals more than doubled during thirteen years beginning with 1991. The per annum growth of respectively 14.3 % and 26.8 % in the year 2003 and 2004 has been particularly noteworthy, indicating towards a much better performance of the country in the years to come. The year 2005 and 2006 has also witnessed 13.2% & 14.7% respectively having recorded 3.92 million and 4.49 million tourists as per provisional estimates. In fact, growth in arrivals in the year 2006 as compared to the preceding year has been higher in case of Indian Peninsula as compared to the average growth witnessed by various regions of the world but except Asia- Pacific. The latter witnessed about 27.8 % growth in 2004 while it was 23.5 % in case of India. China's remarkable performance has largely been responsible for this difference. Traditionally, west Europe followed by North America, South Asia, Southeast Asia, West Asia and East Asia, in that order, have been the major tourism market regions of India, which is a very positive sign in the sense that barring south Asia; all are affluent and fast growing markets.

Country-wise, U.K has traditionally been the largest market for the country, though, of late USA has replaced the former. The touristic significance of these two countries for India is evident from the fact that, together they accounted for over 32.3 % of the total arrivals to the country in 2005. Canada, France, Sri Lanka, Germany, Japan, Malaysia, Australia and Singapore accounting for 3.9%, 3.8 %, 3.5 %, 3.3 %, 2.6%, 2.5 %, 2.4 % and

1.8 % arrival, respectively were the other countries standing on the top ten markets of India in 2005 (Table 1.6; Figure-1.11). Over the years, the top ten tourist markets of the country remained generically more or less same with minor reshuffles in the order of the rank.

Seasonality has remained a grey area for tourism promoters, the world over. On account of the topographic and consequent meteorological extremes vis-à-vis the dramatic diversity in tourist attractions, though India can be considered as 'land of all seasons', the trends clearly indicate that foreign tourist arrival are considerably guided by the seasons.

Month-wise tourist arrivals illustrated in Table 1.8 aptly reveal that autumn, winter and spring months are largely preferred by the foreign tourists to visit India. Maximum influx is during December, generally followed by November, January, February, March and October, in that order. Arrivals begin to decrease with onset of April reaching to lowest level in May, followed by June and September. July and August generally witness more arrivals compared to the three extreme lean months. The reasons for the seasonal changes in tourist arrivals can be conveniently attributed to the meteorological conditions in Europe and North America vis-à-vis India.

Tourist from these affluent markets obviously find the orient to be climatically ideal during winter months when the prevailing climatic conditions in this part are ideal from their own standards while it is relatively too cold for them back home. Tourist visits, during the summer months, despite the scorching heat in majority part of India, are largely due to the soothing conditions in the Himalayan Destinations, as well as, relatively salubrious climate along the vast coastal stretch. Low tourist influx during monsoon months even in southern India, on the other hand, can be conveniently attributed to the poor mobility, flood and flood like situation in majority parts of the country. However, it is particularly intriguing that September, despite relatively better climatic conditions as compared to July and August marks fewer arrivals than the former two. As such, it seems due to the vacation/holiday patterns in the burgeoning markets of the country.

Going by the available statistics for the year 2005, it is evident that India's share in international tourism in terms of tourism receipts (0.8%) has been considerably higher as compared to the tourist arrivals (0.49%). Also, during 1991-2005 periods while the country experienced negative annual growth in 1993, 1998, 2001 and 2003, the negative trend in terms of tourism receipts was prevalent only in the year 2002 and that too by merely

– 1 %. It is also apparent in the Table 1.9 and Figure – 1.13 that this negative growth got effectively countered by the strong growth marked in 2003, 2004 and 2005, which was respectively 15.7 % , 31.5% and 16.5%.

The stronger growth patterns in receipts can be attributed to fact that the average length of stay per tourist (around 30 days) in the country is one of the highest in the world. Increasing tourist expenditure on account of the interplay of rising prices vis-à-vis worldwide growing per capita income too has its obvious impact in this regard. The economic significance of tourism for India becomes all the more vital in view of the fact that, even now, when the country's share in world tourism receipts is merely 0.8 %, it is already acting as the third largest source of its foreign exchange earnings. Further, this smokeless industry, according to conservative estimates, is providing employment opportunities to more than 8 million people in its direct sector.

The employment perspectives become all the more significant since the employment multiplier in tourism sector comes to be about 2.36 i.e., direct employment to one person in tourism industry creates 1.36 additional jobs in other sectors of the economy (Kandari, 1984). Not citing the example of a country like USA whose annual tourism receipts go beyond 90 bn US $, one can conveniently perceive the contribution of this burgeoning industry in strengthening economy of India if its share in world receipts even touches 1 % mark.

International Tourism during 2005 and Beyond:
Available information about inbound tourism in India during year 2006 is still incomplete and largely provisional. But based on the provisional statistics brighter aspect emerge indicating the higher growth rate in case of tourism receipts than arrivals indicating towards considerable increase in per tourist expenditure. One can conveniently perceive from a provisional report of DOT that inbound trends are likely to be sustained during the year.

Based on these statistics, it can be observed that Indian tourism sector has touched new heights in 2007, registering about 14% growth in tourist arrivals and about 20% increase in foreign exchange earnings. One of the major reasons for this growth was the large-scale tourism promotion campaign, called Incredible India, which the government launched in key tourist markets over the last few months. Launching of several innovative schemes like 'Atithi Devo Bhava', 'Priyadarshini' and 'Rural Tourism' too must have contributed in this regard. In order to sustain the growth trends, concentrated efforts are being made by the state and central government to take various strategic steps. In this context, the Centre has asked the state governments to enact tourism trade Acts and set up single-window tourism facilitation centers.

The tourism trade Act is aimed at regulating the tourism trade and protect tourists from unscrupulous elements. The government is also embarking on a plan to train personnel at the airport on the ways to interact with tourists. Besides, steps are also being taken to train taxi drivers and tour guides about etiquette. The World Travel and Tourism Council (WTTC) has recognized India as one of the fastest growing tourist economies in the world, and that, the golden triangle, comprising Delhi, Agra and Jaipur, has become one of the most prominent tourist circuits in the world and almost 60 per cent of foreign tourists arriving in India visited this area. On future perspective, WTTC estimates towards 8.8 % growth in Indian tourism during the next decade.

Outbound Trends:

On account of the open air policy of the central government vis a vis steady increase in the income of the people especially those concerned with the multinationals or working/dealing with exports, the outbound trends have consistently been witnessing remarkable growth, particularly onwards early nineties of the last Century. Unlike the negative growth in international tourism, as well as, in the context of inbound traffic to India, the outbound tourism has never experienced negative growth during last fifteen years though there was zero growth in the year 1994. In fact, the growth has been remarkably high in the year 2004 and 2005, i.e., 16.1% and 15.6 % respectively.

Domestic Tourism:

Domestic tourism, especially in the form of pilgrimages has been a glorious heritage of India. One can finds frequent mentions in the Epics and the scriptures. Thanks to the technological advancements that, it has tremendously increased over the years, despite economic and other constraints.

Though, no authentic data are available in this context, conservative estimates reveal that annually over 430 million people travel from one part to the other parts of the country under different pretexts of tourism. Obviously, pilgrimage had and continues to have the lion's share in domestic tourism in India.

The pace of growth in domestic tourism is evident from the fact that the number of tourists has dramatically increased from 67.7 million in 1991 to 382.1 in 2005 indicating over 5.5 growth in the span of merely fourteen years (Table- 1.16; Figure-1.12). Average per annum growth of over 18 % during the 13 years in question, has nevertheless been remarkable. Statistics available for 2005 reveals that Andhra Pradesh and Uttar Pradesh, each receiving over 24 % of the total domestic tourist continued to retain their position as the leading states followed by Tamilnadu (11.3 %), Karnataka (6.5 %) and Rajasthan (4.9 %) in that order. Uttaranchal, Maharashtra, West Bengal, Bihar, and Gujarat were the other states occupying top ten ranking in this context, though standing way behind Uttar Pradesh and Andhra Pradesh, in terms of the share in total domestic tourist traffic.).

It is quite intriguing to note that despite losing an outstanding tourist destination region (i.e., Uttaranchal Pradesh) Uttar Pradesh has effectively retained its top ranking in this regard. Though, yet to be statistically verified, presence of the two eminent pilgrim canters of the country (i.e., Allahabad and Varanasi), the Taj City, two of the four prominent Buddhist destinations (Sarnath and Bodh Gaya) in the state and its strategic location in transit to Bihar, West Bengal, North Eastern States, Southern India, Uttaranchal, as well as, parts of Haryana, Himachal and Punjab and even Nepal must be proving instrumental in maintaining the status of Uttar Pradesh as one of the top ranking domestic tourist destination state of the country. Somehow, Maharashtra and Madhya Pradesh are yet to perform on the lines of U.P. despite sharing more or less similar generic qualities with Uttar Pradesh.

Summary:

Global tourist statistics in general and tourism patterns in Indian context in particular suffers wide ranging complexities, double or say multiple counting being the major bottleneck. Collection of tourism statistics itself starves for a uniform recording system which in-turn makes the statistical interpretation rather vague. However, relying on the official data of DOT for the period 1999 – 2005, it can be conveniently concluded that Maharashtra, Uttar Pradesh, Karnataka, West Bengal, Kerala, Tamil Nadu, Rajasthan, and Goa are more or less consistently retaining their share, in that order, as much in terms of domestic tourist traffic as in terms of foreign arrivals.

A comparatively higher foreign tourist influx in case of Delhi vis-à-vis its geographic area can be attributed, as much to its being one of the major cultural destination and the capital city of the country, as to its being the major port of entry. Maharashtra, Uttar Pradesh, Tamil Nadu, Rajasthan and Karnataka seem to be popular among foreign tourists, due to their rich monumental heritage. The tiny state of Goa is undoubtedly a popular destination on account its beautiful beaches and colorful culture. Unfortunately, Jammu and Kashmir, despite its distinctive natural grandeur and unique culture is consistently loosing grounds due to terrorism, while the tourist potential of north - eastern state, on the other hand, is yet to be effectively opened for both national and international tourism from marketing, infrastructural and policy perspectives.

On the whole, it appears that the number of domestic tourists as compared to foreign tourist arrivals is almost 90 times greater, which in common parlance should not have been more than 10 to 20 times to the former. However, taking into consideration the vast geographic span of the country, the glorious tradition of pilgrimage, economic backwardness and its huge population, the accepted principle applicable to the countries of Europe and Americas in the context of domestic vis a vis foreign tourists ration, is rather impossible to stand in Indian context, though the existing gap between the two may sound to be narrowing down from a holistic view point.

As such, even a lay man can perceive the fact that India's share in international tourism is too meager, rather dismaying if the prevailing vividly varied and rich tourist resource treasure of the country is taken into consideration. Country's performance appears to be too poor if the international tourism trends to such tiny nations in the close neighbors like, Taiwan, Singapore, Hong Kong, South Korea and Philippines are taken in to consideration, leave aside the example of countries like France, Italy and Spain where the influx of the foreign tourists is considerably higher than their respective population.

CHAPTER XVI

TENDENCY OF TRAVEL

Introduction:

The origin of modern tourism and dramatic growth-pace can be directly attributed to the inter-play of technological and economic development. To quote Singh (1975) 'modern tourism is a direct product of economic and social progress promoted by technological and scientific advances, higher real income, longer leisure time, demographic expansion and increasingly cheaper and varied tourist-plant facilities that provide the essential conditions for the growth of tourism'. 'Thanks to the ever greater automation, particularly on the industrial front, that more and more people have now disposable income and leisure time on the one hand, and strong desire to escape such by-products of industrialization and urbanization like noise, pollution, over-crowding, routine, monotony and boredom on the other, thus making travel and tourism both a 'convenience', as well as, 'compulsion' to the modern society (Kandari, 1984). Researchers have proved that, "the inhabitants of large urban and industrial cities are most eager escapers from their environment on weekends and annual holidays" (Wahab 1971). As a result of the multifold advancements, especially in the field of transport and communication, more and more people have now access to faster, cheaper and safer means of transport and an equally effective communication system. In addition to this, the consistently increasing awareness level complemented by innovative promotional strategies adopted by the destinations is adding further dynamism in travel propensity.

The unprecedented growth in tourism vis-à-vis pace of advancement particularly in transport and accommodation sectors have a close cause and effect relationship. Thus, while the dramatically increasing number of tourists and the consequent strong and varied demand for travel and stay is consistently providing the much needed momentum to the growth and development of the requisite supplies, the sustained qualitative and quantitative progress of the transportation and hospitality sectors is proving instrumental in motivating more and people to travel far and wide for tourism purposes. Putting in other words, the latter two core components of tourism need to be competitively strengthened if tourism is to be promoted in a big way.

Travel Propensity: Net and Gross Propensity:

Propensity basically refers to the capability of the persons to undertake a touristic pursuit that has been converted into practice. In simpler words, the ability of a person or group of persons from specified geographic area, within a given unit period of time is the reflection of travel propensity. As stated earlier, propensity is an outcome of the conditions created by the interplay of the basic four prerequisites of tourism, viz. discretionary time, disposable income, needs or desires and, of course, social sanctions.

Although reference is usually made to travel propensity both in the context of transport and tourism, in the former propensity is generally expressed in terms of travel by any mode of transportation for any purpose; while in the later, the analysis usually indicates relating to the likelihood of traveling for the purpose of tourism for leisure, vacation, business or any other reason.

So, propensity to travel can be understood as the potential of persons, belonging to a defined geographical area, to undertake travel in a given period of time with the objective of satisfying some tourism related needs. One thing that you must understand clearly is that travel propensity is always measured in percentage terms and it is the ratio of outbound tourists (who undertake at least one trip) or cumulative trips and the total population of the place in question. Whatever may be the case; we need to allocate the geographic limits very carefully and must be able to assign a touristic purpose to the persons being considered for our estimation.

Typology of Travel Propensity:

Travel propensity is studied in view of two perspectives, which are a) in terms of the number of persons and b) with reference to the total trips undertaken, and depending upon the perspective is categorized as either Net Travel Propensity or Gross Travel Propensity. The same are being discussed below:

Net Travel Propensity:

Net Travel Propensity (NTP) is measure of the proportion of the population of area or country that undertakes at least one trip for the purpose of tourism in a stipulated period of time, which is most commonly is taken as one year.

Thus,

NTP = No. of persons taking one or more trip/ Total population X 100

Gross Travel Propensity:

Gross Travel Propensity (GTP) refers to the total number of trips undertaken by the residents of a geographical area for any touristic purpose in a unit period of time, expressed as the proportion to the total population of the area.

Hence,

GTP = Total no. of trips/ Total population X 100

Further, it may be noted that GTP/NTP provides an indicator of how frequently people from a geographical area; city, region or country; travel for touristic pursuits. This ratio is termed as Travel Frequency.

So, if, for example, population of a city comprises of 1,00,000 persons and out of these 25,000 persons go out to other places as tourists and, on an average, 50,000 trips have been registered in a particular year, the following would be the NTP, GTP and Travel Frequency of the population:

NTP – 25000/ 100000 X 100 = 25%

GTP = 50000/ 100000 X 100 = 50%

Travel Frequency – GTP/ NTP = 50/ 25 = 2

The comparative position of a country as a tourist generating place is ascertained by determining county's tourism potential generation index. Country Tourism Potential Generation Index (CTPGI) is calculated by a simple formula where in the first step number of trips generated by a country is divided by the total trips generated worldwide (say 'A'). This ratio certainly indicates relative importance of the country vis-à-vis global tourism standings. But, it is difficult to make comparisons because of differences in population size of the countries. Therefore, another ratio needs to be ascertained by dividing the population number of a country by total world population (say 'B'). On an average, 'A' divided by 'B' provides us with CTPGI. The greater the index, the more likely it is that the country is at present, and will continue to be a strong generator of tourism trips. This concept was introduced by A. J. Burkart and S (Rik) Medlik in U. K. in 1970's, but was adopted and applied by many scholars, and that too quite successfully, in different parts of the world.

Factors Affecting Propensity:

Tourism has grown from the pursuits of a privileged few to a mass movement of people, with the "urge to discover the unknown, to explore new and strange to seek changes in environment and to undergo new experiences" (Robinson 1976). Putting it in other words, having had its genesis in primitive nomadic, tourism in the form of travel grew strength by strength through the ages along with the progressive civilization and is now fast heading towards its Golden Age (Kandari 1984).Obviously, due to the "antiquated means of transport", lack of way side facilities, safety and security and, non-availability of "discretionary money and time" during earlier phases of history travel largely remained the privilege of elite and well to do class of society who could afford to buy the conveniences (Kandari, 1984), and consequent to the extremely limited demand, the accommodation sector too remained confined or say, dormant. Subsequently, when Renaissance in Europe followed by the era of Grand Tours followed by the development of modern transport facilities gave momentum to travel and tourism, the accommodation industry also began to prosper, both in qualitative and quantitative terms.

It was the period when, alongside various other types of stay and catering establishments, the concept of hotel and motels came on the fore. Evidently, the period between the two World Wars, when the movement of people remained largely confined to the displacement armies, proved to be a rather dark period with regard to the development in travel and hospitality business. However, end of Second World War not only at once rejuvenated traveling but also institutionalized it in the modern concept of tourism which in turn provided a new lease to hotel and hoteliering. Since then, technological and the consequent economic prosperity are synergistically contributing to the ever faster growth of this multifaceted industry in a sustained manner. As of now the "sporadic travels of the yore have practically transformed into mass movement of people thereby giving way to world's fastest growing industry namely Tourism (Kandari,1998). To quote Singh (1975) "modern tourism is a direct product of economic and social progress promoted by technological and scientific advances, higher real income, longer leisure time, demographic expansion and increasingly cheaper and varied tourist plant facilities that provide the essential conditions for the growth of tourism".

Thanks to the ever growing automation, particularly on the industrial front, that more and more people have now disposable income and leisure time coupled with strong desire to at least temporarily escape physical and psychological problems of noise, pollution, overcrowding, routine, monotony and boredom, etc. prevailing in industrial and urban areas. In fact the interplay of technological advancement and industrialization has made travel and tourism both a convenience and compulsion to the modern society (Kandari, 1984). Researchers have proved that "the inhabitants of large urban and industrial cities are most eager escapers from their environment on weekends and annual holidays" (Wahab, 1971). Consistent development in the field of transport and communications has further contributed towards increasing propensity to travel. Today, people have natural access to faster, cheaper and safer means of transport and equally effective communication system. Time distance gap has considerably narrowed down thereby transforming the world into a close neighborhood. "The spread of education has created cultural awareness and has stimulated desire to travel" (Hellen, 1966). Development of newer attractions and destinations, improvement in tourist plant facilities and services, availability of competitive tourist supplies both in terms of quality and price and effective marketing strategies being adopted by tourism developers and private sector enterprises are further tempting more and more globe trotters to set out on recreational, pleasure, and adventure trips or to explore nature and culture. Consequently, both international and domestic tourism are consistently growing ever-stronger.

After discussing the factors in general, let us now have an idea of these one by one. To simplify the discussion, we will divide these into two major categories; the first one enlists life style related factors, while the later consists of the assorted ones. Let us discuss these factors one by one

Life Style Factors:

Income and employment:

Income, especially disposable income, is directly related to the prospects and frequency to undertake a journey for touristic purposes, which certainly correlates to travel propensity. A close look at the top tourist generating companies reveals the fact that majority of these are economically well off (like UK, USA, France etc.) and are more flexible and adaptable socially. The changing economic scenario, worldwide, has injected a new dimension to many a profession, and this is increased business related traveling. Mutual dependence between the countries, easy access, globalization of business etc. may be cited as examples behind this phenomenon. Obviously such employment opportunities have direct impact on the travel propensity.

Education:

Knowledge, which mainly comes through education, helps us to get extensive exposure of many things and beliefs. Obviously, the clearer the vision, more is the understanding; which, in turn, is somehow assists us to have optimistic outlook and this positive attitude affects our tourism related decision making process, thus, resulting in increased travel propensity. In addition to this psychological dimension, education also improves employment opportunities, which ensures economic freedom, this is accountable for income enhancement resulting in more disposable income......and we have already discussed the consequential dimensions in the previous paragraph.

Household size:

It has been observed that the tendency to travel is more common in smaller families compared to that in larger ones. Quite obviously; on one hand, it is economical to arrange touristic activities for lesser persons and, on the other, the management is more difficult with the increase in the members for a tour. The rapid growth in the number of tourists in past one decade is a testimony to this fact. Even in countries like India, the transformation from joint family system to nucleus one had been a vital factor behind excessively brisk growth of both domestic and outbound travel. Conclusively, larger the household size, lesser is travel propensity and vise-versa.

Domestic age:

One of the most crucial aspects, having a direct linkage with propensity to travel, is a very interesting factor to study. One of the most fascinating fact is that the relationship between travel propensity and domestic age varies with cultural background, social structure & liabilities, economic and physical health. An in-depth analysis of the statistics discloses the fact that there had been exceptional growth, both at National & International level, in the age groups of 25-34 years and 55-64 years due to the above mentioned reasons.

Race & Gender:

Right from the ancient period, some of the races had been more mobile compared to the others. Even during Empire era (1-5 AD), there are records, Romans and Greeks were the most itinerant races, in both intra and inter-regional travels. Even a close look at Indian scenario reflects that the maximum domestic tourists generate from West Bengal and Kerala. Gender also matters a lot, as in some of the societies fare gender is given more liberty and freedom of movement. Such societies have, in general, higher travel propensity in comparison to the orthodox societies. We can see that there is more movement of women tourists from Europe and the America than from Asia or Africa.

Holidays:

It can be easily experienced that propensity to travel fluctuates with the vacation period. In India maximum persons prefer to opt for tourism related pursuits during May-June or October-November mainly because of the summer and Pooja holidays, as the discretionary time increases during these months. In fact this factor gives rise to a phenomenon called Seasonality in tourism. Seasonality refers to the peaks and plunges that are the result of the volume of floating population (tourists). There would hardly be any exception where the destination remains almost stagnant perennially as far as the month-wise number of tourists is concerned.

Other Factors:

Level of urbanization:

Level of urbanization has manifold impacts on the propensity to travel. On one part, urbanization ensures better infra & super structure, hence more mobility. Then there are quick and efficient sources of information regarding touristic pursuits, which enhances the knowledge & eagerness level and, in return, the movement (i.e. propensity). The stress and strain caused by urban life also increases the quest to spend some leisure time in order to relax. There might be a possibility that the urban area is also a commercial centre. In such a case the compulsive movements to meet the business oriented needs may also add on to the propensity.

Economic development:

Simple! The more the economic development, the more would be the capacity to spend on ones' leisure pursuits, and the higher would be the desire to travel and, hence, there would be additional mobility for tourism oriented activities.

Political factors:

If the political situation of tourist generating region (TGR), tourist transit region (TTR) and tourist destination region (TDR) is congenial, the movements would be more. In case of disturbed political situation the tourists virtually cease to move to any place. Importantly, disturbance at any of these three regions hampers the touristic activities. Additionally, the political relationship between the countries is a reflection of the communal tourism equation. Tourism equation means the mutual freedom of movement, the amount of money that one can carry and the simplicity of documentation, like VISA on arrival; to quote a few of the points that are must to inculcate a symbiotic relationship between the countries.

Technological factors:

It is a proven fact that any technological development had been, and will be, supportive to the cause of tourism. May it be betterment of transportation or new developments in information technology & aviation or creative inputs in accommodation sector; tourism has always experienced positive consequences. Simply putting cost effectiveness, swiftness and safety are three major factors to promote tourism and ensure higher propensity and any technological development generally ensures these.

Socio-cultural factors:

This particular factor affects travel propensity in more than one way. Firstly, richness of culture of a destination increases the very tourismagnetism of the place, and works upon the propensity of the incoming tourists in a positive manner. Secondly, a welcoming & tourists friendly society is encouraging for the persons to go to a specific place. Obviously, we want to go to places where we can enjoy the time spent without any fear or tension. The best examples of being tourist friendly Indian states come from Goa, Rajasthan, Himachal Pradesh and, of course, Uttarakhand. And finally, the socio-cultural osmosis (means the inevitable induced change in both the guests and hosts due to reciprocal interaction that affects the social norms & ethics and cultural characteristics) facilitates the mutual understanding (i.e. brotherhood - which is the one and only effective option for global peace), in addition to persuading an informal school of learning, which enhances the knowledge spectrum on one hand, and opens up new vistas of economic gains as well.

Summary:

Let us sum up, friends. Most simply putting propensity is the tendency to travel. This tendency is the directly proportional to few variables, which include economic status (or say spending power), knowledge spectrum (which is the result of education and exposure), accessibility to, both, information and place(s) to be visited, effectiveness of the supply-system and of course, the flexibility of the generating & destination society. Further, propensity is calculated in terms of the ratio of the number of persons who undertake at least one touristic trip and total number of trips to the population of the generating area or region in the given period of time. The results in the first case reflect the Net Travel Propensity and the later reaches out to Gross Travel Propensity. The ratio of GTP and NTP results in what is called Travel Frequency. An idea about travel propensity is helpful in planning the infra and super structure at tourist generating, transit and destination region as the number or volume of tourist traffic is the deciding factor for planning these crucial dimensions. So, the knowledge of travel propensity is incredibly important and you must have a very clear idea about this.

About The Author

Meet the remarkable Dr. Anshumali Pandey, a living testament to excellence in education, hospitality, tourism, and the fascinating world of tribal food. A true polymath, he effortlessly wears the hats of a seasoned educator, esteemed chef, celebrated author, meticulous business auditor, and adventurous culinary traveller.

With a focus on higher education, office administration, HR, labour laws, audit, procurement, and tender processes, Dr. Pandey has gained prominence as a leading hospitality educator, holding a distinguished PhD in the field of Management.

Fuelling his passion for tribal food, tourism, and village exploration, he has delved deep into extensive research, leading to numerous illuminating research papers and publications. Notably, the Ministry of Tourism, Government of India, recognized his expertise and contributions, bestowing upon him a National Appreciation certificate and a cherished memento in 2018.

Drawing from a rich experience spanning over 27 years in the professional realm, Dr. Anshumali Pandey has honed the art of precise and compelling writing. This has resulted in an impressive collection of

99 publications, comprising 77 enlightening books and captivating short stories. His literary repertoire covers a wide spectrum, ranging from culinary expertise to HR mastery, from nurturing young minds through children's books to exploring the realms of spirituality.

Residing with his family in the picturesque Western Indian tribal belt of the union territory of Dadra & Nagar Haveli for more than two decades, Dr. Pandey has wholeheartedly dedicated his time to understanding and aiding the tribal and rural communities of the region. His writings not only showcase his immense expertise but also reflect his profound knowledge of diverse subjects he has thoughtfully chosen for his books.

A true champion of the hospitality sector, Dr. Anshumali Pandey's multifaceted prowess has established him as a reputable and revered name in the industry. His boundless passion and unwavering commitment make him an inspiring figure for aspiring professionals across various fields.

Books written by the Author are –

1. Theory of Indian Cookery (2 Editions Printed)
2. Beauty and Irony of Silvassa Tourism
3. A Short Indian Food Story
4. Be Your Own Guide to Indian Cuisine
5. Cookery Fundamentals
6. History of Indian Food (2 Editions Printed)
7. The Great Indian Story Book for Children
8. Personal Budget: Easy Work Book
9. Online Classes Log Book
10. Dictionary Making Work Book for School Children
11. The Lazy Bed
12. Hindu Dharm (हिन्दू धर्म) (In Hindi Language)
13. Where is my coffee?
14. Your First Job is Never your Last (Volume 1)
15. You are Almost There (Quick Fix Resume and Interview Hacks)
16. Working for the Enemy? - A lesson in Career Management
17. Public Speaking for the Young
18. A Date With Coffee
19. How to be The Best Hotel Front Office Employee
20. Diploma in Food Production, The complete Syllabus
21. Diploma in F&B Service, The Complete Syllabus
22. Diploma in Front Office, The Complete Syllabus

23. The Time to Speak is Now
24. Munshi Premchand (Short Stories in English)
25. The Housekeeping Department, Text Book
26. Hitchhiker's Guide to Trekking in Uttarakhand
27. Uttarakhand, A divine Land for a Reason
28. Bachhon ke liye rochak kahaniyan (बच्चों के लिए रोचक कहानियाँ) (In Hindi Language)
29. Basic Communication Skills of English
30. The Basic Office Organisation Book for Start-ups
31. Hospitality HRM
32. Hospitality Marketing
33. Bakery Ingredients and Tools
34. Human Resource Management for Indian Professionals
35. The process of LAWFULLY operating a Hospitality business in India
36. Indian Classical Sweets: History, Tradition and Recipes
37. History of India's Himalayan Cuisine: Classical Cookery of Kashmir, Laddakh, Jammu, Himachal, Lahaul, Spiti, Garhwal, Kumaon.
38. Vindu: Andhra Cuisine (Part 1 of South Indian Trilogy)
39. Saappadu: Tamil Cuisine (Part 2 of South Indian Trilogy)
40. Sadya: Malayali Cuisine (Part 3 of South Indian Trilogy)
41. South Indian Cuisine - The Researcher's Guide Book
42. The Ramayana for Children and other short stories from Indian Mythology
43. Legends of the Tribal Shiva
44. Third Generation Children's Story Book
45. It's Elementary: The Top Nine Adventures from the memoirs of Dr John H Watson (2 Editions Printed)
46. UNITY IN DIVERSITY, The foundation of Indian Tourism
47. The Thar Express: Culinary History of Rajasthan and Gujarat
48. Basics of Computerized Accounting
49. Impact (Impact of Globalization on Indian Social Life)
50. Vishnu – The Lord of Amazing Incarnations
51. Being a Mahatma in the Freedom Struggle
52. The Culinary Journey of Purvanchal: Lucknow to Patna
53. Culinary History of the Gangetic Plains
54. Indian Culinary Secrets
55. The Story of Jain and Parsi Food
56. The Great Indian Pilgrimage Tourism

57. Introduction to Tourism Studies – Text Book
58. Bread and Rolls (2 Editions Printed)
59. Diploma in Digital Marketing the Complete Syllabus
60. The Theory of Sweetened Bakery Foods
61. Campus Placement Guide for Management Trainee in Leading Hotels
62. Diploma in Housekeeping Management, the Complete Syllabus
63. Jokes and Stories for Kids
64. Demigods of India
65. Practical Cookery Guide Book for Parents and School Teachers
66. Introduction to Cookery for Elementary School Children (Kindle)
67. The Fearless Entrepreneur (Being your own Boss)
68. Culinary Heritage of Bengal's Widow Culture
69. Journey into the Mythological Wisdom of Vedas & Puranas
70. From Stigma to Strength: The Legacy of Bengal's Widowhood
71. HAKKA: Discovering a Vibrant Community in India
72. The Indo Chinese Pot Boiler
73. Bombay Daak: *Discovering the Kolis of the Seven Islands*
74. Speak Your Mind: A Guide to Clear and Impactful Communication
75. Urbanization And Rural Dynamics In India
76. Short Stories from the Animal Kingdom
77. The Short Story Book for Children - Morals and Humour

Connect with me: anshumali.pandey@gmail.com
https://notionpress.com/author/337004

Please scan this QR code on your phone to know more about the latest and complete works of Dr Anshumali Pandey